"This is a book you must read. Against all odds Patricia Wright succeeded in observing the previously unknown behavior of the mysterious and enchanting little owl monkey, the 'monkey of the night.' With the skill of a born storyteller she describes hair-raising adventures deep in the Amazon rainforest—and the problems of raising a child far from civilization. You will laugh and cry and marvel at the determination, courage, and scientific integrity of this amazing woman."
—JANE GOODALL, PhD, DBE, Founder of the
Jane Goodall Institute & UN Messenger of Peace

"Heart-warming, honest, deeply inquisitive, and chock-a-block with the absolutely insane adventure known as field biology. As a conservationist, as a primatologist, no question about it, Patricia Wright is a heavyweight contender. *High Moon Over the Amazon* proves her a great storyteller as well. This is a seriously fun, smart book."
—STEVEN KOTLER, *New York Times*
bestselling author of *Abundance:
The Future Is Better Than You Think*

"A naïve young American woman with a pet monkey goes to the Amazon to find it a mate. This is the improbable beginning of an important scientific career—Pat Wright's. *High Moon Over the Amazon* is a lively, exotic, inspirational tale about dreams that, against all odds, become reality."
—DAVID QUAMMEN, author of
Spillover and *The Song of the Dodo*

HIGH MOON OVER THE AMAZON

MY QUEST TO UNDERSTAND THE
MONKEYS OF THE NIGHT

Patricia Chapple Wright

LANTERN BOOKS | NEW YORK
A Division of Booklight Inc.

2013
Lantern Books
128 Second Place
Brooklyn, NY 11231
www.lanternbooks.com

Printed in the United States of America

Library of Congress Cataloging-in-Publication Data

Wright, Patricia C., 1944–
High moon over the Amazon : my quest to understand the
monkeys of the night / Patricia Chapple Wright. pages cm
ISBN 978-1-59056-421-9 (hardcover : alk. paper) —
ISBN 978-1-59056-480-6 (paperback : alk. paper) —
ISBN 978-1-59056-422-6 (ebook)
1. Night monkeys. 2. Wright, Patricia C., 1944–
3. Night monkeys—Behavior—Research—Peru.
4. Titis (Mammals)—Behavior—Research—Peru. I. Title.
QL737.P957W75 2013 599.8180985—dc23
2012046017

To Amanda Elizabeth Wright

And to Herbie and Kendra, who started it all

CONTENTS

Acknowledgments   ix

CHAPTER ONE

MONKEY BUSINESS
(New York, 1968)

1

CHAPTER TWO

MONKEY MATCHMAKING
(Colombia, 1971)

25

CHAPTER THREE

TROPICAL DISEASES
(Costa Rica, 1972)

57

CHAPTER FOUR

FATHER CARE
(Cape Cod, 1973–75)

80

CHAPTER FIVE

MONKEY IN THE MOON
(Puerto Bermúdez, 1976)

101

CHAPTER SIX

INTO THE AMAZON
(New York and Peru 1977–80)

149

CHAPTER SEVEN

GREEN CATHEDRAL
(Cocha Cashu, 1980)

188

CHAPTER EIGHT

JUNGLE TALES
(Cocha Cashu, 1980)

221

CHAPTER NINE

THE RETURN OF GRINGA VALIENTE
(Cocha Cashu and Puerto Bermúdez, Dec 1980– Jan 1981)

251

CHAPTER TEN

THE LONE RANGER
(Cocha Cashu, Jan–May 1981)

263

CHAPTER ELEVEN

HARPY EAGLE AND BIG FIG
(Cocha Cashu, 1981)

292

CHAPTER TWELVE

DARKNESS BRIGHTENS
(New York, 1982–83)

310

Author's Note   319

About the Publisher   323

ACKNOWLEDGMENTS

My mother, Julia Chapple, and father, Ed Chapple, always encouraged me to follow my dreams and cherish the natural world, and I would like to thank them for providing me with a firm foundation. My daughter, Amanda, has made this story possible by tolerating and enjoying years of jungles and monkey adventures. James Wright, my first husband, chose Herbie to begin with. Jim and Betty Wright, his parents, encouraged us in all endeavors in our early years. Herbie and Kendra were my inspiration to find out why they did what they did. Nancy Mulligan took a chance and funded the first expedition to find out what owl monkeys do in the wild.

Warren Kinzey, my academic advisor, encouraged me at every step of my career. His kindness and patience will never be forgotten. He taught me to look at the whole ecosystem, to never forget what the anatomy can tell you, and that persistence and motivation pay off. John Oates taught me to question everything, and that science and conservation go together. John Terborgh invited me to Manú National Park, and indeed there *is* no better place to raise a child. He also kindly supported us at Princeton. Charlie Janson showed me how to follow daytime monkeys and to observe carefully. Robin Foster inspired me to look at the world from a botanical view. Louise Emmons mentored me on how to trap, track, and study nocturnal mammals. Scott Robinson gave us the birds' eye view.

Charlie Munn taught Amanda to burp and draw birds. Nina Pierrepont was a good friend in difficult days in the rainforest. Anne Wilson Goldizen collaborated on learning why monkeys do what they do. Dave Sivertson is thanked for his assistance with playbacks and recording *Aotus* hoots, and thanks to John Allman for sending Dave to the Manú National Park. Patrick Daniels devoted years of his time to be my field assistant and my friend. Cirilo Lujan is thanked for being my guide in Puerto Bermúdez and then in the rainy season of the Manú. Adremildo and his family were important support for Amanda, James, and me in Puerto Bermúdez. Thanks to Peggy Stern for her assistance following *Callicebus* in 1982 in the Manú.

Mia and Floyd Glenn are thanked for babysitting the owl monkeys while I was in Peru. John Fleagle gave his support and kind encouragement, and took my monkeys into his home in 1981. Fran Jones Frummer and Lisa Forman let Amanda and me live with them in difficult times. Chris and Maureen Chapple, my brother and sister-in-law, cared for Amanda in the second grade. Ted Chapple, my brother, has given his continuous support and advice. I would also like to thank Elwyn Simons for giving me my first job, and Friderun Simons, Verne, and Cornelia Simons Seifert for helping Amanda with her quarter horse and being such good friends.

And to all my friends and colleagues who helped make this owl monkey study and life possible.

For helping with crafting earlier versions of the manuscript I thank Julia Chapple, Maureen Chapple, Jukka Jernvall, and Rachel Ryan, and for guiding the more final versions, Noel Rowe, Wendy Lee, Kara Davis, and Martin Rowe.

Manú National Park

CHAPTER ONE

MONKEY BUSINESS

(New York, 1968)

WAAWWRRKKKK! MY EYES shot up to the bright red and blue giant macaws, preening their feathers and calling for attention. Below them, emerald green and gold frogs shimmered on broad, glossy leaves. A giant, hairy tarantula crouched, immobile, waiting for its next prey. Waawwrrkkkk! The macaws' call pierced the air again. I glimpsed a pair of dark brown eyes wincing and realized someone else disliked the dissonance of the parrot calls.

We had arrived early to the Fillmore East to experience Jimi Hendrix when the rain hit. We burst into the pet shop Fish N Cheeps to escape the pounding rainstorm. The cozy, mammalian scent and raucous parrot sounds transformed the harshness of Greenwich Village streets to the sounds and warmth of the tropics. As I approached the chocolate brown woolly monkey, who had shied from the loud calls, he reached slowly out of his cage to me, as if to shake my hand. Woollys are some of the largest monkeys in South America, and I had never seen one up close before. His round face was very childlike, and his expression disarming. I turned to Jamie, my artist husband, to show him my new friend. But Jamie was intrigued by a small monkey on the other side of the shop.

"This is the one I like," he murmured.

At first, I couldn't tell what Jamie saw in this monkey. The little grayish monkey was asleep, curled up with his head tucked under his knees and his tail wrapped neatly over his head, as if to protect him from intrusion. I poked at him gently, and he awoke with a lunge toward my finger.

"I don't think he likes me," I whispered.

The monkey scowled his annoyance at being woken up at this hour. His huge golden brown eyes were made more dramatic by white patches accented with black triangles for eyebrows.

"What kind of a monkey is this?" I asked the elderly shopkeeper.

"It's an owl monkey from the Amazon. Sleeps all day, that's all I know about it."

"How old is he? When did he come in and how much does he cost?" The questions came flooding out.

But the answers were abrupt. "Young, three days ago, forty bucks."

"Is he destructive, loud? What does he eat?"

"All I've seen him do is sleep, and the monkey chow is gone in the morning."

The two-pound monkey opened its golden eyes again and looked into mine. A charming harlequin face with a droll, built-in smile.

"I need someone to keep me company while I'm painting at

night." Jamie spoke under his breath as he bent over to get a closer look.

I reached timidly toward the cage, and this time the owl monkey extended his hand and grasped my finger, murmuring a soft, contented gurgle. Was he making up for his bad temper at my earlier thoughtless poking? I smiled broadly up at Jamie, pleading and teasing at the same time. I liked this monkey, too.

But neither Jamie nor I had forty bucks. In 1968, forty dollars was a fortune for us, a recently married New York couple. Our ticket to the Fillmore East to see Hendrix was only five dollars, and my yearly salary as a social worker was a little over $4,000. Forty dollars was certainly an unimaginable amount to squander on a pet, especially a pet monkey.

After gazing at the beaded gold and black tegu lizard, and saying goodbye to the woolly monkey, we left the shop to brave the pelting rain once more. As my feet splashed through the puddles, my thoughts were focused on that monkey's little, round face. His smile and shiny eyes beckoned beyond the inconvenience of rain and cold. I wanted that monkey. I really wanted that monkey. My childhood obsession, that to my mother's dismay had previously been fixed on raccoons or wild rabbits, had a new focus. Even the skills and showmanship of Jimi Hendrix couldn't wipe the memory of the monkey out of my mind.

In the weeks after, we took trips to the New York Public Library and brought home to our four-story walk-up Brooklyn brownstone apartment stacks of volumes about monkeys, each of which had only a few lines about the owl monkey.

"'*Aotus* is the Latin name for owl monkey,'" I read out loud to Jamie. "'Owl monkeys are rarely kept as pets, because of their night activity cycle.' That's all this book says about them. But wait, this book, *Monkeys as Pets*, says that 'owl monkeys can be a quiet and clean pet, but can make a loud booming call during the night.'"

"Did you say that book was called *Monkeys as Pests*?" Jamie's eyes crinkled as he looked for my reaction. "All the other books say that monkeys don't make good pets. Monkeys can't be toilet trained, or for that matter be trained to do anything."

I continued to read out loud. "'Although young squirrel and capuchin monkeys are quite manageable as juveniles, once adults, these monkeys often turn vicious toward their owners.'"

Yes, we were forewarned. But both Jamie and I loved animals, especially tropical animals, and our apartment was already home to a large, lumbering, lettuce-eating iguana named Iggy. Our favorite books were tales of the tropics and the adventures of zoo collectors like Gerald Durrell. We had even visited the Caribbean island of Aruba on vacation.

Despite all the reading, we were still intrigued by the fantasy of owning a monkey and decided to ignore the sage advice of the library books. We found the forty dollars, returned to the Fish N Cheeps, brought the monkey home in a cardboard box, and named him Herbie.

On that day I didn't know about the evils of the exotic animal pet trade, and certainly not about the painful trials of owning a monkey. I didn't dream that this monkey could lead me to his native South American rainforest home; and, of all things, inspire me to ask questions that would take me years to answer. After all, I was a social worker caring for battered and desperate human lives in the ghettos of Brooklyn, and not concerned with understanding the reasons behind this monkey's nocturnal rainforest lifestyle. But, step by step, my career in monkey business was being born. It wasn't a difficult birth, but rather a difficult childhood.

My parents met when my mother, Julie, a twenty-two-year-old chemistry teacher, bicycled into the Niagara Falls airport to take flying lessons. Ed Chapple, a thirty-four-year-old Canadian bachelor, was her instructor. After the third lesson a dramatic thunderstorm arose and Ed gallantly offered to drive Julie home in his Chevrolet. She agreed, and Ed packed the bike into the trunk. Once on the road, Ed said he was hungry and invited Julie to dinner. She remembered being very embarrassed when he asked her what she would like to drink, and she said "water." Drinking alcohol was considered social, but she didn't like the taste. Julie was intrigued by this tall, lanky guy with hazel eyes, a shock of brown curly hair, and a shy manner.

They were not alike. Julie came from a well-to-do Springville, New York, family. But her mother disappeared to Detroit when she was eight years old, and her father, an immigration officer, died two years later. Julie and her brother were raised by a maiden Irish aunt. Always the smartest in her class, Julie was a graduate of the University of Buffalo and was bent on a career in chemistry. She was a city girl and loved to go to museums and the theater.

Ed was raised in the small town of Meaford, Ontario, population 4,000, which also boasts of being for a short time the home of John Muir, the famous wildlife author and activist. My father was a country boy, raised on a farm, and loved to hunt and fish in the wilderness of Georgian Bay. An athlete, he was a high school basketball star and excelled at lacrosse, pole-vaulting, and the broad jump. He had started as a forestry major at the University of Toronto, but the economic crash of 1929 ended that luxury.

Ed's mother, Ursula Key Chapple, was a formidable six-foot-tall woman with long gray hair always wrapped in a bun. Ed had two brothers, one older and one younger. His father, a gentleman farmer and dashingly handsome (according to my grandmother), died at fifty-nine of asthma and heart troubles. Ed's youngest brother, Bill, died unexpectedly at age twenty-eight from Rocky Mountain spotted fever two days before Christmas.

The death of his brother put Ed's life into a more focused perspective. This was during World War II, and the war years weighed heavily on everyone. Julie had lost her fiancé in Pearl Harbor. Ed was drafted into the Navy. Since wartime didn't allow for big weddings, Ed and Julie eloped on February 12, Lincoln's birthday. I was born on September 10, 1944, in Doylestown, Pennsylvania, near where Ed was stationed.

Later, we moved to Niagara Falls, New York. I remember our home as a two-story gray wooden house with a big porch and no yard. Dad would take me to the park many blocks away to feed the ducks. On the way home he would ask, "Are you tired, Patty Jo? I can carry you." Indignant at the thought, the two-and-a-half-year-old me exclaimed, "No, no, I'm not tired. My shoes are tired." And I kept walking. My will and determination were clear.

Just as I turned three, my parents bought a partnership in a small airport near Medina, New York, and we rented a brick house across from the Apple Grove Inn. My mother was pregnant again and I remember going to the hospital with my teddy bear clutched tightly. I looked at my mother, pale and frail, peering down at a bundle of blankets.

"Dad, look . . . Mom has a teddy bear just like me."

The little bundle was a tiny boy with a big name, Hugh Edward Chapple II, named after my dad. But his big sister renamed him Ted that first week, and it stuck. I also had a sister who was two years younger, Diane. Three children in four years was quite a challenge for my young mother.

My first pets were two baby raccoons that my father brought back from the airport where he worked. "Sam found the two baby coons on his farm. He thinks the mother was killed to make 'coon pie.' What do you think?"

"Oh Dad, they're so cute! Look at their black masks and wriggling whiskers." I gathered them into my arms.

Cheerful, playful pets, the twins grew up fast that summer. During one of those first chilly mornings in September, the coon twins and I went outside for a romp, and "Zorro" and "Tonto," chasing one another, disappeared into the nearby woods. I sped after them, begging for them to come back, but they were gone. Day after day, my mother, father, and I searched and called, but the coons were never seen again. Devastated by the first tragedy of my life, I was inconsolable, bursting into tears at breakfast and after lunch, sobbing for my lost playmates.

"They're wild animals," my mother explained. "Don't be so sad, they'll lead a happy life in the woods."

That fall, at age five, I started school in Medina. Kindergarten meant new friends, but the boys on the school bus punched my arm after I had my smallpox vaccination, and I refused to ride the bus anymore.

"I can walk, Mom, no problem," I said.

"But it's miles to school—it'll take you over an hour."

Dad took my side. "Let her walk. Walking never hurt anyone."

From that day, I walked to school an hour every morning and never took the bus until we moved to another town three years later.

That was a long winter when I was five. By springtime, I plotted to get a new pet.

"Mom, wouldn't a kitten be nice to have around?"

My mother, her days full with three children under six years, was emphatic: "No."

We never argued with our mother. She was a tiny woman with a large presence, snapping black eyes, and an Irish temper. However, my heart was set on owning another pet. Noticing that one of the barnyard cats was ostentatiously plump, I had an idea. Every day after school I tracked the fat calico cat as she crept through the grass, hunting near the orchard. When she spotted me, I would freeze and then look away, and she would twitch her tail and disappear. Every day it became my favorite game to find her and watch.

"Playing hide and seek with the cats again?" my mother asked, observing the grass stains on my school dress.

One day the calico cat wasn't fat anymore, and my tracking

took a serious turn. I followed her far enough to see her disappear through a jagged hole in the barn wall. One Saturday, I got up at 6:00 A.M. and snuck out of the house before my mother was up. I watched the hole in the barn until the mother calico came out. Then, head first, I squeezed slowly through that hole. It was dark inside, and my hand touched straw. I could hear tiny meows and a spitting, hissing sound. There must have been three or four kittens, but I couldn't see in the dark. I grabbed a kitten and, ignoring the bites and scratches, headed back out the hole, worried that the mother would return soon. Once out in the sun, I looked at the writhing bundle of fur. My hands were bright red from the scratches, but the kitten was orangish yellow, my favorite cat color. I couldn't believe my luck.

My mother was just starting to cook a big pot of porridge for breakfast when I arrived, proudly holding my furball.

"My new pet, Mom!" I proclaimed, beaming. "His name is Yowler."

My mother was astonished, and despite being against cats in the house because of my sister, she didn't have the heart to ask me to return the kitten after all my hard work.

My sister, Diane, was asthmatic. Ever since she was a baby, she had a difficult time breathing at night. Diane and I shared a bedroom. The night I secretly brought Yowler to bed, Diane had a life-threatening asthma attack. Back out to the barn went the cat.

Tragedy struck the next summer. Drivers often speeded in front of our house, as we lived at the edge of town. And one sunny summer morning, Yowler was hit by a car. His skull was shattered, and his intestines spilled all over the road. I screamed with horror, rushed to the smashed body on the road, and became hysterical, knowing that my beloved Yowler was gone forever. The driver stopped to apologize, but I continued to scream. Mom arrived next and held me in her arms. Mrs. Simsik, our landlady, came running to the scene.

"Is Diane okay? Oh, sorry, it's only the cat that's been hit. All that screaming for a cat? I thought your sister had been hit by a car."

I remember thinking with the narrow perspective of a five year old, but not saying, "My sister? I wouldn't be crying this hard if it were my sister."

We moved shortly after that to another rental, a sprawling house with a big porch north of the Erie Canal. It was here that my father taught me about storms. When lightning flashed and thunder rocked the air, Dad would carry me out to the porch and tell me not to be afraid. I trembled at the violence of the storms and he held me tight, telling me to count between the lightning and the thunder. "One one thousand, two one thousand, three one thousand." We were taking data on how far away the storm was. "Face your fears, never be afraid of nature," he told me.

I had a gray tabby cat this time, which lived outside the house, and a collie dog named Duffy. Then one day, Dad's best friend gave us an unusual pet. It was a black and white calf that we staked out in the backyard and named Buckingham.

My job was to feed him hay and brush him. All three of us kids loved the baby bull.

My mother felt lonely in this neighborhood, as all her friends lived on the other side of town and she couldn't drive a car. She often complained about the housework and childcare. Television had been invented by then, but we didn't own one, so Mom was often glued to the radio, listening to speeches by Harry Truman. I preferred the dramatic stories like *Stella Dallas* or the exciting tales of *The Lone Ranger.*

To make the week pass more quickly, Mom installed a family tradition. Wednesdays were "fun days" when she would give us each a quarter, and we all would walk hand in hand down the sidewalk to the corner candy store. We were never allowed any sweets except on those days. Ted was three and Diane was four, and we loved this tradition. Ted really liked reaching up to put coins in the machine and hearing the *ka-ching* of the bright blue globes coming through the metal hole. Diane preferred cinnamon sticks, and I chose chocolate.

One day, I came home and asked Dad, "Peter told me to be afraid of dragonflies. He said they were 'darning needles' and they would land on me and sew up my mouth. Is that true?"

"No, Pat, dragonflies are good because they eat mosquitoes," my dad replied. "They can't sew up anything. Maybe Peter was hinting that you were talking too much."

Peter was nine years old and lived eight houses down the street. One day my friend and next-door neighbor—who was also named Patty—and I were playing dolls on the porch when

Peter rode by on his bike. Patty said, "Peter's a sissy, he's riding his sister's bike."

Peter turned around and came back, angry at the taunt. He dared Patty to come down the steps and fight him. She just laughed at him.

Then Peter shouted, "I double dare you. Patty, come down those steps and fight or I will go up after you! I double dare you!"

Peter was threatening my friend, and he was bigger than us. My name was Patty too, and I was sick of his bullying. Peter started up the steps and when he nearly reached the top, I said, "I'll take that double dare," and shoved him hard. He tumbled down onto the sidewalk. One of his teeth broke and blood came out of his nose. He began screaming, our mothers came out and shouted at one another, and he was carried home in a trail of blood. My mom gave me a lecture about not resorting to physical violence, even if somebody double dares you. She explained that negotiation was an effective tool to resolve conflict. To tell the truth, I learned my lesson well at six years of age and have never resorted to physical violence again. Even on a double dare.

I don't know if it was because of this incident with Peter or not, but my father started talking about buying a house in the countryside. He believed that children should be raised outside in nature and with the freedom to explore.

Buckingham, now a big bull, was escaping more often and Mom was having a difficult time pulling this giant beast back to our yard. One day, we came home from school and Buckingham was gone. Mom said Dad had sold him. All three of us kids were very sad.

Peter came by on his sissy bike to say, "Your stupid cow was sold to become steaks. Next time you eat steak or hamburgers or meatloaf, you're probably eating your pet!" I just laughed, as if he were making a joke.

I was eight years old when our family moved to a farmhouse three miles from the small town of Lyndonville (population 499). This town, halfway between Buffalo and Rochester in upstate New York, was located near fertile land that in ancient times formed the lakebed of Lake Ontario. The excellent sandy soil inspired farming, primarily apple, peach, and cherry orchards. We owned three acres of tree-shaded lawn.

My mother, who could pilot a plane but still didn't drive a car, felt stifled and trapped so far from friends and stores. Three more children were born in short order. The work of raising six children without even a washing machine was pure drudgery. My father worked long hours at the foundry where he was supervisor, and my mother was left home alone to cope with us. She was bitter and angry, and we felt her despair. She had been the valedictorian of her class and had given up a promising career in chemistry for us. I vowed that I would never be trapped by motherhood. Never.

The winters were long in Lyndonville, and snow fortresses and snowball fights had a limited appeal for me. In a world without television, I escaped from the brutal winters into a different reality, reading books about warm places or furry animals. *Lad: A Dog* by Albert Payson Terhune was one of my favorites. Every winter, all winter, I dreamed about traveling away from that ice and snow. I dreamed of traveling south, where it was warm.

Because there were eight of us, our family rarely traveled, and when we did, it was north to Canada. Several Sundays a year, we loaded up the family car, squirming children and all, and rode two long hours in the blue Chevrolet for Sunday dinner with our aunt, uncle, and two cousins in Niagara Falls. The adults talked endlessly while we played ball with our cousins. Then, after dinner, my aunt loudly played the piano. Tunelessly, we all sang "(How Much Is) That Doggie in the Window?" and "Amazing Grace."

For our annual week of summer vacation, we traveled even farther north to our Canadian cousins' retreat, a cabin on Bruce Peninsula, on the beaches of Georgian Bay. And sometimes my father, an ardent outdoorsman, would take me, the eldest, farther north on a fishing trip to his hometown of Meaford. I was only five or six when I learned to spear carp and fly cast for trout in streams with my father. It was up there in the north that I learned about the adventure of small planes, fast boats, fish fried fresh over the campfire, and the beauty of the wilderness. Dad, who had spent months learning skills from the Chippewa Indians before he was twenty, taught me how to walk quietly in the forest toe to heel and to observe every nuance of nature carefully. I treasured every trip, and continued to dream that when I grew up I would travel to wild places. But I wouldn't go north, with its two-month window of good weather. I would travel south. Maybe I would even go as far south as Sunnybrook Farm, the home of Lad the dog, in New Jersey.

True to my dreams, I went south to college, even farther than New Jersey, all the way to Frederick, Maryland. At Hood College my curiosity for woodland and wilderness evolved into a major in biology. My favorite course was ecology, which involved class field expeditions to the estuary at the mouth of the Patuxent River. Once again I was in my element, immersed in mud, chasing copepods and shellfish and other such animals. In addition, college involved other kinds of wildness. These were the Kennedy years, and trips to art galleries in Washington, DC, were interspersed with weekends dancing to rock 'n' roll and drinking beer until dawn in Appalachian Mountain cabins. But despite all those parties, I didn't fall in love with an Annapolis cadet or a fraternity brother.

Love is often serendipitous. Like the proverbial lightning, love struck on my first summer home from college, when I went for a swim in Johnson's Creek by the Lyndonville dam. Jamie Wright had just emerged from the water after a daring dive. "Great dive," I said, smiling, already bronzed from the southern sun.

Jamie had always been shy and multitalented, even in high school. His cousin was in my sister's class, but since he was in a class below me and therefore an inferior being, I had never associated with him. He was known as an artist who drew clever cartoons on the blackboard after class. His grandfather owned the biggest business in town—an applesauce factory—and his grandmother taught seventh grade math. Jamie didn't say anything to my comment about his diving, but in response glanced down at his feet.

"I just came home this week. From college in Maryland. We just had exams. I passed them all." My idle chatter resounded off silence.

I continued, "I see that things haven't changed much around here. Except maybe for that red Renault. Whose car is that?" It wasn't that I really cared about cars, but I was grasping for conversation.

"Graduation present from my grandfather. Want a ride?" Jamie looked up slowly, and I could see his steel-blue eyes were intense and crinkled in a smile.

It was on that ride that he discussed Iggy, his pet iguana, and his longtime pursuit of raising tropical lizards. That summer, I met Iggy, Chuck (the chunky chuckwalla), and the foot-long, nocturnal Tokay gecko named Topaz. And later that summer, Jamie disclosed his latest oil painting, tropical wildlife immersed into a surreal world. Jamie's paintings were a circus of life, bright colors with realistic images of nature reminiscent of Salvador Dalí or Pieter Bruegel. This latest painting was simple, bright butterflies, gleaming foliage, and hummingbirds.

And that same summer, I fell in love with this quiet artist with the wry sense of humor. In September, Jamie started Brown University in Providence, Rhode Island, far from Maryland. His frequent letters were clever and textured with his cartoon drawings and cryptic poems.

The following spring, I cut classes to go with him to New Orleans for Mardi Gras. With two friends he drove his Renault from Providence to Maryland, where I joined him, and we continued south through the night. We didn't sleep for days, carried by the music, magical floats, and beer of the French Quarter. A few months later, going north to Providence, we stopped in New York City, attracted by a blimp advertising "Meet the Beatles," and bought tickets from a long-haired girl in front of Shea Stadium. The Beatles arrived just as we entered the stadium, and we were engulfed in the screaming crowds.

Jamie and I shared a sense of adventure, a love of animals, wildlife, rock music, and modern art. At twenty, that is enough to build a life together.

Nervously standing outside the Methodist Church in Lyndonville one day in June, adorned in white lace, I had no idea what was going on. At the moment he was supposed to be waiting for me at the end of the aisle, Jamie had disappeared. Mike Barros, his best man, looked worried. Our college classmates had gathered from across the country to see us, the first couple they knew to get married. Both sides of our families had come for the first family wedding in decades. My six bridesmaids stood beside me, dressed in blossom pink and apple green and expectantly holding pink roses and baby's breath bouquets.

Anxious ushers in gray tails paced in the antechamber while Jamie's father and uncle hastily left the church to search for him. Somebody had seen Jamie and Ross Marlay, his college roommate, on a motorcycle heading north, but that was hours ago. It was Jamie's uncle, Harry Maines, the mayor, who found the motorcycle by the side of the road with the two young men pushing it. "It ran out of gas," was their sheepish explanation. It has never been explained to me what Uncle Harry said in reply, but I can guess it wasn't phrased in wedding prose. The rest of the wedding proceeded according to Emily Post.

After a five-dollar-a-day, two-month honeymoon visiting Europe, Jamie and I moved to New York City. I was to be the breadwinner while Jamie earned his masters in fine arts at Pratt Institute in Brooklyn. However, there were no jobs in "mud and animals" in New York. Being practical and getting hungry, I accepted a job as a caseworker for the Department of Social Services, also known as the Department of Welfare. Equipped with only my long brown hair, deep brown eyes, broad smile, and a romantic view of humanity, I began to visit 125 homes of people in need, living in the center of the concrete jungle called Brooklyn.

The cultural leap from small-town life in western New York to the urban problems of central Brooklyn was a big one. I had a bachelor's degree from Hood College, but I was about to receive an education in real life. I was assigned to Brownsville in Brooklyn, a mixed black and Hispanic neighborhood with high crime and frequent homicides. At twenty-two, I learned about inner-city teenage pregnancies and the cascade of misfortunes that locks women into a lifetime of struggle and pain. My "clients" described lives of desperation, the punishing effects of alcohol and drugs, and the fear of waking up in the morning facing a gun or hearing that a child—your child, your sister's child—has been injured. Danger lurked outside and behind the door. And sickness: many people on welfare are in poor health, with tuberculosis, diabetes, and depression, often living alone in a hostile world.

The contrasts with Lyndonville shocked me out of my Pollyanna naïveté and into action. Each morning, it became a challenge to solve these people's problems with the tools the US government had given me: "on the job training courses," "daycare advantages," and "new health programs." I visited every one of the homes on my caseload and listened to what these people had to say. I would sit in their kitchens sipping coffee, listening to their problems and their life stories filled with heartbreak, fear, and drama. I listened and learned. I learned that poor people are just people—often people born into a tough situation that spirals into a worse situation. The challenge was immense, but I was willing to dig in and give it a shot.

In the late 1960s in New York City, Andy Warhol was jolting the art world with images of soup cans and Marilyn Monroe. The East Village was filled with long-haired youth in bright tie-dyed clothing and bare feet. Head shops were mixed with record shops, and the smell of marijuana mingled with the beat of The Doors, The Stones, and Frank Zappa.

Thus, it wasn't so strange that Jamie and I ended up with a monkey as a pet.

The addition of a new species to our household changed our lives in ways we could never have dreamed. We had planned to put Herbie in a cage, but Herbie believed in the primate rule that home is where your family is, and that meant your parent's head. From the very beginning, he preferred Jamie's copious head of unruly brown hair. Jamie was also six and a half feet tall, the kind of "canopy" height that appeals to a monkey. At night, while Jamie painted, Herbie would quietly munch on apples or investigate under the bed where I slept. Occasionally, he would scamper to the kitchen, especially if I was preparing him a tropical snack. His decision to ignore the cage was definite. No matter how many fuzzy hats and security blankets we put inside the cage, the little monkey refused to go in. But what about the toilet training? Monkeys are impossible to toilet train. When a monkey is in the trees, fertilizing the ground far below is not a problem. However, in our apartment it *was* a problem. We trained Herbie to perch and aim for several key spots where newspapers were placed on the floor, but the training was not perfect and I spent most mornings cleaning up.

There was a creeping feeling that Jamie and I had lost control over family decisions. We were sixty times heavier, and in total control of the finances, but the rules that governed our lives were becoming "Herbie's rules."

Herbie didn't mind me going off to work all day long, as he was in deep sleep. But New York was a showcase for new bands like Cream and Pink Floyd, and for five bucks you could sit in the tenth row center while B.B. King, Janis Joplin, Bob Dylan, or Eric Clapton played at the Fillmore East. Not surprisingly, these concerts were at night. And Herbie objected to being left alone at night. Abandoning your offspring in the territory was not "acceptable" parental behavior. During an ordinary day, Herbie was not in the least destructive or difficult to live with. But when we returned after an evening away, the apartment was in shambles. Salt and pepper shakers overturned, potted plants toppled to the floor, drinking glasses shattered, runners thrown off the tables. Herbie would greet us at the door, looking quite innocent.

After one such spree, I had had enough. "Jamie, the choice is simple," I said. "We either stop going out, or we get rid of Herbie." Even before the threat had been uttered, a lump swelled in my throat and tears rimmed my eyes. We both were in love with our little companion.

"He needs company. Can't we find him a wife?" Jamie suggested.

This seemed like the perfect solution to a happy couple. By this time, Herbie must have been almost three years old, and based on what we had read, he was mature enough to begin his own family. It seemed obvious that once Herbie had his own family, he wouldn't be as concerned with our whereabouts. The next morning, I phoned every pet shop in New York, requesting "an owl monkey female (OMF)—attractive, young, and in good health." Alas, there were no *Aotus* females to be found in New York.

Then I had an idea. "If we can't find a wife for Herbie in New York, can't we find one in South America? We can travel as tourists to the Amazon and bring back a wife for Herbie.

We've always wanted to visit the rainforest. Yes, we can do that . . . yes, we can do that. . . . Let's go!" What can I say? It was the sixties.

We binged on guidebooks that told us how to travel in Colombia, Ecuador, and Peru on five dollars a day. Like most US citizens, we knew about Europe but hadn't a clue of what South America had to offer. The sudden revelation of the Indian handicrafts, museums, and rainforests that lay to the south whetted our appetite for adventure. I mustered the courage to tell my boss that I had to quit my job to travel to South America. After a long discussion, we agreed on a two-month leave of absence. It was time to buy the tickets.

The tickets weren't the problem, but babysitting was. If we'd had a human child, our relatives would have been fighting over the opportunity to babysit. But Herbie was a monkey, and there were no volunteers. In fact, at the mention of the possibility of babysitting for months, the responses from both sides of the family were quite rude, and it was good that Herbie didn't understand English that well.

It became obvious to me that we would have to take Herbie with us. After all, if we were going to South America to find him a wife, he should really have some choice in the matter. But when I called the airline, the employee responded with a chill in her voice. The company did not allow the shipment of monkeys, or any other wild animals, on their planes. Later, in a subsequent call, when I asked if I could take my "cat" on board an international flight, the answer was much warmer: "As long as your cat is in a regulation-size, under-the-seat pet carrier, no problem. Don't forget the health certificate."

The international health certificate was likely to list the species on it. When I called the veterinarian, he reminded me that the laws were changing, and that the US Department of Fish and Wildlife would have to check the monkey when he reentered the country. It seemed strange to me that a cat could move freely across borders, while a monkey would be questioned at every stop.

I was at the Colombian consulate in New York filling out visa forms for Jamie and me when I had an idea. In a sincere and knowledgeable voice, I said to the woman behind the glass window, "I have two owl monkeys, both born in New York, who are going with me on vacation, but they'll need some sort of paperwork to come back to the States with me. Cats can reenter with a health certificate, but monkeys need a special visa certifying that they originated in the US. Can I purchase one here?"

The sudden realization that one administrative paper would probably solve many future problems had inspired me to bend the truth a little. The woman seemed momentarily puzzled, left the window for a few minutes, and to my surprise, appeared with a visa form, which I filled out with the names, sexes, and species of my two monkeys (one male, one female). I paid twenty dollars, official stamps were applied, and I walked out of the consulate with a guarantee that there would be no border hassles. I practically skipped down the street, eager to tell Jamie about my brilliant strategy. I had just achieved my first end-run around international bureaucracy!

But, of course, that was just the beginning of the quest for a wife for Herbie. The itinerary was simple enough: travel south to the Amazon with stops in Barranquilla, Bogotá, and Leticia in Colombia, and then return through Miami to New York. We bought an under-the-seat cat carrier and packed our bags. We included oil paints for Jamie, flashlights in case we had to venture into the jungle to find this monkey wife, a raincoat for the rainforest (of course), and sunglasses for those days off. Our flight was set to leave on June 6.

CHAPTER TWO

MONKEY MATCHMAKING

(Colombia, 1971)

OUR PROBLEMS STARTED at JFK Airport, when we made the mistake of arriving early, before Herbie had gone to sleep for the day. Just as the airline agent was about to approve his under-the-seat status, Herbie pushed his little brown hand out of the end hole of the cat carrier. "That is not a cat!" the airline agent declared. No amount of pleading would convince her to let us go, and we had to take our bags back home, an hour by subway, with Herbie in the carrier.

The next day, we arrived an hour later, when Herbie had settled down for his deep daytime sleep, and we were greeted by a different agent. This time there were no little brown hands in sight, and we boarded the plane with our "cat" under our seat. Because it was daytime, Herbie slept all the way to Barranquilla, and Jamie and I reread our guidebooks.

Before long, the stewardess announced that we were about to land in Colombia. I looked down at the turquoise-blue waters of the Caribbean, the white waves smashing against forested cliffs, and felt the warm exhilaration of adventure. Once we were out of the plane and waiting for our luggage, however, the realities began to sink in. Everyone spoke Spanish. We couldn't understand anyone, we couldn't read any signs or forms. The frustrating feeling of isolation, the alarm of being from another world, the helplessness of trying to communicate . . . and people just shaking their heads, not understanding, in response.

My panic was not helped by the mouse-sized cockroach that scuttled by me. Having a monkey in a cat carrier was a pretty minor problem compared to changing dollars into pesos, and figuring out how to cheaply get to the pension circled in the guidebook. Crowds jostled us, and I clutched my purse and passport firmly. Finally, our luggage arrived, and we made it out into the night air of South America. Herbie had returned to his homeland! A momentous occasion, I thought.

Herbie didn't seem to share this view. At the pension, we let him out of his cat carrier. He had fared better than we had on the trip, having slept soundly. He looked around at the less-than-luxurious surroundings, smelled the stale, humid, mildewed air, and moaned an "I'm not very pleased with this place" sound. It was too late to get dinner at the pension, but I'd saved Herbie some grapes and a banana from my airline meal. After his breakfast, he investigated our new surroundings. The tiny room with its rhythmic fan was weakly illuminated by one bedside lamp. The stuffiness couldn't be alleviated by opening a window because Herbie might take the opportunity to explore outside. The room was sparse, with a bed and a half-painted wooden chair with a cracked leg. Mosquitoes buzzed ominously. Jamie lit the mosquito coil and, discouraged and depressed, I drifted off to sleep.

In the morning, the reality of downtown Barranquilla matched our dreary hotel room. A large port town known for its hustlers, traders, and thieves, it didn't seem a likely place to find Herbie a wife. We needed to get to the Amazon, which meant we would need to fly through Bogotá, the highland capital of Colombia, and then south to Leticia, a village on the edge of the second largest river in the world. We started that journey on the following day.

The Amazon rainforest looked like a nubbly green carpet from the air. Occasionally, the green was broken by a meandering ribbon of river. For hours and hours we looked down at the forest, the vastness humbling and awe-inspiring. The airplane droned loudly as the hours continued, and then we began to descend. Closer and closer came the greenness; then the huge river, magnificent in its size, filled the airplane window. The dirt strip of a runway loomed ahead and then we were down on the ground. Everyone on board clapped.

Airport procedures were now routine for us. I had learned to substitute sign language and shrugs for Spanish. The airport building was a simple, thatched structure with the atmosphere of tropical decay. Men, casually dressed in short-sleeved shirts or T-shirts, greeted the plane's cargo and passengers with languor. There were no women in sight. Outside, the humid air was alive with an orchestra of birds and insects. Herbie's brown hand came out of his window and we knew he was anxious to explore. We hefted our luggage into the back of a battered pickup truck and, along with five other passengers, headed down a dirt road into town.

After locating a hotel room that didn't have easy avenues for escape, we opened Herbie's carrier and offered him bananas and papayas, which he agreed were a good breakfast. Herbie seemed to like this place better than our residence in Barranquilla. This room in Leticia had concrete walls and floor, a palm-thatched roof, and a screened window. In my first glance around the room I spied five huge spiders over the bed and apprehensively motioned to Jamie. Herbie's keen eyes were also riveted to the eight-legged creatures looming over the pillow. Before we could stop him, he lunged toward a spider, grabbed it with two hands, and ate it. I shuddered, but Herbie just plucked the next one, and munched on spiders like they were Godiva chocolates.

After we unpacked and got settled, it was time to explore the town. Always reluctant to leave Herbie behind, Jamie tucked him under his shirt, with Herbie's little round face peering out between the buttons. Eventually, the sunshine proved to be too bright so he tucked his head inside and went to sleep.

Leticia was an Amazon port at the border of three countries: Colombia on the north side and Brazil and Peru across the water. With contraband and desperadoes, Indians and colonists, Leticia had the culture of any frontier town. We dodged puddles and mud as we strolled down the unpaved "main street" that ran parallel to the Amazon, and turned left at the road that bisected the main street and ended a few hundred yards later at the river. That "T" was the total extent of the town's infrastructure; the real main street was the river. The only ground vehicles in Leticia were three dilapidated pickup trucks, relegated to the chores of airport and Amazon shuttle service.

Leticia bustled in the early morning, but sweltered to a halt by noon. As we meandered down to the river, the thatched stalls and tin-roofed, clapboard stores looked haphazard and chaotic—a jumble of color crowded with loud, jostling people. Bare-footed Indians bought rum while bearded settlers stocked up on supplies to take downriver. We had arrived late and the shops were beginning to close for hours of afternoon break.

As we approached the port, it too was slowing down for lunch and siesta. Most boats were giant wooden canoes with thatched canopies and shields from the tropical sun. The Johnson motors attached to the sterns vibrated noisily and churned the muddy water. Boats were the only way to travel and move goods. Indeed, a man was as strong as his Johnson motor. In our best Spanish, we asked the boat owners where to find a monkey, and their answers were all the same. If we came back early in the morning, about 5:00 A.M., the animals would be coming in off the river.

The next morning, our ritual began, a before-dawn scramble to get to the docks when the first boats arrived. They had traveled for days down or up the Amazon, filled with cargo, oil drums, bananas, palm nuts, dried fish, and live animals. There were crates and crates of them: capuchin monkeys, woolly monkeys, squirrel monkeys, snakes, cranes, scarlet macaws tied by their feet, and occasionally a jaguar.

I asked the unloaders of each boat if they had an owl monkey—*mono de la noche* in Spanish, or "the monkey of the night"—but the answer was always negative.

"Where are these animals going?" I asked innocently.

"To Mike Salakis." Each answer was the same. "Mike will buy them."

We found Mike's place a short walk from the center of town. It was a large house, one of the few in town with a generator for electricity and running water. To the east of it was a warehouse teeming with the stench and screams of captured prey. Crates were stacked up outside the building. We could see the pathetic squalor of wild animals crammed into tiny spaces. A squirrel monkey had a bloody nose and cuts on his tail from trying to escape his prison. He looked at us with glazed eyes, as if he had given in to his pain. A green parrot, beak open, was panting in a crate, hot and thirsty, standing on five of his dead friends. The smells made me gag, and I was about to tell Jamie we had to leave, when Mike sauntered out of the warehouse to see what we wanted.

Mike was about forty years old, a Greek-American from Tarpon Springs, Florida, who'd moved to this Amazon outpost about twenty years previously. Like many foreigners, he'd taken an Indian wife and lived in a modest house with few modern amenities. He was short in stature and casual in a loose Tarpon Springs T-shirt and jeans. My first impression was he seemed like an uneducated man, maybe a high school dropout who, having been an outcast in his own society, sought refuge here. He seemed to be doing well at his chosen occupation, which we suspected was running contraband across borders. His conversation was interspersed with cursing and Camel cigarettes, and although he was willing to discuss business with us, I felt that he was always thinking about something else as we talked.

"Jamie and I have just arrived from New York." The words sounded naïve as they escaped from my lips. That it was our first time in the Amazon was obvious.

Mike just nodded and continued to draw on his cigarette.

"You've a lot of animals here." I smiled as innocently as I could. "Do you have any *monos de la noche,* owl monkeys? We have a male, but we need a female."

"Small, red-brown, big eyes? None this week. Maybe tomorrow, next week. They come in." Mike shifted his attention to an Indian carrying another crate and motioned for him to take it to the warehouse.

"Those animals, the ones in the crates, where are they going?" My voice was as nondescript as I could make it.

Mike looked up at Jamie, back at me, and then spoke defensively. "I take good care of my animals. They got food, they got water. Some of them die, but most of them make it to Florida. My operations are in Florida, Tarpon Springs. Ever been to Florida?" His eyes riveted on me.

"Yes, once. To Fort Lauderdale," I murmured, remembering a college spring break.

Mike continued. "Other dealers here, they don't have my kind of money. They can't feed the animals, they don't build regulation crates. Most of those animals they get . . . their animals just die. But my animals have it good. Yeah, they do fine."

Feeling that we'd exhausted our welcome, I looked for a way to retreat. "Thank you for your trouble. We'll be in Leticia a couple of weeks, and we'll check back here from time to time."

Mike nodded and ambled toward the house. We walked back to town, trying to shake off the sounds and smells of Mike's operation. We both knew that some of those animals would end up in our New York pet shop. We had met the other end of the reality of the pet trade, and it was not a pretty sight. We hadn't known about this cruelty when we bought Herbie. The fact that we had unconsciously contributed to this industry made me sad.

I was depressed. Day after day, the squalor, the mud, the crates of animals, the oppressive heat, and the dawning realization that we wouldn't find a wife for Herbie were beginning to wear on me. Herbie actually fared better, settling into his routine of tropical fruits, freshly caught insects and spiders, and two strolls a day around town in Jamie's shirt. In the afternoons and evenings, Jamie unpacked his briefcase of oil paints, meticulously bringing to life the jewels he collected around Leticia: frogs, butterflies, and beetles. Each painting was more vivid than the last. Herbie busied himself near Jamie, picking up brushes, chewing on fruit, and hopping in and out of Jamie's shirt. Some of the paintings were so realistic that Herbie would pounce on them with the alertness of a hunter. Then Herbie would look up at Jamie, sheepishly acting as if he'd known it wasn't a real spider or insect the whole time.

The evenings passed by quickly for Herbie and Jamie, but I was tired of writing letters. I wanted to leave Leticia—this manmade, muddy, filthy, stinking purgatory—and see the rainforest, but boats were prohibitively expensive. Even for an hour or two, the price was over a hundred dollars, and on our budget that was impossible. We were trapped, and our time in the Amazon was running out.

The third week that the boats arrived without owl monkeys at the docks, my frustration and disappointment reached new levels. We had tickets to leave in a few days, and our Leticia trip had been a total failure. Jamie's first painting was nearly finished, but now even his patience had worn thin and he grumbled about getting out of town. Hoping a strong cup of coffee would help, we went out for breakfast. As we reached the port, a slight, round-faced Ticuna Indian, dressed in patched and muddy jeans, timidly stopped us. He smiled, looked at his feet, and asked us if we wanted a boat ride up the river. We would see monkeys. His Spanish wasn't much better than ours. He hadn't been the first person to ask if we wanted to go on a boat trip, and the next step—negotiating the price and discussing how expensive gasoline is on the Amazon—usually ended the conversation. This man, however, mentioned a price of about ten dollars. I hesitated, surprised at how low it was. He then lowered it to eight.

"We're ready," I said.

Jamie and I followed the Ticuna down to the dock. As he began untying his boat, we glanced at each other as we realized why his offer was so inexpensive. His motor wasn't a Johnson but a paddle. We delicately boarded the very small dugout canoe and the Ticuna paddled us upstream with the skills of one born to the job. The noise, bustle, and squalor of Leticia drifted into the distance, and a celestial calm enveloped us. The oars dipped into the water, almost silently propelling us along close to the shore. The current was weaker near the riverbank, and we could nearly touch the vegetation. A chorus of birds signaled that it was still early morning. Pairs of scarlet macaws flew high above the canopy, raucously chatting even in flight. The mysterious green tapestry of intertwined vines and river-side vegetation guarded the secret world within. Occasionally, a cascade of flowers, like a grandiose wedding bouquet, spilled out into the water. Jewel-like, iridescent hummingbirds sipped from it, one blossom at a time. Butterflies glimmered in the sun as they, too, tasted the sweet nectar.

The river was so high and broad that the other side was barely visible. Huge uprooted trees struggled in the middle, like toothpicks carried out to sea. Our canoe, fashioned from a similar tree, moved slowly ahead. The muscles of our guide bulged with years of fighting this river. We had confidence in his skills, but our fragility was humbling. One false move, a sudden start to see a caiman or one clumsy lurch to avoid a branch, and we'd all be prey to the river. But a spell had fallen over us, and we sat silent and still, enraptured by the jungle that we had dreamed about.

The clear sunlight began to remind us that we were in the tropics, and we hadn't brought sunscreen, hats, mosquito repellent, water, or food.

We'd been traveling for nearly two hours when the dug-out began to turn right. The green wall opened, and a smaller stream split the greenness like a machete opening a trail. Our Ticuna kept paddling and was silent as we looked back for some signal. Then the front of the canoe glided to the water's edge. Jamie agilely jumped to shore, but I wobbled and lunged toward the muddy bank. The guide smiled at my lack of coordination and tied the boat. He moved ahead of us onto a trail, swinging his machete, leveling overhanging branches with the pinging noise of a professional.

The trail was wet, and my flip-flops, which had done perfectly well in Leticia, sank into the ooze. There was a snap and my bare foot lunged into the air. Embarrassed, I pulled the shoe out of the mud and snapped the toe-thong in place. Two steps later, I was stuck again. The Ticuna had stopped, amused. Jamie, who of course had worn proper shoes, looked annoyed, then gave a wry smile. "Cinderella?" he asked.

After one more attempt to walk in the mud, I took off both shoes and put them into my sack.

"Barefoot," I said to the Ticuna.

He shook his head. *"Spinas,"* he said, referring to the thorns. He offered to give me his rubber boots, but they were much too small for my oversized American feet.

"My feet are too big!" I told him.

"Cinderella's sister," murmured Jamie.

"Barefoot," I said again and began to walk confidently without shoes, mud oozing up through my toes.

My attention was pulled to a Morpho butterfly the size of my fist, lazily flapping down the trail, its iridescent blue wings glinting in the sun that splashed through the canopy. The clear, loud birdcall of the screaming piha, like a wolf whistle, dominated the air and then the harsh din of what I knew must be parrots and macaws joined in.

Our excitement increased as the dissonant calls became louder. Then the Ticuna stopped, pointing to a giant 130-foot-high strangler fig tree just off the trail. I had read about strangler figs, but to see this monster, its trunk braided a hundred feet up to the canopy, was something else altogether. This giant had started from a seed, dropped on a broad branch in the canopy by a bird or monkey. The seed had grown down slowly, embracing an adult tree with its tendrils, squeezing and draining its life until the parent tree died. The strangler, without a backbone of its own, had literally overcome the parent tree in a transformation that had taken more than fifty years. Despite the horror of the botanical bodysnatching, there are benefits. Once or twice a year the adult strangler fig produces millions of bright red and yellow blueberry-sized fruits that are feasted on by hundreds of species, mostly birds and monkeys. The one we saw was providing a feast for a flock of green Amazon parrots and a giant toucan. At least, those were the birds we could identify without binoculars or a bird book.

We'd been staring up at the circus of movement, entranced for over half an hour, when the Ticuna said softly, "*Monos.*" His keen ears had picked up a signal. We began to move quietly up the trail. Or tried. Even barefoot, despite my father's instructions when I was a child, I walked with the stealth of an elephant. The Ticuna pointed up to the canopy and kept moving. The small shadowy figures jumping high in the trees were indeed monkeys. Small, fast, black monkeys, fast monkeys, dancing away from us. The last in line hesitated for a

minute, curiously looking down, tilting his elfin face nearly
upside down to get a good view. His alert eyes sized us up. He
grimaced like a naughty leprechaun and chattered menacingly.
And then they disappeared into the greenness. We'd seen monkeys! Glowing with happiness, I turned to our guide.

"*Mico*," he said matter-of-factly. "*Blanco*," and he pointed
to below his nose.

"Marmoset," said Jamie. "Some kind of black marmoset
with a white mustache."

"They're fast," I said, thinking how hard it would be to follow them.

I could see the Ticuna was amused by our intense enthusiasm. For him, this must have been everyday life. For us, expe-
riencing the smells, sounds, and sights of the rainforest for the
first time, it was like falling in love.

After a few hours, our guide turned around: it was time to
head back. In our enthusiastic delirium we had not noticed
the huge black clouds. We were out on the Amazon heading
downstream before the rain hit in sheets of gray, pounding
us relentlessly. I was blinded and chilled by the force of the
water. By the time we reached Leticia, the thunderstorm had
passed, but we were drenched, shivering, sunburned, hungry,
exhausted, muddy, and happy. Totally happy.

After washing my very muddy feet by the pier, I put on my
flip-flops. We paid our guide ten dollars, and he grinned his
thanks and disappeared into a bodega. We were heading up
the road for food when we heard someone speaking English
to us.

"Find your monkey yet?" Standing in front of us was Chip,

a red-haired American college student from Boston who had arrived at our hotel the day before. He was spending a week on the Amazon getting "experience in jungle ways."

"I've been looking for you," he said. "I was hoping you'd want to share the cost of a boat trip downriver. There's a cool ceremony going on this afternoon at a village. We'll be the only white people there but my friend here, Mico, speaks Spanish and knows this village. He'll take care of us."

He pointed to an Indian man who stood in a blue painted boat with an ancient lawnmower motor attached to its keel. I forgot how wet, hungry, and cold I was. I was eager to visit an Indian village. The Ticuna had settled here thousands of years ago and lived mostly by fishing. I wanted to ask my Ticuna guide questions about his culture, but without a common language, that was impossible. Jamie, a little begrudgingly, reached in his pocket for the twenty-five dollars for our share of the boat. I gulped water from Chip's bottle, not realizing it was our afternoon's supply. The sun had returned with scorching heat, and the drone of the motor added to our exhaustion.

Half an hour downriver, the boat stopped at a cluster of wooden dwellings on stilts. All jungle villagers cleared the vegetation down to bare earth in order to rid their living space of tarantulas, scorpions, ticks, chiggers, and biting ants. Each house was thatched with palm, was open from the sides, and had hand-woven rope hammocks strung from the rafters like large, tattered spider's webs. One long, open house with a thatched roof was decorated with palm fronds and flowers. Resident Ticunas and their relatives milled around the village's central courtyard. Their faces were painted with bright red lines and black dots, and their long vest-like clothes were covered with hand-painted animal designs.

We nudged Chip, and he leaned over to Mico. Chip translated that the red paint was made from achiote, a bush with spiny pods filled with red-orange pulp. After the ripe pods were harvested, the pulp was removed and mashed together to make body paint. The black dye came from a peach-sized fruit borne by a canopy tree called a *Genipa*. The clothing was made of bark pounded into fabric.

As we approached the central square, we could hear drums throbbing rhythmically and women chanting. In the middle of the group was a young girl of about twelve years of age, sitting on a mat. An older woman, perhaps her grandmother, her face heavily painted with black dye, was chanting loudly, and six other women, perhaps the mother and sisters, also chanted. The girl was dressed in a bark cloth sarong stained with red. The red was blood. As I peered through the crowd trying to get a better view, I realized that the grandmother was plucking strands of hair out of the girl's head, one by one, while the girl sat stoically without flinching or crying out, her head bowed. Tears were running down the girl's face as the chanting increased in volume. Nearly all her hair was gone, the last few strands still on her bloody scalp.

I was so delirious from exhaustion and hunger that the scene seemed surreal. I was in shock, never having even read about this custom and now so near, wincing at every hair plucked. Feeling faint, I reached over to Jamie for reassurance. But Jamie was not looking like a pillar of strength either.

I nudged Chip. "What is happening to her?"

Chip spoke with Mico and translated. "It's a puberty ceremony marking the passage into adulthood. The girl was kept alone in that hut over there with no food for three days. Only her grandmother could go in and talk to her and tell her the secrets women are supposed to know. And then this morning at dawn she was carried out here. The grandmother will pluck out every hair on her body, and then the girl will be washed. When all her childhood is washed away, she will be an adult and she will meet her new husband and the festivities start."

It looked like the festivities had started a little ahead of schedule. A crowd of a couple hundred people were standing in a circle around the main event, talking, jostling, and apparently ignoring the ceremony. Their focus of attention was a large round gourd, hollowed out like a bowl, which was being passed around. The gourd was filled with three or four cups of a bubbly, custard-like liquid. Each recipient took it with both hands, drank the whole gourd at once, and returned it to a wooden canoe, where it was filled and given to the next person.

Chip's voice broke into my trance again. "That wooden canoe is filled with *masato*, a cassava root mush that the women in the village chewed and spit into that canoe days ago. Then it was covered with palm fronds and allowed to ferment until it's alcoholic enough for this ceremony. It won't ferment unless it's mixed with saliva, and men's saliva won't work."

The haphazard milling of the crowd gave me the impression that the gourd had made several rounds. When the gourd arrived, Jamie drained it easily. My turn was next. My head was pounding like the drumbeat, and I hadn't eaten lunch. I was about to decline the frothing gourd, but looking up I recognized smiling eyes. It was our Ticuna guide from the morning. This must be his village, his family, I thought, and I felt to refuse the masato would be very rude. I took a deep breath. The drink was bitter and frothy, with the sting of alcohol. I drained the bowl, smiled weakly to hide the waves of nausea that were flowing over me, and handed back the gourd. As our guide disappeared into the crowd, the ceremony began to crescendo.

Chip found us again. "The hair thing is over," he whispered. "Now the women from the family will wrap her in that mat and carry her down to the river to wash and dress her."

Just then, a roar of human voices came from behind us, and twenty or more masked men came out of the shadows, shouting. The masks and costumes were made of hand-painted bark fabric and hid the fact that their wearers were very drunk. All the women in the village clasped hands in a circle around the girl to ward off this invasion of demons. As the men charged the women, I could see bulges pointing out from under their costumes. Were these phallic symbols, or not symbols at all? I clung to Jamie as the drunken men charged to the drumbeats, trying to break the chain of intertwined women. Unsuccessful, they retreated to the back of the houses, as the ritual demanded, before returning for a second and third time. Again and again, the women rebuffed them. The demons staggered menacingly, intoxicated with masato, the music, and the rite itself.

Abruptly, one masked demon broke away from the others and charged toward me, growling. I realized the below-the-belly bulges were wooden sticks tied around their waist with vines, symbolic of the occasion. Jamie stepped between me and the demon and it returned to the others. My heart was joining my stomach in its rebellion as I reeled.

"I want to go back," I whispered to Jamie, as the women lifted the girl over their heads, still chanting, and carried her toward the river.

Jamie hesitated. "Let's wait till after the feast."

Although I was feeling faint and had a splitting headache, I was also very hungry and the smells of smoked meat were tempting. The girl's family was already distributing huge portions of roasted dried fish and meat and cassava. The food tasted smoky, salty, and good. Then the gourd full of masato returned and the music became louder and more dissonant. The sun was setting, and an evening chill set in.

By this time, the girl had returned in her new robes, and her father began making a speech. The older man, with red achiote stripes on his cheeks and forehead, his head adorned with a crown of toucan and macaw feathers, handed a plate of food to a young man who also had a painted face and bright red macaw feathers in his black hair. The young man gave the girl what must have been her first meal in three days. She took the meat with head bowed, and moved away from him. At first, I thought he was her fiancé, but it appeared she didn't like him. He approached her, coaxing her in a low voice. She rebuffed him and ran to her grandmother's side. The father began to talk again.

Chip whispered his interpretation from Mico. "That young guy wants to marry her, but the girl doesn't want to marry him. The father is saying she needs more things: a house, more clothes, maybe a bushpig. She isn't ready to promise him anything yet. Now the young guy is saying he'll get a house, more clothes, and if the spirits of the forest are willing, even a bushpig."

This time the father seemed happier, but the girl just started eating. The crowds returned to their drinking and eating and the drums began again. "Is that it?" I asked. "Is that the beginning of their romance?"

And then I realized how exhausted and confused the girl must be. As for her suitor, well, he had drunk enough masato to soothe the pain of a rough beginning to the relationship.

Filled with bushmeat and crunchy fried cassava, Jamie and I walked away from the crowds to view the sunset. The sun was like a red wafer dipping into the Amazon, streaking the sky with blood-red lines. The disturbing events of the ceremony dominated my mind, but the scene was softened by the sound of frogs and insects, the rising full moon, and the breathless beauty of the moment. Jamie and I convinced a Ticuna to paddle us up the Amazon to home and Herbie. Chip stayed on until dawn.

The next morning, we got up late in a panic. Our timetable was running out—our flight for Bogotá left in two days. We'd slept in and were late for the boats. By the time we made it to the docks, there were no animals at all coming off the water. Dejected, we were walking back for coffee, barking at each other for oversleeping, when Chip appeared, looking like he'd had a sleepless night.

"Did you get your monkey? It had big eyes and was small."
His words blurred together and I asked for clarification.

"An Indian brought it in this morning. You weren't there. I think the Indian took it to Mike. All the animals go to Mike. . . ."

Before Chip could finish, both Jamie and I started running toward Mike's warehouse. We rapped anxiously on the door and Mike appeared, cigarette in hand.

"Yeah, I think we did get one of those night monkeys this morning," he said. "Let me see. Must be in Shed Three." And he spoke in Spanish to some of his workers.

Holding our breath, we waited for the Indian to return from the shed. There in his hands was a sleepy little red-chested owl monkey, with big, amber eyes blinking in the tropical sun. "It's beautiful." I sighed in disbelief. And as I took the owl monkey in my arms, I stroked its dense fur to reassure it. It was like holding a baby for the first time. "Is it a male or female?" I asked.

Then realizing how silly that sounded, I checked. "It's a girl. We've found a wife for Herbie!"

Then I looked up and saw Mike's face. The ruthless businessman cracked a smile. "How much is she?" I asked, realizing a little late that my honest eagerness to own this monkey might have increased the price.

"Well, I'll give her to you for the same price I paid the Indian who brought her this morning—two dollars."

I couldn't believe our good luck. The monkey was shy but not afraid, and she nestled into my shirt out of the sun. We joyfully set off for her first meeting with Herbie. She was beautiful, but not the same color as Herbie; none of his muted browns and beiges. Her eye patches were whiter, her black eyebrows were darker, and her underside from her throat to her tail was a rich pumpkin orange, offset by her deep brown back. Her long sleek tail was jet black. Since the books had said there was only one species of owl monkey, I knew she was the right species. Herbie was probably just from a different region.

"Let's call her Kendra," Jamie suggested, and Kendra she became. The truth was, I'd never seen any animal as beautiful as Kendra, and we could tell by her sharp teeth and her sweet face that she was young, maybe just over a year old. Wait till Herbie sees his wife, I thought.

As we entered our room, Herbie was asleep, curled up on a pillow under the blankets. Hearing our voices, he popped his head out and opened his eyes blearily. Like anyone woken in the middle of the night, he wasn't too pleased.

"Maybe we shouldn't spring her on him too fast," Jamie said, trying to mellow my matchmaking enthusiasm.

I wrapped Kendra in my sweater with her head peeking out and placed her on the table near the window. She seemed very worried about her unfamiliar surroundings and glanced around apprehensively. Herbie's eyes were closed against the brightness of the daylight. He hadn't seen whom we'd brought. He hadn't seen his beautiful red-chested bride.

After about half an hour of patient waiting, we decided to give our new pet a piece of banana. As we approached the window, talking softly to her, she nestled into the sweater for protection and Herbie opened his eyes. He looked toward the window, his black pupils the size of pinpoints. He blinked and looked again, as if not believing what he saw. We held our breaths in anticipation of this romantic first meeting. What was Herbie thinking? It must have been over two years since he'd seen another owl monkey. He would be thrilled to see one of his own kind again, and she was such a beauty!

Kendra reached out to sniff the banana we'd left on the edge of the table, and Herbie sprang into motion. Suddenly, there were two balls of fur racing around the room, hitting the floor and bouncing off the walls. This was no courtship ritual. Herbie was chasing the invader with the fury of an assassin. His hair was on end and he made a loud vibrant noise we'd never heard before. Kendra was terrified and running for her life.

Jamie joined the chase around that small room and I screamed and clapped and tried to distract Herbie. Finally, Kendra ran under the bed out of sight, and Herbie leaped onto Jamie's head, puffed up like a pompom. The chase had lasted only moments, but we were all out of breath.

"Not exactly the best way to begin a relationship," I said. "What happened? What went wrong? She's young, beautiful. What's his problem?" I couldn't keep the discouragement out of my voice.

"We haven't learned how to think like an owl monkey yet," replied Jamie. "We don't know the rules. We don't know what makes one monkey choose another for a wife. We just don't know what we're doing."

"I think they just need more time," I said. "It's all been too abrupt. He resents being dumped into this relationship."

"Herbie doesn't know he's here to get a wife," Jamie protested. "He thinks he's in the Amazon on vacation."

I shook my head and sat down on the bed. I thought of the Ticuna girl. "Relationships take time and patience. And they need that special spark."

"Well, this relationship has plenty of sparks," said Jamie sarcastically. "He hates her."

I had to agree.

I prepared two bowls of food and slipped one under the bed. The plate was empty in the morning. As long as Kendra stayed out of sight, Herbie didn't attack her. But we had serious scheduling problems. Our flight was leaving Leticia the next day. We needed to settle our bills and pack. There was no time to find Herbie another female that he might like better, and we couldn't carry those two owl monkeys in the same cage. With little problem, we bought a suitable piece of carry-on luggage. However, getting Kendra into the cage was another story. After two hours of struggle, both monkeys were in their separate carriers and we were packed. We bid goodbye to Leticia.

There was a large crowd at the airport. Even though it was still morning, it was hot and humid. Although we'd come to learn that in South America lines are unknown—everyone just pushes and shoves in one undulating mass to the counter— the pressure seemed particularly urgent on flights like the one we were taking. Small planes flew to Bogotá once a week and were often overbooked. The fact was that those at the end of the line often didn't fly that day. When I reached the ticket counter, I noticed my wallet was gone. My tickets were in my hands but our passports, our cash, our traveler's checks had all disappeared. I searched my purse over and over with the same result. Gone. I'd been pickpocketed.

The ticket agent was patient. "Passports are often stolen here, especially US passports. You should've been more careful. Yes, you can go to the authorities, but they will do nothing. What can they do? Anyone could have taken it, and it's already gone downriver, probably to Brazil."

Angry at my carelessness and our helplessness, I was overwhelmed. The thought of being trapped on the Amazon for who knew how long terrified me. Tears welled up in my eyes.

"Calm down," the ticket agent comforted me. "You lost your passport. It's not the end of the world. You will have to go to the embassy in Bogotá and they will give you a new passport. You can go on this flight; you don't need a passport for internal flights. Go ahead to Bogotá, you can get money, and a passport at the US Embassy."

Just then, I remembered the monkey visas from the Colombian embassy. Had I lost those, too? I leafed through my documents and to my relief found that I'd tucked the monkey visas into a pouch separate from our US passports. Thankfully, they were there. The US Embassy in Bogotá wouldn't have been able to replace those two priceless documents.

Jamie, Herbie, Kendra, and I were soon flying over that green nubbly carpet heading north to the mountainous capital of Bogotá. We were much wiser than we'd been two months before. This time, we knew the beauties that lay under that canopy. We'd seen the magnificent Amazon, the second largest river in the world, and we'd found a female owl monkey, although the jury was out on whether Herbie would ever accept her as a mate. Even with the recent events of the theft, we felt the trip had been a success.

In Bogotá, we checked into the cheapest hotel we could find, Maria's Hotel. We explained to Madam Maria that we might have to stay a week or so while we waited for our passports, and we had very little money. Very little. We agreed on the price of a dollar fifty a week for the room. The madam was quite a big woman, about fifty years old, with an abundance of makeup and very long, black hair. But she loved animals and was pleased to have two monkeys as her guests. She didn't seem bothered at having two gringos either.

The room had only the price to recommend it, being small, dirty, and infested with cockroaches, and far from the honeymoon suite it had been advertised to us as. Since we didn't know how long we were going to be there, I decided I'd better do some cleaning. After all, this was Kendra's first experience in civilization, and under the bed was her only refuge.

We visited the American embassy downtown that afternoon. The building was imposing from the outside, and the bright red, white, and blue flag in front reminded us of our homeland. The US Marines, clean-shaven and short-haired, were quite a contrast to disheveled and long-haired Jamie and me, as they asked for our passports inside the door. Our explanation was met with a distant stare, and a Marine motioned us to sit down and wait. We filled out forms for new passports.

After almost an hour, the Marine signaled us to enter the consulate's office. The consul official, dressed impeccably in a gray suit, sat behind his desk. He looked at our forms, noted that we were from New York, and asked if we had a photocopy of our original passports with us. We said we hadn't. Then the official explained that it would be a two-week wait before our new passports could be issued. I was stunned. We couldn't stay in this capital, penniless, for two weeks

The official, polite but firm, explained that the paperwork took that long, and there wasn't anything we could do about it. I objected, saying we had no money to eat. "You can call New York," he continued. "Your parents can send money to the embassy." As we left his office, we saw four other American tourists telling the Marines that they had been pickpocketed in downtown Bogotá. We weren't the only victims; lifting American passports seemed to be a Colombian national sport.

"Two weeks," I kept muttering. "What can we do broke in Bogotá for two weeks?"

The hotel didn't have central heating, and the chill of the Andes set in early that night. We had a giant wool blanket, but Kendra had never been in the mountains before, and she was under the bed instead of the covers.

Worried that Kendra would freeze, Jamie and I plotted our strategy. We decided that one reason for Herbie's violent negative reaction to Kendra could be jealousy. So we totally ignored beautiful Kendra and only paid attention to Herbie. The second part of the plan was not to put Kendra's food dish under the bed, but place one large plate filled with tempting foods on the table in the corner. We arranged a little cave of blanket at the foot of the bed and snuggled under the covers, leaving one dim light on. Herbie eagerly leaped to the food dish and gingerly chose the best grapes, the finest piece of papaya, and a crunchy green bean. When he'd finished feasting, he joined us under the covers, out of the cold.

About an hour later, Kendra slowly moved from under the

bed and carefully, stealthily, made her way up the chair, over to the table, and next to the dinner plate, keeping a watchful eye on Herbie. We could see her shivering from the cold. Herbie opened his eyes and watched her delicately eat several grapes and a piece of mango before he dashed toward the table, sending her scrambling under the bed. Then he returned to the pillow and went back to sleep. Our evening's sleep was less than restful. The hotel guests were talking loudly in the halls, banging on doors, and making noise until the early morning hours. It seemed that our "hotel" was particularly active on the weekends. Sometime before midnight, startled out of my sleep again, I noticed a bulge at the foot of the bed. The ruse had worked. In the morning, Herbie was asleep on our pillow, but Kendra was warm, snuggled in by our feet.

The couple's relationship seemed to be improving. Perhaps it was the chilly mountain air that brought them together, but on the second night in Bogotá, we caught them eating on the table at the same time. By the third night, Kendra was sleeping on our bellies, and on the fourth night, we woke up with two contented monkeys curled up between us. "This is a honeymoon suite, after all," I exclaimed, maybe too romantically.

Jamie, consistently skeptical, muttered, "At least they're not trying to kill each other, that's the first step."

From that moment on, however, the two monkeys were inseparable. Kendra followed Herbie's every leap and nuzzled close to him at every opportunity. They exchanged low, warm murmurs as they chatted. Kendra's new surroundings, as unlike the rainforest as I could imagine, were fine with her now that Herbie had ceased trying to kill her. I had learned another primate rule: A lone monkey is usually a dead monkey. Since predation is high in the rainforest, more eyes and ears to spot danger are very useful. Monkeys instinctively stay together for survival and even to stay warm on chilly evenings.

As soon as our passports arrived, we booked a flight out of Bogotá. Our tolerance for this cold highland city had ended long ago. We eagerly paid the madam and explained that we were on our way to Miami in the morning. Updated on the monkey romance, the madam was glad to hear that this time we only had to take one carrier on board. When we asked if she had an alarm clock to wake us for our early flight, she signaled to her son, who was sort of the receptionist, and instructed him to knock on our door at 7:00 A.M.

He didn't knock on our door at 7:00. At 8:00, I awoke with a start, and we jumped into action to get to the airport as quickly as possible. The thought that we might have to spend up to a week more in Bogotá because we'd missed our flight was intolerable. With monkeys in tow, we arrived at the Avianca counter almost exactly one hour late. I sighed, internally furious that we'd missed the flight, and asked when the next flight to Miami was so we could reschedule. The man behind the counter waved us away impatiently. I didn't understand and asked him again. His annoyance increased and he told us to get in line over there, and pointed us to a very long line at the next counter.

Discouraged, I waited in line. However, I was too patient. Everyone seemed to push in front of me, as was the custom. I'd lost my will to battle for position, and I was the last of the crowd to reach the agent. I laid our tickets on the counter.

Before I could ask about rescheduling, the agent gave me three passes: one for supper, one for breakfast, and one for a room at the Hotel Presidente. I blinked in amazement, not understanding the generosity. Then I looked at the board above me. Our flight to Miami had been canceled. The airline was required by law to put us up for the night because of the inconvenience they'd caused us. We hadn't missed the flight, it had missed us!

The four of us boarded the airline bus headed downtown. The Hotel Presidente was elegant and our room was palatial— a suite with a bed, covered with a rose-colored satin spread, that was three times the size of our previous one. The room was warm, with green wall-to-wall carpet, a phone, and a couch smothered in puffy pillows. There was an antique wooden desk, a giant brown leather chair, and a spacious green tablecloth with a vase of fresh pink roses. The bathroom was wonderfully modern, with a flush toilet, a large sink adorned with a fragrant bar of pink soap, and a bathtub with hot water. The contrast between the Hotel Presidente and Maria's Hotel, or, for that matter, our simple Amazon lifestyle, couldn't have been greater.

We opened the carrier, and Herbie and Kendra hopped out and carefully inspected their new home. Then they both made a bubbling purr that meant they really liked the place. Herbie moved to the bed to explore, then hopped to the table with Kendra following right behind. I touched Jamie's arm to be sure he was watching. Herbie was smelling the roses. How romantic! I thought. Then, Herbie delicately nipped off a petal and ate it, and to my horror Kendra joined in. Four roses had been demolished before I could stop them. I set out a plate full of papayas, mangos, and greens and shut the remaining roses in the bathroom.

After lunch, the monkeys continued their exploration. Kendra especially liked the soft pillows, and she and Herbie bounced up and down on the bed. The rest of the day Jamie painted, I wrote letters, and Kendra and Herbie just hung out. The night was peaceful, with no noisy guests. We'd decided to take advantage of staying at a fancy hotel and asked room service to send us breakfast at six in the morning.

At 6:00 A.M. a knock came at the door, and a woman dressed in a black-and-white, freshly ironed maid's uniform cheerfully wished us *buenos dias* and brought in a huge tray filled with papaya, mango, and pineapple slices, pastries, orange juice, and coffee. I motioned for the maid to put the tray on the table next to the bed. Just as she was about to set it down, off the curtain rod shot a furry little monkey, landing right on the maid's shoulders. Terrified, the maid dropped the tray on the table and ran out the door screaming in Spanish.

"Herbie!" I scolded. But Herbie and Kendra, grateful for their breakfast, were dining happily. "I guess they thought that breakfast was for them," I added.

"I guess it *was* for them. All we have left is the coffee!" Jamie pointed out.

Our next task was to get packed to go to the airport. We were eager to return to New York, having grown tired of hotel rooms, cheap restaurants, and transporting our bags everywhere. We were ready to settle down, at least for a while. But on that flight our anxieties were still high. Would customs let us return with both monkeys?

At the customs counter in Miami, the Fish and Wildlife authorities were at first puzzled by our monkey visas. "Both of the monkeys are healthy, have no problems, and they've just been on vacation with us for the last two months. Here, look for yourself." And I opened the carrier to reveal two very sleepy monkeys.

"They're so small," said the young Fish and Wildlife inspector. "I thought they'd be bigger. Beautiful eyes. What do you call them, owl monkeys?" He signed the form and we were free.

Before we knew it, we were back in our Brooklyn apartment. The familiar old couch, the stereo's well-known records, the faucet that ran clear water, the refrigerator that could keep beer cold and milk and meat from spoiling. It all was quite a treat. Everyone spoke English, even on television. And we could read the newspaper. Sometimes you have to go far away to realize what you have at home.

Herbie seemed to remember the apartment too, leaping to his favorite spots with Kendra following behind. She seemed to approve of her new home, lounging on the couch pillows, running along the curtain rod, and exploring the spacious kitchen with all its good smells. She was affectionate and liked to snuggle on our laps, nuzzle our shoulders, and be petted like a pampered housecat. Mango juice and avocado slices were her preferred delicacies. And when Kendra purred and looked up with those giant amber eyes, how could anyone refuse?

Kendra's personality was quite different from Herbie's. She didn't seem to take life as seriously as he did. He had his rules, which he imposed on her with the same severity as he had on us. He got up at dusk, went to bed at dawn, and held to a strict schedule with a sense of responsibility that contrasted with her relaxed demeanor. But now he was much more content to stay home when Jamie and I went out for the evening.

It all could have ended there: two happy couples living together in New York City. But it didn't take us many months before our longing for the rainforest became impossible to bear. The next step in my quest to learn about owl monkeys beckoned. This time, the question had to do with where *Aotus* was found. The books said there were owl monkeys in Panama, but not in Costa Rica. However, the rainforest was continuous between the two adjacent countries. Monkeys couldn't tell political borders, I was pretty sure of that. Why would the monkeys not be in both countries?

And so we bought more guidebooks. This time for Costa Rica.

CHAPTER THREE

TROPICAL DISEASES

(Costa Rica, 1972)

ONCE AGAIN WE found ourselves in a plane at JFK Airport, buckling our seat belts with a cat carrier full of monkeys underneath us. Our planning for this trip to Costa Rica had developed over a year and we felt quite organized. I'd taken a night course at New York University in Spanish and was well prepared for conversations. We'd land in San José, the mountain capital, and take the train east to the Caribbean coastal town of Limón. We'd hire boats up and down the coastline, diverting into the rainforest interior whenever possible to search for owl monkeys. Our goal this time was to document the northernmost forest where owl monkeys live. At the end, we'd planned a trip to the beaches of a Caribbean island. There was to be no monkey business there, just sun and piña coladas. The reason we had our two owl monkeys with us was simple. On the last trip, we'd had difficulty finding a babysitter for one monkey. This time, there were no volunteers for double the trouble.

We stayed only one night in San José. We were eager to see

the rainforest as quickly as possible, as we had only four weeks before I had to return to my social work job. The train ride was an all-day affair, starting from San José in the highlands, moving through cloudforest, down through the mountains, until we reached the valleys where the houses were thatched and on stilts. By the afternoon, as we looked out of the train window, the bananas declared we were in the lowlands; and by evening we'd reached Limón, the Caribbean port.

Our negotiations to go north began at the sea in the morning. Jamie and I approached a group of long dugout canoes docked at a river that was protected by a sandbar. Nearby, the Atlantic Ocean heaved its whitecaps defiantly at the beach, which was covered with black sand, spills from the central volcanoes, and accented with poisonous, translucent jellyfish shimmering like cupfulls of spilled Jell-O. The sea's vicious temperament was compounded by the abundant sharks and the hungry undertow. Although fishermen braved the Atlantic to bring back tuna and swordfish, those Costa Ricans who wanted to transport people and goods north or south avoided the seacoast and journeyed using a combination of inland canals and rivers.

Walking along the river's shore, we chose a long canoe, which had once been painted blue. More importantly, it had a twenty-five-horsepower Johnson motor adequate to travel up the canal. John, the owner, who was aged somewhere between fifty and sixty, was a dark-skinned, coastal Costa Rican, and he even spoke English. He would take us up to Tortuguero, near the Nicaragua border, for less than fifty dollars. We could stay at the Tortuguero research station and go into the forest.

The station's scientists were there now, he said, because it was the season.

"The season for what?" I asked John.

"The turtles are laying eggs on the beaches."

It dawned on me that the name *Tortuguero* meant "the place the turtles go." Tales of sea turtles migrating from remote islands to lay eggs on even more distant shores had always piqued my curiosity. Here was an opportunity to see this phenomenon in person.

We agreed to leave at dawn the next morning, and John chuckled when I told him about our monkeys. "Had a little monkey once," he remembered. "Kind of yellow-colored with a reddish back. Chittered all the time and ate rice and bananas. Nice little animal. Only bit me a couple of times, but then one day broke the string tied round his waist. Ran off. Never saw him again."

From my library readings I knew there were only four species of monkeys recorded in Costa Rica: mantled howlers, Geoffroy's spiders, white-headed capuchins, and red-backed squirrel monkeys. The small monkey John described must have been the red-backed squirrel monkey, the rarest of the group. We hoped to glimpse one on this trip, but the squirrel monkeys left in Costa Rica only numbered in the hundreds.

The next morning, Herbie and Kendra were sleeping in their carriers when we loaded up the boat. John was talkative. He lived alone, and it seemed like he'd been saving up his conversation just for us.

"My father was a Black from Belize. That's how come I speak English. First he came to Nicaragua fishing. One trip he came down this river to trade turtles and met my mother. My mother's mother had a bodega in Limón. And my mother sold him a case of beer. That's how it all began. I had three wives over these years. Maria, my first wife, was a real good-looker. Met her in Limón when she was visiting her cousin. We fell in love at first sight, but. . . ." His voice trailed off. Then he sat up, realizing he'd stopped. "Maria died birthing our first child. She was too young, only nineteen years old. Still remember her smile." And again his voice faded as the boat revved around a bend.

As the day wore on, the sun rose high and the stories of John's life and wives continued. His second wife lived in San José, and the third had disappeared with his best friend. He had ten children, all grown now and living in San José. There was more, but most of the time the motor made so much noise that we couldn't hear a word he said.

Jamie and I sat together staring at either side of the river, which was about forty yards across. John drove straight down the middle, checking ahead for fallen trees or other obstructions. The motor drowned out the sounds of birds and insects, but the sights were quite delightful. A glossy green and rusty red kingfisher darted low over the water, dipping dramatically into the river, then returned to the bank with a silvery fish dripping from its beak. Then, in one gulp, the fish was gone.

The straight white trunks of the *Cecropia* trees lined the banks like soldiers at attention. *Cecropia* are light-loving, fast-growing trees that prosper along edges such as riverbanks. Their canopies, like green umbrellas, are an uneven patchwork of large, lobed leaves. The fruit on the ones I saw looked like dangling earrings and reminded me of elongated green gum-drops speckled with black seeds. When we veered close enough to the banks, John pointed to the *Cecropia* trunks swarming with ants.

"Careful of that tree," he warned. "Those big black ants attack anything that touches that tree. Can kill you if enough of 'em get a chance at you. Latch onto your skin, hold on like a vise, inject their poison. Even if only one bites you, the pain lasts hours. You can get covered by hundreds of 'em. God help you then. That happened to my friend, José. He was in hell before we got those ants off. Delirious for days, almost died. Can still hear him screaming."

Not willing to let the topic drop, he continued. "Nope, nobody bothers those trees. No monkeys, not even vines touch those trees, 'cause if they do thousands of ants storm out of the trunk, ready to sting. Just like people, those ants have to protect their property.

"You see those leaves?" John meant the dead, brown, crumpled elephant-ear leaves caught in the crotches of the *Cecropia* tree branches. "Those leaves are sometimes not leaves. Look close. You seen a perezoso yet?"

Had I heard him right over the motor? Had he asked if I'd seen a lazy thing yet? I bent down, squinting into my dictionary. Yes, I was right, *perezoso* did indeed mean lazy.

"Look careful at them."

And then I saw one. It looked like a dead leaf, curled up in the crotch of the tree, but my binoculars revealed it had hair, a very small head, no ears, tiny eyes, and two claws at the end of a hand. What kind of a creature was this? A two-toed sloth, the closest thing to a plant that the animal kingdom has been able to produce.

"Mostly those perezosos sleep. But even perezosos gotta eat. So, once in a while, the critter slowly reaches out and eats a big green leaf. Just sits and reaches out. Real slow it chews the leaf, closing his eyes, enjoying the taste. Could take most half an hour to eat one leaf. And then when the leaf is finished, he closes his eyes and sleeps. The critter lives in one tree for months, waking up to eat a live leaf, looking like a dead one. Look, there's another one," he said. And we realized that almost every *Cecropia* tree had its own sloth.

"But what about the biting ants?" I asked.

"Ants don't care a bit about him. They probably think he's one of the leaves in the trees. I hear there's one strange thing they do. Never seen it myself, but my friend Ricardo saw it once. Saw one of those perezosos climb slowly down on a vine, claw over claw, very slowly. Took hours to make it all the way down to the ground. Then it dug a hole in the ground with those claws. When the hole was done, that critter turned round and sat in that hole, looking like it was thinking real hard. Well, it took a long time, but that sloth left a neat pile of crap in that hole, and then it used its claws to cover up that pile, just like a kitty-cat. And then it climbed back up into the same tree. That's what Ricardo said. Never seen it myself."

"John, that doesn't make much sense," I responded skeptically. "A animal that slow would get eaten on the ground."

"Could be the perezoso only shits a couple of times a year." John laughed, enjoying my amazed expression.

Jamie, who had been lulled into a nap by the motor, opened

his eyes. "Sloths must be great pets. Very low maintenance and no cleaning up. Maybe we can make an exchange: our monkeys for two, two-toed sloths."

"Jamie, go back to sleep," I muttered.

The sky overhead was blue, and the breeze created by the boat felt good in the hot sun, as hour after hour we droned on down the river, hypnotized by the world around us. It was late in the afternoon when the motor started to sputter.

"Looks like we're running out of gas just in time," said John. "My house is right round this bend. We'll eat some supper. Don't have much there. You like rice and beans? We can stay the night and get an early start for Tortuguero in the morning."

My head was throbbing from the motor and the sun, and my legs were cramped from a whole day on the wooden bench. Walking on land would be a welcome change.

John pulled into the bank, and as he tied up the boat we jumped ashore. As we climbed up to the house, I noticed a few chickens diligently scratching and pecking in the yard. A bare-dirt yard surrounded an unpainted wooden shack. The tin roof was rusted and the wooden porch railing was missing some pieces. Several steps were also missing, and we had to maneuver carefully into the house.

"Sorry, it's a simple place," John apologized as he heaved a burlap sack filled with rice onto the floor inside. "Haven't been here for a couple of weeks."

It might as well have been two years. As John swung open the shutters, the shabbiness of the interior struck me. Gray, weathered walls flanked unpainted wide-plank flooring. A calendar from three years ago, with a sun-faded Chinese woman holding a parasol and smiling seductively, curled down from the wall. The long, coppery antennae of a cockroach waved from behind her and disappeared. The smell of chickens melded together with the scent of mildew. The beds were simple wooden platforms, with no mattress or springs, and the table was accompanied by four handmade chairs, rungs askew. There was a woodstove, but no refrigerator. A Singer sewing machine with a hand crank reminded me that there had been wives here once, but it had rusted in spots. It shocked me to see how simply John lived every day.

Jamie and I helped build and fan the fire. Although it took over an hour before it was ready, our dinner of rice and beans, steaming on the tin plates, tasted warm and good. John boiled water and brought out green plastic cups, instant coffee, and condensed milk. He then reached into his travel bag for the last course, which was a large bottle of Guaro, the local rum. We toasted to the night, and with the hum of crickets and the buzz of cicadas chorusing in the background, John continued his story.

"My oldest daughter, Liliana, married a rancher. Moved near Santa Rosa to raise cattle. It's drier over there. Liliana had three children in three years, but I haven't seen them yet. She never writes, but my cousin visited her once and brought back the news. The first, a boy, was born with a crooked leg. Never will walk right, but the second son is strong and smart."

"Could the lame son be helped by an operation?" I asked.

"Don't know."

"Maybe an operation in San José?" I was trying to be optimistic.

"Maybe. It's far from Santa Rosa." He sighed deeply.

Lulled by the day on the river and the soothing rum, Jamie began to nod off. I yawned and was about to search for our sleeping bags. But John wasn't ready to retire yet.

"It's lonely here. Out in the bush. Not many women like to stay on the river. They want to be in the city with the bustle of markets and the chatter of friends. They don't like the isolation, the quiet."

"But it's so beautiful here with the river and the forest," I said. "Away from the pollution, the noise, the traffic. Much better than the city." As the words slipped easily from my lips, I hesitated.

"You like it here on the river, I can see that," John said. "You should stay." For a moment, I rolled that idea slowly around in my mind. Yes, I loved the forest, the wildlife, the peacefulness of the river. That was true. But could I really live this quiet life of cooking rice and raising chickens? Could I live with wooden benches and no electricity? Without flush toilets, hauling up buckets of water from the river, pounding mud-stained clothes in the streams? Never hearing the news, or going shopping? Day after day, year after year?

Rats began scurrying up in the rafters, quarreling and squealing. I glanced into the kitchen, happy to see that John had tied up the food. I brought the monkeys' carrier closer to our sleeping bags, and gave Herbie and Kendra some bananas to eat. I didn't dare let them out. This house had no screens, and once the monkeys escaped, who knows if we could ever get them back into the carriers?

My mind returned to John's question. Deep inside where the

real decisions are made, I realized I didn't want to live here. I realized that I didn't want to deal with the realities of everyday frontier life.

"Sorry, John, we have to go back to New York. But right now we need to get a good night's sleep." And I crawled into my sleeping bag.

The next day, we reached Tortuguero Research Station. John helped us unload and introduced us to Bob, the interim station manager. Tall and tanned, Bob was a research assistant there and was pleased to show us around. More scientists were arriving next week, he told us, but this week he was in charge. The small research station had dormitories for guests with screens on the windows. Bob was amused as Herbie and Kendra hopped out of the carriers. A quick glance around the room to size up the place and the agile team was busy cleaning up all the insects and geckos they could find. We added a dinner of tropical fruits and left them to finish their exploration, carefully locking the door of our room.

Bob offered to take us on a tour of the beach and told us about the turtles.

"Sea turtles are ancient creatures that spend most of their life swimming in the ocean. The female sea turtles over age twenty-five years swim up to 1,000 miles to return to the beach where they were born to lay their eggs."

The black sand was hot under our feet and I rushed to get near the wet rim of the sea. "You're lucky," said Bob. "The female turtles have just arrived. Why don't you come out with me tonight to tag them?"

Eager to be part of the research, that night we accompanied

Bob out on his beat with our flashlights in hand. Bob, wearing cutoff jeans and a blue windbreaker with a daypack slung casually over his shoulder, continued his stream of information from the afternoon as we left for the beach.

"There are seven species of sea turtles alive today. Often specialist feeders, the hawksbill dines exclusively on sponges, the leatherback eats primarily stinging jellyfish, and the young green turtles prey on jellyfish, small mollusks, crustaceans, and even sponges. But larger adults are strict herbivores, consuming seagrasses and algae. We'll see green sea turtles on the beach tonight."

The black sand beach and the thunderous whitecaps brilliant in the full moon made a marvelous background for the gigantic lumbering turtles as they pulled themselves up over the sand. First we saw one, and then two, and soon realized that there must be eighty turtles within sight, all plodding out of the waves onto the shore. Many had started with the first step of creating a nest site by removing the dry sand with their front feet and rotating their shells to tamp down the damper sand. Then, with her back flippers, each female began to dig a deep hole in which to lay her eggs.

"Each female will lay hundreds of ping pong ball–sized eggs in her hole, then cover the nest with sand," continued Bob. "Not many of those eggs will actually hatch, since turtle eggs are very tasty—for people, dogs, raccoon dogs, anything that can dig in the sand. And of the pocket-sized turtles that do hatch, the birds eat a lot of them." Bob was peering into the dark with his funnel of light, checking for tags on the glistening carapaces.

"But it's not just the young ones that are preyed upon. Adult sea turtles are hunted for their meat and to make tortoiseshell jewelry. A large green sea turtle can be over a hundred years old and weigh a quarter of a ton, maybe even 400 pounds, but the big ones are becoming rarer and rarer." Bob sighed. "Look, that female is tagged. I've got to record that number."

We would have wandered on the beach all night watching turtles and recording their tag numbers, but just before midnight the moon disappeared and sheets of rain sent us racing back for shelter. We were quite soaked and chilled when we returned to our monkey companions.

It rained all the next day, and the next. The novelty of our location wore off and Bob became engrossed in analyzing his data and trying to make the shortwave radio work. A rainy beach had no appeal, and my head was throbbing, probably because of the high humidity. To top it off, my usual cast-iron stomach decided not to get along with all that rice and beans, and I was spending extra time in the outhouse. Jamie didn't want to go exploring in the forest alone and tried to convince me I was feeling better. All I did was moan.

"Get up," he said. "I have to find John and ask him about this place. Don't just lie there. You'll feel better if you move around." I rose, dressed, and followed him down to the dock. We found John in the shed, tinkering with one of the station's motors with his friend.

"We were wondering about the forest around here. Are there any monkeys?" Jamie queried from the doorway. "Can we go into the forest?"

John looked up slowly, shaking his head. "That forest is

filled with terciopelos. You can't go out for even a short walk without risking your life."

My damp dictionary was stuck in my pocket, and I quickly flipped to the t-section. *Terciopelo* meant "velvet" in English.

"Terciopelos look like a black velvet ribbon with a beige diamond pattern on its back. Beautiful. But don't be fooled, because they are the meanest, most aggressive, most poisonous snakes in the world. These big snakes, they chase you down, and attack like fury. After they bite, it's only a few hours before you're dead. An awful, agonizing death. My brother was killed by a terciopelo."

"Must be a fer-de-lance," Jamie muttered. "It's a pretty deadly snake."

"They're abundant in these forests?" I asked hesitantly.

"Everywhere," replied John. "I don't like to go out in the forest. I stick to the river and the beach. I don't know if you can even find a guide."

I was getting discouraged about wandering around in the jungle looking for owl monkeys at night. A combination of the torrential rains, my illness, and the tales of velvet, deadly snakes convinced Jamie and me to return south and try to get closer to the border with Panama. The next day, we packed up the monkeys and started back to Limón. At the port, we bid John goodbye and boarded a bus south to the coastal town of Cahuita.

Cahuita was a small town at the end of the road south from Limón. Built on stilts for the hurricane season, it had about 500 inhabitants. We chose Cahuita because it bordered a huge expanse of rainforest reserve that extended down into Panama. If we were going to find owl monkeys in Costa Rica, this would be the place.

All the business in this coastal town was owned by one Chinese family, and that included the new hotel. Wooden, on stilts, and basic, it had screened windows and met our needs. We tried unsuccessfully to locate a guide in town. The Costa Rican Indian groups had been exterminated nearly a century ago, and not many of the coastal colonists knew the forest. As a result, we bought our first machete.

At dawn the next day, we went out on the edge of the reserve and walked along the beach. The sea was brutal here, too. Uprooted trees had been heaved onto the shore, breaking the beauty of the shoreline with haphazard debris. But some of that beach litter consisted of colorful shells that showed an impressive diversity of invertebrate architecture. The luxuriant rainforest melted tantalizingly into the shore. There were no trails into the forest so we proceeded slowly. As luck would have it, we heard monkeys. The rustling of branches was our first clue, followed by the long, low whistles and loud chucking noises. They were approaching us, and we waited expectantly in silence, binoculars ready.

Then we had our first glimpse. White heads and chests, organ grinder–monkey faces. Capuchins! The smartest monkeys in the Americas. Weighing about five pounds, the females led the pack, intent on finding palm trees and other delicacies. Behind these five females was a central male, slightly bigger and burlier, with decidedly longer canines protruding from his mouth. When the male saw us, he gave us a warning smile, showing how very big his canines were. The group of about twenty monkeys did not seem afraid of us; in fact, they were noisy and playful and seemed much more intent on ripping apart palm trees or play-wrestling. Most began hanging by their tails while reaching out with their hands for the tiny red fruits suspended like Christmas decorations at the tips of branches. We watched every move in their daytime drama, fascinated by their activity, as they descended to some fruit trees at the edge of the forest near the beach.

"Jamie, this is paradise—the beach, the forest, the monkeys," I said. Just then, I caught sight of a shadowy male figure, nearly naked, coming out of the forest. He had long hair and a shotgun.

"Hey, what are you doing here?" He spoke to us in English.

"Watching the monkeys," I replied. "What about you?"

"I live here. I've lived here for almost five years. I eat things from the forest, not monkeys, but peccaries and birds. Where are you from?"

Confused by his train of conversation, I replied, "New York, Brooklyn."

"Do you want to buy some grass?" the man asked next. "I've some pretty good stuff here. Panama Red. Have you heard of Panama Red?"

Jamie's shoulder-length curly hair, cutoff jeans, and T-shirt had probably given this man the confidence to broach the subject. But we were very cautious about this kind of activity. The joys of a Central American jail, or even stiff fines, didn't appeal to us. After all, we were monkey parents, with all the incumbent responsibilities.

So we declined, but instead sat on the beach and chatted

with the man, whose name was Joe. We realized that he was representative of a growing set of refugees, far from the constraints of the American law. Drug-dealing kept them in cash, but cultural isolation took its toll. At least Joe wasn't making much sense. He talked about sharks, and how he never bathed in the sea, only in the forest streams. He talked about eating parrots and turtles. He talked about buying more shotgun shells in Cahuita, a trip he made every month or so. We nodded and watched the monkeys until late in the afternoon.

"Ever seen monkeys at night?" I asked, breaking into his monologue.

"Once," said Joe. "There were two small ones with giant eyes. They looked like owls as they came down over the hut, tilting their heads from side to side. No ears, just round faces with big eyes. Curious guys. Like Halloween spooks. They were monkeys or demons, I don't know. I scared them away and they never came back."

Jamie and I were excited. This was our first evidence that there were owl monkeys in Costa Rica. But could we trust what Joe, a man surely prone to hallucinations and delusions, said? We needed to see for ourselves.

Joe wandered off, and we sat on the beach watching as a boat materialized on the horizon. The sun was low and drifting into oranges and reds, outlining the tiny craft against the line between sea and sky. As it came closer, we could see a single man paddling in the vicious sea. The whitecaps tossed the prow of the little boat high, then dropped it. With binoculars we could see a huge disc in the front of the boat.

"He must have a sea turtle," I said.

Indeed, when the man in the straw hat beached his hand-hewn dugout, a huge marbled brown and black carapace turned out to be the cargo. The sun was dipping into the sea, the darkness settling over the beach, and the sight of the magnificent turtle, maybe a hundred years old, resting in the boat with its throat cut made us sad. We knew she had been on her way to the beach to lay eggs. Seeing my expression, the fisherman explained that he had ten children, and he could sell this turtle for a good price. We decided to get back for dinner and walked solemnly along the beach to the hotel. When I unlocked the door to our room, I knew something was wrong. Kendra was looking morose and Herbie was nowhere to be found.

"Where is he?" I asked Kendra in vain. "The window, Jamie. He's weaseled his way out of the window screen."

Both of us were out the door in a shot, then I ran back in to tape the screen shut and close the door so we wouldn't lose Kendra as well. By the time I found Jamie, he had Herbie in his arms.

"Is he dead?" I burst into tears at the sight of his limp little form. Next to him was a sticky flypaper strip. After escaping from our room, Herbie must have begun to explore other chambers. Nobody was in this room, so the door must have been left ajar. The gummy strip must have been there for a while, since it was covered with insects. We could imagine Herbie jumping on this banquet. But the toxicity of the pest strip would have been too much for him. My sobs were uncontrollable. Why hadn't we come home earlier?

Just then, Herbie opened his eyes, glazed with poisons. At least he was alive. We carried him, limp and comatose, back to our room. Once inside, he roused a bit but started to vomit. Big, violent heaves, and then he collapsed again. It was a difficult night, and both Jamie and I sat by his side, cleaning him when he vomited. By dawn, Herbie had become less limp and sat up with his head tucked over his knees, as if sleeping normally. The vomiting had stopped, and his big round eyes were swollen, red, and miserable. He looked gratefully up at us, and we gave him a sip of water.

Although I hadn't been chewing on pest strips, my stomach problems were getting worse as Herbie's got better. I began vomiting every time I ate, and my diarrhea was back again. The tropics are well known for malignant diseases, and I worried that I'd drunk the wrong water. Two days after Herbie's near-death incident, while he had begun eating again, I was too sick to get out of bed. My head was swimming and my weakness made me feel that my spirit was being sucked into a whirlpool. I couldn't lift my head from the bed.

"Jamie, we have to go home early. I'm sorry we haven't found the monkeys, but I can't go into the forest like this. I can't even get out of bed. I'm really getting scared." And I closed my eyes.

"You don't have much of a fever," Jamie pointed out. "It's just that the humid lowland air has gotten you down. You should drink more Coke, it settles the stomach."

I just stared into space.

"Tell you what," he continued. "We'll go back to San José. You'll feel better there. And then we'll go to the beach on San Andrés—that's a tourist paradise. Sun and beach and coral reef: nobody can feel sick there."

We had purchased a side trip to the island of San Andrés, to lay on the beach for a week at the end of our trip. Jamie convinced me the seaside resort would cure me, and we were on our way to San Andrés.

But I didn't get any better there. I didn't care that San Andrés was one of the most beautiful islands in the world. I was miserable, and didn't leave the bed my first morning.

"Jamie, I'm just so feeble," I moaned. "I can hardly walk. I can't eat. I'm even throwing up Coke."

The second day on San Andrés I went out for a walk on the beach for only half an hour and then had to go back to our room, while Jamie went snorkeling. That night, I told Jamie that I couldn't even hold down water. My face was white through my tan, and my eyes were sunken, watery, and bloodshot. I was almost as thin as Jamie himself. "I have to go home," I said. "I mean home to New York."

Jamie sighed. He was not a bit ill and was completely enjoying the sunshine, the coral reef, and perfect surf. He reassured me that I'd be better the next day. If I wasn't, he'd check the international flights. I thought Jamie wasn't being fair not to respond to my illness, but I was too weak to object. Sure enough, I didn't improve, and Jamie went to the airport, only to return with bad news. "Well," he said, "it turns out San Andrés is an island without many scheduled flights. In fact the next plane off this island won't leave till Thursday. I hope you can wait two more days. I changed our tickets for the Thursday flight."

He looked at my ashen face. Even though a doctor might be expensive, it was time to get professional help. "Let's go down to the hospital and ask a doctor what to do," he continued. "You do look awful." I could see the concern on his face. When we reached the small hospital at the edge of town, we found the doors closed with a sign that said HUELGA! Nobody was to be seen. The hospital was abandoned.

"I guess that means 'gone to lunch.' On islands like this they take long lunch hours." I stopped my translation to look at my watch. "It's almost four, so they must be opening up again soon. Find someone to ask when the doctors will be back." In my delirium, I continued to be my overly optimistic self. I couldn't believe the hospital was closed that day.

Jamie approached a young woman with a child and asked when the hospital would be open. Seeing my drained face, she realized I was very ill.

"*Huelga* is 'strike,'" she said. "Everyone, all the medicos, doctors, nurses, secretaries, are on strike for higher wages. Nothing is open. No clinics, no other hospitals. You have to wait. Maybe next week the doctors will be working again."

Tears began to run down my pale face. I moved quickly to the side of the street and heaved again, trying to relieve my stomach of its distress. There was nothing we could do but leave the abandoned hospital. The sun beat down relentlessly as we searched for a nonexistent taxi. I collapsed by the sidewalk. Jamie picked me up and carried me back to the hotel. By this time, his nonchalance had vanished. He was really worried.

Trying to help our situation, the hotel manager lent us a book about tropical medicine. Jamie thumbed through the book. "Let's see. The nausea, weakness . . . you could have malaria or dengue fever. But no, your fever isn't high enough and you don't have chills that make your teeth shake. This must be it—*Giardia*, or maybe amoebas, both of which have symptoms of slight fever, nausea, diarrhea, and weakness."

I groaned. Herbie and Kendra nestled next to me purring, trying their best to comfort their ailing mother.

I stayed in bed all the next day trying to read, and that night a tropical storm hit. Like a dagger, the lightning lit up our room as if it were day, and only a second later the thunder boomed. The hotel quivered. Herbie and Kendra retreated under the bed.

The storm continued all night and by dawn we could see torrents of muddy water swooshing down the streets. It was Thursday, and, not believing the gravity of the situation, we took a taxi to the airport with Herbie, Kendra, and our luggage.

The cabdriver was discouraging. "No planes today, no planes tomorrow. Planes can't fly in this weather. I hear the whole airport is flooded. I heard on the radio it is the worst storm in a hundred years. No flights today."

I switched into desperation mode. I was sick. I had to get out. Surely the airplane pilots would understand that.

"Worst storm in a hundred years," the cabdriver repeated in response. "Leaving will be impossible today. Impossible."

We were insistent, and so he drove us all the way to the airport, the water parting beneath the wheels. Once we were there, we could see that our cabdriver had been right. The airport would have worked better as a harbor. We could see the roofs of the hangars, the departure gates, and the cargo building, but everything else was underwater. The water in the waiting room was up to my knees. I sloshed about holding the monkey's cages above my waist, frantically asking for news of the flights. The only person we could find just shook his head and said, "*Mañana.*"

Back at the hotel, I collapsed into bed. I didn't care what happened next. I was just happy to be in bed, and then asleep.

In the morning, the sun was blazing and the water had begun to retreat. Once again, we packed up for the airport. We arrived to a buzzing of other passengers, anxious and wanting to leave. Within three hours, the runway was dry enough for takeoff. When I woke up, we were at JFK. New York. Home. Jamie collected our luggage while I sat on a chair, weak and pale. We headed by taxi directly to the emergency room of New York University Hospital. I hadn't eaten for days, and I was badly dehydrated. The nurses put me on intravenous rehydration immediately and then, ironically, all my fluids were taken for testing. The next day, still wired up to the fluid-giving IVs, I felt weak, but better.

The doctor came in with the verdict. "Mrs. Wright. We've finished the first round of tests. We looked for malarial parasites in your blood, but so far we haven't detected any. It also looks like you don't have *Giardia* or dengue fever. We did find evidence of *Entamoeba histolytica* but that wouldn't be producing most of your symptoms. Mrs. Wright, there is one more thing." He hesitated, ominously, and my heart began to beat faster in apprehension. "We ran an extra test, and we have a definite diagnosis. Our tests show that you are pregnant. Congratulations!" And his seriousness gave way to a smile.

I was stunned. Having resigned myself to having a severe, maybe fatal, tropical disease, the news that all my illness had been caused by severe morning sickness was quite a shock.

Pregnancy was not exactly what we'd planned. I turned to Jamie, who looked very relieved, and then it began to dawn on him. A baby, after five years of marriage. We were about to have an addition to our family. A baby, a human baby. Hmm, we thought. What would Herbie and Kendra think of that?

CHAPTER FOUR

FATHER CARE

(Cape Cod, 1973–75)

AMANDA ELIZABETH WRIGHT was born on April 3, 1973, weighing in at eight pounds, eight ounces. Jamie made history by being the first father allowed into the delivery room at New York University Hospital. After the panting and pushing and the process of childbirth, I was exhausted when I first met Amanda, and looked up to see Jamie holding our daughter adoringly in his arms. I reached up for her and gathered her close to my heart for the first time. My fatigue evaporated into mist and the whole world went pastel.

"I'm going to be a mother now," I explained later to the nurse as if that were a profession, and as if I knew what that meant. The concept was a traditional one, but it rang foreign to me. I'd been working since college and had never stayed home. I loved my job as a social worker and had worked up until the day before Amanda was born. Jamie had always been the one who'd stayed home to work on his paintings. But now it was Jamie's turn to take a job in a photography laboratory to support the household, and I came home to a new lifestyle. Our household was still not exactly traditional. There were monkeys in it.

At the insistence of all four of the grandparents, Jamie had built a gigantic cage for the monkeys. It was as high as the ceiling, painted green, and filled with a variety of mobiles, perches, trees, and trapezes—a veritable jungle gym. Amanda's crib was filled with bright toys, too, and another gift, a new rocking chair, was waiting for the parents.

I had experience as a monkey mother, but the monkeys had never been this helpless. Human infants can't cling or even see very well. It was amazing that despite all these handicaps, Amanda could get her will across as efficiently as our monkey children. Neither owl monkeys nor human babies sleep through the night, and for those first weeks Jamie and I were hollow-eyed zombies, dealing with the demands of three nocturnal children. Finally, we all settled into a routine.

Herbie and Kendra, pleased with the jungle gym, didn't object to being locked in during the day, which we attributed to our expert interior decorating. After supper, when Amanda was sound asleep, the cage door was open for the rest of the evening. Both Jamie and I were surprised at the monkeys' easy acceptance of this new time-sharing routine.

One thing was puzzling to us. Amanda was a good baby, and Herbie and Kendra ignored her those first few weeks. But if she cried in the night, Herbie immediately went over to Jamie and bit him. The total significance of this gesture was lost on us, but it was obvious that Herbie felt it was Jamie's responsibility to stop the baby from crying.

Then pieces of the puzzle began to fall into place. Three and a half weeks after Amanda came home from the hospital, we had another surprise. I had woken up early in the morning to prepare the monkeys their meal of raw egg and milk poured over banana slices. Usually Herbie and Kendra were right at my elbow waiting for their morning treats, but neither monkey was to be seen. I checked in the living room and they weren't in their usual places. I carried the bowls to the cage. To my surprise, the two monkeys were inside the nest-box with the teddy bear pillow. Why had they gone to bed so early? Then I saw a skinny little string of a tail. It came from underneath Herbie.

"Oh no, it can't be true," I gasped. Herbie had this protective, almost sappy look on his face. Kendra had her eyes closed, obviously exhausted. "Jamie, wake up!" I called. "We have a new monkey. Kendra and Herbie just had a baby!"

And Amanda had a new sister, named Mango. The little furred owl monkey at first could do nothing but cling, squeak, and suckle, and Amanda could only wave her arms and legs, cry, and suckle. And at this point, both newborns were much too small and helpless to comprehend one another.

The two couples were both preoccupied with the business of raising these helpless new family additions. In the human family, I suckled Amanda, changed her diapers, washed her in her bright blue plastic bathtub, read *Goodnight Moon* and *The Very Hungry Caterpillar*, played Joni Mitchell and Bob Dylan records to her, and rocked her while watching the Watergate scandal unfold on TV. Jamie cooed at Amanda in the evenings after he returned from work and occasionally picked her up and bounced her on his knee for five or ten minutes. But the job of caretaking was mine.

In the owl monkey family, things were different. Mother Kendra was showing a harsher side that was out of character for her. Yes, she suckled the infant about once every two hours, but for a maximum of three minutes. Then Kendra would nip the baby, Mango would squeal, and her father would bound over to take Mango from her ill-tempered mother. Herbie crouched close to Kendra, pushing his back conveniently next to the baby, and Mango eagerly climbed onto his back. Kendra scampered off to nibble fruit or lounge on the pillows while Mango was with Herbie. The monkey infant rode on Herbie's back, was washed by Herbie, played with Herbie, and eventually learned to eat solid foods from Herbie. Every few hours, Kendra would return to suckle Mango, or if she forgot, Herbie would go find her.

Herbie took his responsibilities as an owl monkey father very seriously. I'd never imagined that male primates were capable of those caretaking skills. He was totally devoted to his fatherly duties, quite the reverse of what I expected. In contrast, Kendra took it easy, occasionally coming to the table to eat grapes and avocados. As the days progressed, exhausted by my one-sided parental duties, I realized that there might be something to learn from the owl monkey parenting style.

I watched carefully. I began to understand why Herbie had bitten Jamie for neglecting the crying Amanda. The owl monkey rule is that all responsibility for childcare rests with the father. This includes protection, babysitting, playing, and teaching foraging and feeding skills—everything except giving milk, which by definition all mammal mothers do. The laissez-faire attitude we'd always seen in Kendra might be because her only job was to eat those mango bits and avocado slices, and make milk. All the other trials and tribulations of parental life rested on Herbie's shoulders.

As our infants became older and more independent, my observations continued to astound me. Herbie was totally dedicated to that baby monkey. Every waking moment, he was watching, protecting, carrying, and playing with tiny Mango. I assumed, having been raised in the fifties and sixties, that mothers were programmed for childrearing, not fathers. This mothering instinct was part of our biological heritage. Now it was becoming clear that this was not true in all primates.

Hoping to find out more about primate behavior, I once again trekked to the public library, this time transporting Amanda in her infant carrier. The Brooklyn Public Library was a massive cathedral with oak walls, rows of wooden card catalogs, and a big imposing desk, behind which sat an equally imposing middle-aged woman. I approached the desk and asked politely where to find the books on primate behavior. The librarian, at first concerned that the baby might cry, had to be reassured that Amanda would stay asleep. It was obvious that she thought babies should be left at home and not brought to a library. Finally, the librarian focused on my request.

"How our primate ancestors affect our behavior? Yes, come over to the Anthropology section. We should be able to find something there."

I followed obediently behind her, carrying the sleeping Amanda. The librarian pulled out two volumes. One was called *The Territorial Imperative* and the other *African Genesis*, both by journalist Robert Ardrey.

"Yes, this is just what you want," the librarian said. "Mr. Ardrey gives fascinating accounts of how our ape ancestors make us what we are today. Yes, you can check both books out for two weeks, then they have to be returned on time." Her voice took on a stern tone. "And don't let the baby near them."

I took the books home and read them when Amanda napped, which at this young age was quite often. It was true the books were entertaining, but the message I found inside was not quite what I was looking for. Ardrey interpreted recent studies of baboon behavior and ape-like fossils to explain how our primitive ancestors programmed us to make war, and that our earliest human ancestors from Africa were club-bearing predators. Both books boldly suggested that our biological destiny came from our primate heritage. Underneath our human exterior, Ardrey suggested, lurked beasts from the past, guiding our footsteps into war and hunting. To my dismay, the primate heritage he was describing bore no relationship to what I was observing at home.

I returned the books to the library on time. The middle-aged librarian wasn't there, so I felt free to explore the Anthropology section myself. This time I found a book by Jane Goodall, *In the Shadow of Man,* about the young biologist who had been the first person to follow chimpanzees in the wild. Another find was by the prestigious British professor Desmond Morris. The title, *The Naked Ape,* looked promising, and Amanda and I took both books home.

After dinner, I would read Jamie passages. Jane Goodall

wrote that female chimps were close to their infants, but males were distant fathers. Desmond Morris was adamant that, from their primate heritage, human females were programmed to be mothers and their whole life was geared to childrearing. Males were born to be hunters, protectors, and to fight to attain high ranks in relation to other males. That was the human destiny.

"Jamie, what's going on here in our house?" I asked. "These little monkeys are doing something that these books don't explain. Is this father care just a Herbie specialty or are all father owl monkeys this dedicated? If all owl monkeys have developed this system of father care, why don't these primate books say a word about them? They only describe baboon and chimpanzee behavior. Don't these owl monkeys count? They are part of our legacy, too."

Jamie just shook his head, as puzzled as I was.

Late spring arrived, and our Brooklyn apartment was cramped for the six of us. In previous years, we'd spent summers in Aruba, Colombia, or Costa Rica. I still longed for the green of the tropics, but now we had two families with young babies. Traveling would be a logistical and financial nightmare. There was no question that exotic trips to the south were out. But each day the temperature was hotter and more stifling.

"I can't take it," I said to Jamie one day. "We don't have air conditioning. This place is like an oven. Amanda had heat rash yesterday, and she sweated and screamed all afternoon. In this humidity the monkeys stink. You're off at work in an air-conditioned office. You don't understand."

Tears streamed down my face. I had become a nagging housewife. Amanda started fussing, and I went to the bedroom to pick her up. By the time I returned, Jamie had drawn a cartoon of three monkeys in a tree and a family in a sailboat. I smiled with relief. I understood his cartoon. Within a few days, we packed up and moved to his family's cabin on Cape Cod for a three-month vacation. The fact that the cabin was a little over a four-hour drive from New York meant that Jamie could still work and visit on weekends.

Cape Cod is a large boot-shaped peninsula of sand left bordering the Atlantic Ocean by the force of a glacier from the last Ice Age. For us, it was a far cry from the Amazon, but its scrub oak, pine, and cedar forests were forests nonetheless. And there were some real advantages to these woods. There were no dangers like stinging ants and fer-de-lances, which made it better for Amanda's grandparents' fears for their only grandchild.

Jamie's grandfather had been a whaler with a large family, and the shorefront of Punkhorn Point near the town of Falmouth was entirely populated by the Wright family. These eight brothers and sisters all had cabins on the point overlooking Popponesset Bay. The Mashpee Indians owned the interior forests, but they lived on the other side of the bay.

Jamie's father, Jim, the youngest of the siblings, had inherited the three-bedroom cabin built by his grandfather fifty years previously as a retreat and fishing lodge. The gigantic fieldstone fireplace was the focus of the living room. The front deck, encircled by a railing, looked off to the wooden pier and the expansive bay. We moved into one of the bedrooms and left the others free for guests like Jamie's younger sister Carol and her photographer husband, Craig. Cousin Connie and her husband, Bill, loved to sail, and they arrived from Boston on weekends. Our friends from New York, Lady Lothar and Norman and Chantal Schiller, joined in. In fact, the summer was a hive of social activity.

Amanda had no problem sleeping through the raucous all-night parties, but we were concerned about the social stress affecting our monkey family. We couldn't prohibit our family and friends from visiting. We had to find a solution. Because Punkhorn Point was a forested peninsula, Jamie and I made a major decision. We never liked confining our monkeys, but in New York City we had no choice. Since we planned to spend three months on Cape Cod this summer instead of visiting the rainforest, we would give our owl monkey family the opportunity to explore the northern woods.

At dusk, when the warmth of summer peeked through the spring, we opened the door and encouraged the monkeys to explore. Herbie and his family peered out into the blackness of the night, their pupils dilated to gather all the starlight. Peering to the right and then the left, they didn't move past the doorjamb. The medley of crickets and spring peepers was loud and alluring. Herbie looked back into the cabin, then peered again out into the darkness. A low rumble started in his throat, and then a clicking sound we hadn't heard before. There were things out there in the darkness that he didn't know about. He turned around and leaped back into the cabin with Kendra following, and the two nestled together on the back of a chair in front of the giant stone fireplace.

I shrugged my shoulders and turned to Jamie. "Well, the cabin is their territory. They feel safe inside their territory. Perhaps Herbie remembers the last time when he forgot the 'territory rules.' Remember in Costa Rica when he discovered the pest strip and nearly died? Maybe he remembers that lesson."

Whatever the reason, Herbie did not want to exit the cabin.

The second night of the experiment, Herbie was riding on Jamie's head when Jamie walked out onto the deck. Clinging to Jamie's long hair like a security blanket, Herbie peered anxiously into the darkness. For almost a week, the only way we could get the monkeys outdoors was riding on our heads. After a week of these evening deck tours, we came up with a new strategy. We'd take our evening stroll onto the deck, then quickly take the monkeys off our heads, toss them onto the railing, run into the cabin, and slam the door.

The scheme worked. After looking upset and bewildered, the monkeys gingerly walked along the railing and stared into the darkness of the wilds of Cape Cod. The Cape evenings were alive with the tantalizing sounds of crickets, frogs, whippoorwills, and the fresh smell of the sea. Herbie, with Mango clinging to his back, took the challenge and jumped off the deck into an oak tree. The branch swayed, and Herbie gripped with both hands and feet, using his tail to keep his balance. He moved unsteadily along the branch until he reached the trunk, where he sat and called to Kendra.

Like a diver making a false start, Kendra ran along the rail, looked as if she would leap, sized up the distance, and then stopped. Herbie called again. This time, she ran along the rail and made the big leap out onto the tree. Like a child learning how to dog paddle, she kept on scrambling until she was next to Herbie. After ten minutes, Herbie ran along the same branch and tried to return. But branches bend, and Herbie didn't quite judge the spring. He missed the railing and hit the porch floor. He sat, stunned, getting his bearings. Kendra crash-landed next. After a short pause, the monkeys galloped back into the cabin and didn't go out again that night. Learning to leap and balance in the trees took practice, and the monkeys improved their skills each evening, spending longer and longer off the porch.

Then one night, the monkeys didn't come back after their usual hourly tour, and we were as worried as parents of teenagers. Jamie and I searched the forest with a flashlight, looking without luck for our little companions. Our grand scheme of having our monkeys enjoy "nature walks" now seemed very reckless indeed. We walked into the woods, calling, but all we saw were katydids and mosquitoes.

I tossed and turned all night, jolting awake at any little sound. At dawn, this time the noise was genuine. Clip, clip, clip, like miniature reindeer running across the roof, our owl monkeys arrived at the door, visibly eager to return to our bed for a long day's sleep.

"Where did you visit?" I asked them. "And how far did you go?" The monkeys gave no answers. Kendra and Herbie smelled fragrant like cedar, and they certainly were tired.

The next morning, Jamie's Uncle Everett arrived on our deck with a glass of lemonade in one hand. Everett worked for the local newspaper and lived in town, and this weekend he and his wife Helen had driven to Punkhorn Point to open up his cabin for the summer season.

After the yearly greetings, Uncle Everett pointed at his glass. "I'm drinking lemonade."

That might not have seemed like a statement worth much notice, except that Uncle Everett always drank beer or gin and tonic.

"Everett, what happened? Do you have a health problem? Aren't you feeling well?" We knew that there must be something seriously wrong to cause such a change in behavior.

"Well, everything has been going just fine," he said, "until last night. Last night, Helen and I were relaxing in front of the fireplace, enjoying our third gin and tonic when, well, I guess it was a hallucination. I don't know what it was, but both Helen and I saw it. Some sort of leprechaun peered at us through the window. No ears, big eyes, and round faces all painted white like a ghost. We ran out onto the deck but the spooks were gone. That's when Helen and I decided to quit drinking. No more alcohol for us, just lemonade."

Jamie and I looked serious, then cracked a smile. "We have a surprise for you. Come look in our bedroom!" Uncle Everett gazed in at the three little faces, eyes scrunched shut, sleeping huddled on our pillow. "They're monkeys," we explained. "Our pet owl monkeys, not spooks. They were out enjoying Cape Cod by night and just stopped by your place for a visit. Shhh, they're sleeping now."

"Those were your monkeys?" Uncle Everett was visibly relieved.

"Yep."

Uncle Everett, grinning broadly, spilled his lemonade onto the ground and picked up a Budweiser.

That summer, the neighbors looked forward to our monkeys' nightly visits. The monkeys had a regular route, often using the shortest path between the cabins. This meant walking the electric lines like tightrope artists, tails moving from side to side for balance. Once they reached the deck, they would station themselves at the spotlights above the window. This was the best hunting spot for moths, beetles, praying mantises, and all the insects that the night had to offer. The old Cape Cod families had live entertainment every night.

Once they had visited all the cabin decks, the monkeys took off into the forest. What were they doing out there in the night? Curious about their wanderings, I decided to follow them. The pines and oaks on Cape Cod are short, perhaps because of the sandy soil. The edge of the forest can be forbidding, tangles of wild grapevines, poison ivy, or greenbriar and blackberries, armed with thorns. But once inside the forest, the shade of the oaks and pine limits the undergrowth.

At first, I was skeptical about being able to track our three monkeys. It was dark out there in the forest. But luckily, when the monkeys moved through the trees, they jumped noisily from one tip of a branch to another. I could follow underneath the rustling of the leaves. Herbie and Kendra also talked to one another. The quiet murmurs echoed back and forth like a beeper signalling system. They seemed to want to keep track of each other, and those contact calls clued me in.

When the moon was bright, I could often see monkey silhouettes against the moonlit sky. I could always tell Herbie, because of Mango's extra little head, glued solidly to his back. Herbie and Kendra did a lot of exploring, but then, suddenly, they were quiet. The three of them often chose a dense cedar tree, curling up together near the trunk for a two-hour siesta, before they jumped off again. It took me a long time to figure out that trick. It was Mango who tipped me off, since she left her parents for a bit of play while they napped. She never went farther than a foot away, hanging by her feet, biting the branches, pouncing on an imaginary insect. But at the least sound, she jumped back onto her father, clutching him as if her life depended on it.

Early one evening, near the cabin where the illumination from the spotlights helped my view, I saw the monkeys for the first time meet a creature that belonged in these forests. A flying squirrel in a tall pine tree spotted Herbie, who had Mango on his back as usual. The South American monkey and North American rodent moved toward each other at a height of twenty feet until they were nearly touching noses. Herbie blinked, perplexed. The squirrel, half the size of the monkey, scampered off to the edge of the branch, looked back at the monkey, and flicked its bushy tail as if offering a challenge. Then it jumped, spreading its limb membranes like a parachute, and gracefully glided to the trunk of an adjacent tree. Herbie watched him as if amazed at the squirrel's abilities. The flying squirrel came back to the tree to stare at Herbie, then glided away again. Herbie, very confused and concerned, left the tree from the other side and joined Kendra in an oak. Intuitively, he knew he couldn't compete with this native acrobat.

The three monkeys had an alarm call, a series of staccato clicks and chucks punctuated by a burbling hum, which alerted the family to dangers. One night, I heard *Chuck, chuck, hmmm! Chuck, chuck, hmmm!* coming from the trees. Looking around, I spotted a family of black and white skunks ambling below on the forest floor, looking for fallen fruit and insects. I knew the dangers of these mustelid scavengers and was grateful to our monkeys for the warning. I cautiously kept my distance, but the monkeys did not. Apparently lacking any skunk training, they kept moving lower and closer to the strange furry creatures with the bushy white tails, until they were positioned only a foot above the skunks' heads. Continuing to scold the skunks with the *chuck-chuck* vocalization, in synchrony the monkeys began to urinate on the backs of these terrestrial mammals.

Now they're in trouble, I thought.

I waited for the skunks to become annoyed and punish the monkeys with a blast of their own fragrance, but the skunks didn't seem to notice and continued to trundle along. The monkeys tired of the game and bounded back in the trees to catch some katydids.

In September, back in Brooklyn, Herbie's whole life was occupied by the needs of his daughter. By Thanksgiving, the burden of carrying Mango on his back was weighing heavily on him. Mango was now about one third Herbie's body weight. She began to look absurd clinging to her father's head, and her ever-patient father was getting tired and irritable. We began to see conflicts that suggested it was time for Mango to show a little independence and responsibility. Herbie began to reach back with his right hand and push her off. If this didn't work, he tried to unhinge her grip on his fur, finger by finger. Mango scrunched her eyes shut and held on tight. Nothing was working very well for Herbie, and his giant off-spring rode on.

Finally, the frustrated father had a plan. He ran into the cage and proceeded to rub Mango on the side of the wire mesh until she let go of his fur. Then he escaped outside the cage and slammed the door before she could follow. It became a new ritual, leaving Mango in the "daycare" cage to play by herself with all the toys. And Herbie and Kendra at last had some time to themselves.

Meanwhile, I carried Amanda everywhere on my hip and was beginning to have a constant backache. Then one day in January, at the tender age of nine months, Amanda took her first steps. Then she learned to run. The weeks zipped by and soon it was spring.

Spring in the city for a Brooklyn mother means trips to Prospect Park. Amanda's best friends Laura and Mathew joined her on the swings and in the sandbox while we mothers chatted about our husbands' jobs, a new recipe, and the accomplishments of our kids. The success of Mathew putting together his first jigsaw puzzle, or Amanda's first word being "shoe" instead of "mama," became major news items. My worldview had narrowed with this motherhood thing, and at first I didn't mind. However, despite my motherly exterior, I was still a young New Yorker, and I began to long to expand my world again. Then an invention occurred that changed my life. Foldable infant strollers replaced the bulky prams of the past, freeing mothers to hop the subways to go to the city, kids in tow. But while the Children's Zoo in Central Park and the toy section of Bloomingdale's were exciting at first, they couldn't replace the physical and mental freedom of the wild. Jamie agreed it was time to go to Cape Cod for the summer.

That summer was a repeat of the previous Cape Cod experience: swimming and sailing by day, and monkeys in the forest by night. Except now, Mango followed her parents instead of riding Herbie's back, and Amanda was walking and running in stiff-legged little steps down the forest trail. Having Amanda on her feet meant the whole year was on fast forward. Then it was spring and time for the Cape again.

The third summer was different. Kendra had a second daughter, which Amanda promptly named Flower. Amanda was talking in sentences now, making definite decisions, and making sure we understood them clearly. She finally had hair, which was very blonde and soft, and she still had her sturdy baby frame.

As with Mango, Herbie assumed his paternal caretaking responsibilities the second day after Flower was born. However, when Flower was about a month old, he also allowed Amanda to carry the new infant on her head. For two-year-old Amanda, this was a real treat. Wearing a yellow sundress, dancing down the forest trails, picking berries for herself with a baby monkey on her head, Amanda had a wonderful summer. That third summer there was a surprise in our family, too. I hadn't planned to get pregnant again, as Jamie thought that one child was enough, but it had happened. I lumbered down the trail with Amanda during the day, but my nocturnal forest wanderings were curtailed. Our baby was due in September, and at the end of the summer Labor Day gathering, the grandparents, aunts, and uncles chattered about name choices and whether the new Wright would be a girl or a boy.

Back in Brooklyn, we'd moved into a brownstone apartment with a second bedroom, and Amanda's crib was ready for the new occupant. On September 27, I went into labor and Jamie drove me frantically to New York University Hospital. Things happened at lightning speed, and I was worried Jamie wouldn't finish signing me in and filling out the paperwork before the baby was born. He made it to the operating room just in time to see the birth. The doctor held up a beautiful daughter with a heart-shaped face and light brown hair.

Looking up at the doctor's face to thank him, I saw that something was wrong. The baby hadn't cried. The next minutes are a blur in my memory as the infant was rushed to a table nearby and four doctors were surrounding her. In my dazed, exhausted state, I knew the baby was in danger, but I also knew she would be all right. She had to be all right. Jamie was still by my side and looked white as a sheet.

It seemed like hours before the doctor, eyes bloodshot and face drawn, returned, telling me our baby had gone to the intensive care unit. They were doing everything that could possibly be done for her, and I would be taken to my room now.

The darkness of the hospital room and the turmoil in my brain made the remaining hours of the night very long. Jamie had returned home and was back in the morning. Our infant daughter was still in intensive care and had not stabilized at nine in the morning when the doctor gave me the report.

"The baby has a diaphragmatic hernia," he said. "This means the diaphragm, the partition which separates her lungs and heart from the intestines, never formed. During her development, the intestines drifted up into her lung cavity, and her lungs had no room to develop and expand. She was fine, until she was born and had to breathe. Her lungs had no capacity. She has had two operations to right the situation. At noon, she'll have another operation. I must be honest with you, her chances are not good."

The words came from another world. The doctor, fatigued and pale, tried to be reassuring. But when he left the room, I was in a trance of shock and disbelief. Of course she'd be okay, I thought. Of course my little baby girl would recover. Of course she would.

Jamie had been up to intensive care to see her, and he didn't say very much, just shook his head, his eyes red with tears. We sat there, hands clasped, in silence. The nurses shooed him out for lunch.

At 2:00 P.M. the doctor came in to tell me that my daughter had died a half hour ago. I stared beyond him. It couldn't be true. The horror of the truth was unreal to me. Jamie came into the room an hour later and we both sobbed. There was little to say. He left for the apartment to take care of Amanda.

The social worker came later and sat down next to my bed. "It's not your fault," she said. "Diaphragmatic hernias are congenital problems, one infant in two thousand is born with one. Few of these infants survive. We don't know why this happens, but all studies show this problem is not inherited. That means that the chances of this ever happening again to your future children are minuscule. That means that nothing you did in your pregnancy caused this problem."

The social worker knew I needed to know all the facts and details. She knew the guilt that lurks in every mother's heart. She knew I needed to think beyond this day to a brighter future. "You already have a wonderful daughter," she said to me. "You must treasure her even more. But I would recommend that you have another baby as soon as possible. The easiest way to forget this tragedy is to have another baby in a year or so."

Her words anchored me. I had been a social worker. I remember the thanks, the gratitude I'd received from people, but I'd never really understood how important my contribution had been to their lives. On this day, I knew how important a social worker can be. I also knew that her solution was well-meaning but not possible for us. Jamie had been adamant about no more children. He wasn't willing to take a chance with tragedy again. And I knew him well enough to know that he wasn't going to change his mind.

The rest of that day and on into the night, my mind churned with disbelief and bitterness. I felt sorry for myself, for Jamie, for all of our family. I had to rethink our future again, and the aching and the emptiness were everywhere.

By midnight that same night, I still hadn't slept. I stared numbly out the hospital window into the darkness. I gazed at the Chrysler Building. The city felt totally distant and indifferent. My fist gripped the chair. "Damn it!" I heard myself saying. "Damn it. If I can't do what I want to do most—to be a mother to that little baby—then I will do what I want to do second most. I will go to the Amazon. I will find out what the night monkey does in the night, why it has this father care. I will." And a kind of fire burned inside of me, a fire of defiance and conviction that never dimmed from that evening on. It was a mission, a passion, a promise to that little baby girl, and to myself.

I would go to the Amazon to solve the mysteries of the night. I would make that dream come true.

CHAPTER FIVE

MONKEY IN
THE MOON

(Puerto Bermúdez, 1976)

B ECOMING A PRIMATOLOGIST was a challenge. If one has no academic connections, what is the first step? Inspired by both her book and *National Geographic* articles about her pioneering chimpanzee studies in Tanzania, I wrote Jane Goodall asking her advice on funding my proposed study on wild owl monkeys. She never replied. Perhaps my letter never even reached her, since I addressed it simply to Jane Goodall, Gombe Stream, Tanzania.

Next, I read *The Year of the Gorilla*, the first account of tracking wild gorillas in the volcanic mountains that rise out of the Congo Basin. I wrote to its famous author, mammalogist George Schaller, this time including Jamie's drawings of Herbie and Kendra. I addressed that letter to the New York Zoological Society, Bronx, New York. My letter did make it to the Bronx, because Dr. George Schaller wrote back a handwritten letter.

Dear Mrs. Wright:

I was pleased to receive your letter describing your experiences with owl monkeys and your aspirations to study them in the Amazon. Little is known about this species in the wild, and your research goals are important. Unfortunately, according to the funding guidelines, the New York Zoological Society will not be able to sponsor your research. Priority for funding is given to endangered species and Aotus, with a geographic range from Panama to Argentina, is not endangered. However, I am forwarding your letter to my friend, Dr. John Eisenberg, Director of Research at the National Zoo in Washington. He has a field station in Venezuela and might be interested in a study of Aotus.

Sincerely,

George Schaller, Director of

Field Research Program

New York Zoological Society

Not an endangered species! No funding. But still encouraged by hearing from such a famous scientist, I next wrote to Professor Eisenberg and received a reply a few weeks later.

Dear Mrs. Wright:

Owl monkeys are some of the most charming of primates and no one has been able to study them in the wild. I fully support your ambitions to study them in their natural habitat, and would sponsor you and your husband to come to my research site in the pantanal of Venezuela, but unfortunately Aotus does not occur at this site. Your husband's drawings

*capture the charm and spirit of owl monkeys, and I wish you
well in your endeavors.*

*I am passing this letter on to my friend Dr. Richard
Thorington, Curator of Primates at the US Natural History
Museum in Washington. He has recently begun a study of
Aotus in Panama, and may be able to incorporate you in his
study. My heartiest best wishes in your future research.*

Sincerely,
John Eisenberg
Director of Research,
National Zoological Park
Professor of Biology,
University of Maryland

Not in the geographic range of Venezuela! No funding.
I immediately wrote several letters to Dr. Thorington, but I
never received a reply.

I was getting discouraged. There didn't seem to be any way
that I could get money to fund my study of the owl monkey in
South America. Everywhere I turned was a dead end.

Then one day, a letter arrived from my mother with a clip-
ping from *The Buffalo Evening News* about monkeys. A young
medical doctor from Buffalo, Dr. Jeffrey Trilling, had accompanied a primatologist to his field site in the Peruvian Amazon
to study the feeding behavior of *Callicebus* monkeys. Dr. Trilling had accompanied the expedition to help with the medical
problems of the researchers. The professor's name was Warren
Kinzey, an anthropologist from City College, City University
of New York.

There was a photo of the monkey in the center of the newspaper article. I stared at that black-and-white photo. The previous year I had seen a *Callicebus* monkey in the Bronx Zoo and pointed out to Jamie that it was a day-shift version of our owl monkeys. It had similar body weight, a similar pair-living social system, and almost the same fur color as Kendra. The obvious difference was the large eyes of the night monkey. If this professor was studying *Callicebus*, maybe he could give me some advice.

I dialed the phone number of City College information and to my surprise reached Professor Kinzey. I began to explain, "My name is Pat Wright and I'm very interested in monkey behavior. Presently I'm a housewife living in Brooklyn, and I want to study *Aotus* in the Amazon. But," I continued, realizing how naïve I sounded, "I need some advice on equipment and methods. And I wondered if I could make an appointment to discuss your monkey research in the Amazon."

Professor Kinzey sounded skeptical on the other end of the line, and I tried to reassure him that yes, I knew owl monkeys were nocturnal. He agreed to an appointment the following Thursday.

That day, Professor Kinzey arrived late at his office after class. His briefcase was brimming with notes, and his desk was piled high with books on monkeys and human anatomy. His gray hair and short beard framed his face and reminded me immediately of a *Callicebus* monkey. His blue eyes sparkled as he listened, rather amused, to the stories of my pets.

Next, Professor Kinzey launched into a lecture about methods and equipment. "A telescopic camera lens is essential to film the monkeys, and a powerful long-range flash, of course, for

Aotus. A camera macrolens would be needed to get color photos of the fruits the monkeys eat. The Halliburton case is completely waterproof and will protect your equipment in the rain. Silva compasses are the most accurate and reliable. The more expensive compasses have a clinometer, which will help measure tree height. Bright orange forester's flagging tape is the best to mark the trails. Notebooks with waterproof pages are expensive, but can be purchased. Justrite D-cell headlamps with the battery pack attachable to your belt are the best. But be sure to have a smaller flashlight, too, to carry in your pocket always, in case the headlamp's batteries run out. The most important purchase is binoculars. Leitz 7x35 is what I use, but you need better light-gathering capabilities. Leitz 10x40 is the best for you."

I wrote down every word and turned his hour of information into a grant proposal that I sent off to the National Geographic Society. Alas, in the return mail, I received a thin envelope. The letter inside said,

Dear Mrs. Wright:
The National Geographic Society has received your request
for funding research on owl monkeys in the Amazon.
Although your research goals are laudatory, we regret that
The National Geographic Society can only fund researchers
who have received their PhD.

My family, hearing of my failures to launch my studies, suggested I speak to Nancy Mulligan from Rochester, New York.

Mrs. Mulligan, a wildlife enthusiast, owned eleven farms in the Genesee River Valley. Her husband had invested in George Eastman in his early years, when he was establishing the Kodak Company. Mr. Mulligan was now deceased and Mrs. Mulligan lived in an elegant old white New England–style manor house, perched on a hill and surrounded by cathedral-like barns. She still maintained full command of the farms' decisions even though she was over eighty years old. She agreed to see me.

On a crisp Saturday in April, Mrs. Mulligan invited us to sit at the dining room table, and Jamie, Amanda, my brother Ted, and I were served a gracious lunch. We chatted politely about the farm and my brother's construction business. After finishing off homemade sugar cookies, we retired to the living room for coffee and discussions about the monkey project. Amanda's eyes wandered to the large oil paintings of sleek horses and the hunt, and she spotted a saddle in one corner of the living room. Amanda, now aged three, loved horses.

Mrs. Mulligan seemed fascinated by my research questions of why some monkey species have father care of infants, and the lifestyle differences between the only species of nocturnal monkey and all the other species of monkeys in the Amazon. She was pleased by my motivation and Jamie's artistic skills, but reserved about making any promises about funds. "Let me talk to my lawyers first, and give me a call in a week or two," she said. I left a copy of my research proposal with her.

I waited a week and then phoned Rochester. Mrs. Mulligan did not have good news. "My lawyers explained that since you do not have a university affiliation, a donation to you cannot be considered a tax exemption. So I am sorry, but I cannot fund this project."

Unable to accept the bad news, I asked, "But if I obtain a university affiliation would it be possible to fund my monkey research?"

She said yes.

My mind was racing when I put down the phone. I dialed Professor Kinzey, but the Anthropology Department secretary curtly told me that he was doing research in Brazil and to call back in a month. Crushed by that news, I had another idea. I picked up the receiver again and called my friend Fran Frummer. She called her friend, the secretary for the dean of undergraduates at the New School for Social Research. The next day, I had an appointment with the dean.

The portly dean of undergraduates sat behind his enormous desk, swiveling in his chair, listening attentively to my explanation.

"Owl monkeys with father care? Field work in Peru? I visited Cuzco once. I'll need your proposal. You have one, right?"

I handed him my typed document already returned by the National Geographic Society.

The dean stared long at my paperwork, nodding and thinking. Then he looked me straight in the eye. "Yes, I think an affiliation can be arranged. The donor's check can be sent directly to the New School, but 25 percent of the grant goes to overhead."

I didn't know what "overhead" was, but I knew I wasn't going to let it interfere with what I wanted from that dean. I walked out of that office with a university affiliation as "adjunct researcher." Bursting with the news, I called Mrs. Mulligan, who immediately sent the check to the New School. They issued a check and within a week I had $3,800 in my hand.

But not for long. My first stop was AeroPeru. Jamie was taking a six-month leave of absence from his job at the photography shop. This time our good friends from Philadelphia, Floyd and Mia Glenn, had the room and patience to take our now large family of monkeys. But I couldn't leave Amanda behind, even though her grandparents had insisted she stay with them. I had learned from Herbie that primate children should be attached to their families. So I purchased three round-trip tickets to Lima for two adults and one child, leaving from JFK June 22 and returning on December 22.

Next stop, 47th Street Camera, owned and run by families of Hasidic Jews, which Professor Kinzey had recommended for the best prices. There were long lines leading to the counter. Above the din of conversation, orders in Yiddish whizzed over customers' heads to the back stockrooms. Then it was my turn. The clerk grabbed Professor Kinzey's shopping list from my hand. "Canon F-1 camera, Vivitar close range lens, I have a better buy on this Canon lens, telefoto lens 80-200, yes, no problem." I had to strain to understand him through his rapid fire. "Why this flash? You need a flash this powerful?"

I shot back, "Yes, I need to take pictures of night monkeys in the Peruvian rainforest. The trees are high, the forest is dark."

"Monkeys in the Amazon? Now I've heard everything. Can't you just go to the zoo? This here is the best flash on the market. Minolta puts it out. Fits easily onto your camera like this, and it's durable. It's a little bit more expensive, but we have a good price. Let's add it all up. Camera body, close-up lens, telephoto lens, and a flash. And Leitz binoculars 8x40. That's all you need, right? $1,429. Here's the bill, pay at the cashier. Need film? Step into that other line. Next customer." He was finished with the monkey lady.

Next stop was Hammacher Schlemmer on Fifth Avenue, where I was served by a tall, gray-haired gentleman with a crisp English accent.

"One medium-sized silver Halliburton case. Fits easily under the seat on any airline. Yes, our cases are waterproof and will float if the canoe overturns. Which river did you say? The Amazon?" His bushy gray eyebrows rose, but the smoothness of his voice did not lose a beat. I could tell he wasn't accustomed to serving wilderness explorers.

"Yes, it will keep your photo equipment dry even in the Amazon. Lifetime guarantee. The foam inside can be cut so each piece of equipment fits precisely for added safety. In case you drop it, let's say, in the rainforest. And this combination lock is an important safety factor. Safety is an issue in South America, I have read. Here, let me show you how it works." I couldn't wait to get away from his condescension.

Last stop, the Army Surplus store on Forty-Second Street. Most of the customers had military-style haircuts and none were women. A young clerk asked if I needed help, and I showed him my list: Army pants, shirts, and jackets in 50 percent polyester and 50 percent cotton for quick drying, Silva compass, Swiss Army knives, flashlights, raincoats with hoods, Vietnam jungle boots, sleeping bags, backpacks and foam mats, and a big waterproof tent.

"We got all that here," he said. "You going to the Amazon? I been to Nam. Saw some action, been back a year. You like the jungle? Mosquitoes, the sweating heat, the swamps, the bugs, you like that?" He was admiring and skeptical at the same time. "God, I hated it, couldn't wait to get out. But if you like the jungle, that's fine. This tent is a great buy. It's going out of stock but it's big, lightweight. A Eureka eight-man tent, big verandah, you can even stand up in it. Mosquito netting on all the windows and doors. It'll be like a jungle palace. Green, a nice color for you." And I added the Eureka tent to the pile.

Within two days, I had accomplished all the shopping. Jamie and I had everything packed by June 20.

Two days before takeoff, I telephoned Professor Kinzey, who had returned from Brazil, to thank him. But I was in for a surprise.

Instead of the congratulations and well wishes I had expected, Dr. Kinzey said quite the contrary.

"No, Patricia. You can't go. It would be foolish to waste your time."

I was silent, not knowing how to respond.

He continued, "I have an article in front of me, written by Dr. Richard Thorington of the Smithsonian Institution, regarding his study of owl monkeys in Panama. Dr. Thorington states it's impossible to follow *Aotus* in the rainforest without radio collars. Radio collars and a receiver cost an additional thousand dollars. You don't have that kind of money. You can't go to Peru with just the equipment you've purchased. It'll be a waste of time and money. I'm sorry to tell you the bad news."

I politely hung up the phone, Professor Kinzey's words echoing in my ears. Impossible in the rainforest without radio collars

... a waste of time and money. ... Tears rolled down my face as I understood the true meaning of those words. Professor Kinzey had said that I shouldn't go to study owl monkeys in Peru.

But the airline tickets were not refundable. The equipment was purchased, much of it on sale, and not returnable. And the overhead! I couldn't get back the New School's overhead. I couldn't call Mrs. Mulligan up and say we had decided it was impossible to study the monkeys in Peru. I couldn't do that. Professor Kinzey had said the research was impossible, but it was just as impossible for me to not go.

But maybe there were things that Professor Kinzey hadn't understood. I had successfully followed our pets in the forests of Cape Cod. I knew what their calls were, what their habits and behaviors were. I knew how they thought. I knew what the rainforest was like. Maybe he hadn't understood how stubborn I was. I would follow the monkeys in the forests of South America without radio collars. Maybe others couldn't do it, but I would.

We departed from JFK in late June as scheduled. The AeroPeru flight touched down in Miami, Bogotá, and Quito, and finally delivered us to Lima. This was three-year-old Amanda's first international flight and her photo was wedged between Jamie's and mine in our family passport. Amanda was excited to buckle her seat belt but fell asleep shortly after takeoff and woke up nine hours later as we were descending into the Lima airport. "As easy as traveling with monkeys." I smiled at Jamie.

Lima, a city of three million people, is sandwiched between the beaches of the Pacific Ocean and the snowcapped peaks of the Andes Mountains. Ringed with shacks without electricity or water, the center is a thriving capital city. Elegant buildings, fine art museums, and bustling traffic give it the flavor of modern life. But the history of this ancient Incan nation can be seen in the Quechua Indians, conquered in 1533 by the Spanish on horseback. Like the other highland Indians of South America, they have long, straight black hair, aquiline noses, and high cheekbones. The Quechua often carry heavy weights on their backs or heads to and from the market. In fact, their everyday lifestyle may not be much different than those of their ancestors, although now they spread piles of woven wool tapestries, turquoise earrings, replicas of llamas, wool blankets, and handwoven sweaters on sidewalks or in makeshift stalls along the main boulevard in the center of town.

The Chanchamayo Valley in central Peru, nestled in the foothills of the Andes east of Lima, was our destination. I had chosen the field site from a gigantic book that I found in the New York Public Library entitled *Primates: Comparative Anatomy and Taxonomy IV—Cebidae, Part A*. The author, W. C. Osman Hill, a British anatomist, described all the old sites where the early *Aotus* had been collected. The Chanchamayo Valley would probably have a more temperate climate than the lowlands, and lower rainfall and colder temperatures would be a better climate for a child's health. I didn't want Amanda to catch those tropical diseases that her grandparents feared.

Very early the next morning, our family boarded a collective taxi to travel over the Andes to our destination: the small city of San Ramón in the Chanchamayo Valley. The paved road ended shortly outside of Lima, and the next twelve hours were long and bumpy as the *collectivo* dodged holes in the muddy road. Amanda didn't seem to mind as she watched eagerly out the window.

"Those llamas are nice. Like furry horses with long necks. Wait till I tell Grampa about them. Look there's another one." Amanda shared my father's love of horses, and this long-necked creature might be even better than a horse.

Outside the window, traditionally dressed Quechua Indians walked to market, carrying firewood or infants on their backs. The layers of red and yellow wool that they wore, cheerful to the eye, kept them warm in the chilly mountain air. Their hats were good protection from the tropical sun but also spoke of hometown origins through their color, shape, and texture. The plaster white hats with a black ribbon distinguished the Arequipa group, the black felt hats were from Ayacucho, and the brown hats with upturned brims and handwoven bands designated the wearer to be from Cuzco. The Quechua men from the mountain villages all wore handknit wool caps with earflaps called *chullos*. As we moved up into the mountains, we realized why these earflaps were essential. It was getting cold.

Going over the pass at sixteen hundred feet was tough. Most passengers were vomiting, and I had a splitting headache from the thin air. Amanda slept through most of the pass, but her stomach was definitely suffering, too. The wind blew, the snow was high, and it was very, very cold. The collectivo stopped abruptly, and everyone stumbled out. I picked up Amanda and we took refuge in some sort of restaurant. Jamie joined us on a

wooden bench and we huddled with the other zombified passengers over a table filled with bowls of soup and steaming
coffee. Out in the frozen air again, we gazed over snow-covered peaks. Shivering, we piled into the car again. After that
stop, we started to descend the backside of the Andes, through
the cloud forest, and into the warmth of the tropics.

Nestled in the center of Chanchamayo Valley's rolling hills
was the small city of San Ramón. We checked into a hotel,
unloaded our considerable baggage, and began to ask about
monkeys. The elderly hotel manager laughed at us.

*"Solamente café aquí. No hay el bosque. Finido. Veinticinco
años pasado. Finido. No hay los monos. Nada."* He shook his
head to emphasize his point.

I translated for Jamie as the meaning of the words began
to dawn on me. "This is a coffee town. Our rainforest was
cut long ago and replanted with coffee trees. There are no
monkeys here. We haven't seen monkeys in these regions for
twenty-five years."

I was bewildered. I had read every word of W. C. Osman
Hill's 1960 volume. I had chosen a site where this species had
been first discovered. It had never occurred to me that a place
where there were monkeys in the 1800s might not have any
monkeys today.

I sat there in that hotel with thousands of dollars worth of
equipment, oil paints and canvases, my husband, my daughter,
and no hope of finding monkeys. We sat down at the hotel bar
and Jamie ordered a beer, and then another.

"¿Donde estan los monos?" I asked the bartender. Where
are the monkeys?

"*No sé. Pregunta en el aeropuerto. Los pilots conocían.*" Again, I translated for Jamie.

"'I don't know, but they must know at the airport. Go out and talk to the pilots at the airport.'"

The next morning, after several confirmations of the lack of monkeys in the Chanchamayo Valley from other people, we went up to the small bush plane airport. A small man with a mustache was sitting behind a desk, and several other men, perhaps mechanics, were joking together.

"*¿Donde estan los monos de la noche?*" I asked, pulling one of many photos of Herbie and Kendra from my pocket. "*¿Donde? Por favor.*"

The airport crew stared at me. There I was—a gringa dressed in a camouflage shirt, green army pants, Vietnam jungle boots, and Leitz binoculars, asking where the monkeys were. The five of them clustered around me to see the monkey photos and talked at once, very loudly, for about fifteen minutes. Finally, a pilot said definitively, "Puerto Bermúdez." That was where we could find owl monkeys.

At that point, it was clear to me that we had better go where the monkeys were. I asked when the next plane left for Puerto Bermúdez. The small man with the mustache said there was only one flight a week and that flight would leave today at noon. There were seats available, he said, but I would have to pay full fare for Amanda. I nodded and slowly counted out the Peruvian money, called *soles*, for our tickets.

When we returned to the airport at eleven with our fifteen bags, the agent shook his head. Too much luggage. I looked out at the plane, a little six-seater Cessna. The agent motioned for us to weigh in on an ancient scale. Jamie was tall but very thin, and Amanda and I didn't weigh much. One seat lacked a passenger. I looked up at the agent with pleading eyes. He relented and decided our extra luggage would still be within the allowance.

Soon our seat belts were fastened and we were cruising low over coffee plantations that promptly transformed into the Amazon forest. The expanse was unbroken by roads, and after an hour and a half, we began to descend. Filling up the plane window was the meandering, muddy Pichis River, one of the headwaters of the Amazon. It flows lazily into the Ucayali River and then into the Amazon west of Leticia in Colombia.

Then I saw the straight line of bare earth that was the airstrip. The little Cessna bounced to a stop, and then the propellers slowed and the motor's deafening roar went silent. When we descended from the plane the hot, humid air of the lowland tropics rushed over us like a steam bath. Staggering, almost incapacitated by the stifling heat, I set Amanda down on the runway. I could see her face getting red from the heat as she looked around. She started screaming and grabbed at my legs for protection. I followed her gaze about fifteen yards and there was a Campa Indian chief, his face painted with red streaks. He wore a headdress of parrot and toucan feathers, and a ceremonial brown robe with bows and arrows attached to his back. I had read that the Campa were fierce warriors.

Amanda continued to scream and Jamie gave me a "What in the world have we gotten ourselves into now?" look. I picked up my little girl and held her tight. "He's the chief. He won't hurt you."

Amanda quieted down as the Campa chief continued on his journey.

We were indeed at the end of the earth this time. Puerto Bermúdez was a tiny village with a few thatched huts, its only link to the outside world this tiny airport. *"¿Donde está el hotel des turistas?"* I mustered up my best Spanish to ask the pilot.

This request must have been unusual because he shared our request with several other men nearby and they all burst into laughter. I was pleased that we could bring such joy to their lives, but with Amanda whining, and Jamie getting more and more annoyed, I really needed to find a hotel.

The crew regained their composure enough to instruct us to go to the Pichis River, where there was a small place with rooms to rent.

When we reached the river, I understood why asking for a tourist hotel had been amusing. The rooms in this place were sparse and contained wooden beds with no mattresses. There was no bathroom or running water. No screens on the windows to keep out insects. We moved the bed to the center of the room, hoping to discourage the three-inch-long brown spiders that clung to the walls. Amanda slept between us, but Jamie and I only dozed.

Just one night was enough to convince us to leave Puerto Bermúdez as quickly as possible. We walked down to the river. This port was small, in contrast to bustling Leticia on the Amazon, and clearly not driven by the market economy. I saw one small dugout canoe with a Campa Indian poling his wife and a carefully centered pile of bananas. The only other vessels were slightly bigger boats with motors owned by *campesinos*—

settlers from riverside farms. Mostly of Spanish descent, these settlers from Lima and Huancayo earned a living by clearing land along the river for growing cassava and corn and raising cows for milk and meat. Without any way to transport animals out to the international market, there was no trafficking in wild animals.

At breakfast, I asked the hotel owner where to find owl monkeys, bringing out the photos of Herbie and Kendra. He thought for a moment, then walked outside and motioned for a man down by the pier to come over. Adremildo, a short, slight man in his mid-forties, looked like he could have been a bank clerk in the United States. He took the photos gently and nodded. I could understand only fragments of what he said, but he seemed to recognize these monkeys from the forest behind his house. He volunteered to take us to his *chacra,* or "farm clearing."

Within half an hour, we had all our belongings and Amanda packed into a dugout canoe and were poling downstream to Adremildo's chacra. The current was gentler than the Amazon, and the river was about thirty yards wide. Amanda, comfortable with boats after Cape Cod summers, sat between Jamie and me. Above us, cottonball clouds were sprinkled over the blue sky. The rainforest closed in on either side of the river, the peaks of the Andes still in view behind us.

After an hour, we could see the thatched roof of Adremildo's wooden hut up on the bank on stilts. A parade of shouting, barefoot children scrambled down the bank to greet us. Adremildo's tiny wife, Josefina, appeared with his oldest daughter, Julia, who was seventeen. After an introduction, we unloaded the boat and carried our fifteen duffels, backpacks, and boxes up to the house.

Adremildo's five younger children, dressed in woven gowns of rough brown cotton, surrounded Amanda. They touched her long blonde hair and laughed at her short flowered dress. Although Amanda was hesitant and shy at first, her flashing brown eyes betrayed that she was enjoying the attention. One little girl took Amanda's hand, and the children went off to see the chickens pecking and shuffling near the pepper plants while Julia kept a watchful eye on them.

Relieved to see the children getting along, I turned my attention to the reason we had come. Were there really owl monkeys in these forests, and if so, how soon could I see them? Adremildo explained that his neighbor, Lujan, knew the forest well, and maybe he would agree to be our guide. He sent the oldest boy off in a canoe to find Lujan and motioned for us to sit on the bench near the fire while Josefina prepared *café con leche*.

Adremildo began to talk, and we learned that this quiet man was pleased to explain his world and its history. He spoke in slow and simple Spanish as I tried desperately to understand.

"Soy uno colono de Lima. No conozco del bosque yo llegara aquí quinientos años ante."

Adremildo had been a settler from Lima who knew nothing about the forest when he had arrived in Puerto Bermúdez fifteen years ago.

"Llegado por trabajo, pero caí en amor totalmente con una Ameushe."

He had come to find work, but fell in love with a beautiful

Ameushe Indian—he pointed to Josefina. I could see that Josefina was still very beautiful, petite with delicate features and long black hair, even six children later.

"*¿Quien son los Ameushe?*" What does Ameushe mean? I asked.

Adremildo told me there were two tribal groups that lived in this region: the gentle, fragile Ameushe and the fierce, warrior-like Campa.

When the Campa arrived generations ago, they murdered all the Ameushe men and took the women as wives. No wonder Amanda screamed at the sight of the Campa chief, I thought.

Just then, Lujan appeared. A man of about thirty years of age, stocky, bearded, and muscular, he carried his machete like a man who knew how to use it. Rhett Butler immediately came to my mind. His wavy black hair framed a handsome face with high cheekbones, which suggested a highland Quechua Indian ancestor. After the introductions, he told me he had seen seven kinds of monkeys during his hunting trips. Yes, there were many owl monkeys in these forests, but they moved only during the night. The Indian name was *musmuqui*. He could take us to the forest tomorrow to search for monkeys and set up our tent.

Although the Indian custom is to take their siestas in hammocks during the day, at night the entire family huddles together for warmth. So our small family of three slept together on the palm-trunk floor of the thatched hut, separate from the other family pile. In addition to Adremildo's snoring, I could hear the throbbing of insects and the booming of frogs in the nearby rainforest. I was as excited as a ten-year-old child the night before going to the circus. Tomorrow I would walk in that forest. In fact, even now, owl monkeys could be right on its edge, in a tree, looking over at us. I listened hard for the owl monkey's chucking call, but began to drift off to sleep.

The following day, I realized Amanda was as happy as I was. She stayed behind to play with the children while Jamie, Lujan, and I looked for a campsite in the rainforest. It was beautiful, with a canopy over a hundred feet high, and it was undisturbed even by any human trails. Crystal-clear brooks gurgled through rolling hills and bright-colored birds flickered through the foliage. We decided to establish our campsite near one of those streams.

The day after that, we erected our deluxe canvas tent under a giant fig tree. The US Army Surplus clerk knew what he was talking about when he said our tent was a nice one. The square green bedroom had large screened windows and an enormous front flap that extended out like a verandah. We laid out our Therm-a-Rest mattresses and sleeping bags. Lujan macheted some branches and lashed them together to make tables and benches, using vines as twine. I set up a washing area down by the stream. The next morning, Jamie, Amanda, and I moved in.

In the beginning, Lujan took me out in the forest during the day while Amanda stayed with the Indian children and Julia, the oldest daughter. He moved first in line, armed with a machete and an ancient sixteen-gauge shotgun, just in case. He seemed to know the birds fairly well, and back at camp we compared his names for them with the Latin ones in the bird book. The big birds were easier, like the toucan, large and bright-colored in the canopy, and green Amazon parrots, noisy when aloft but invisible when they landed in a fruit tree.

On the third day in the forest, we spotted two huge birds as big as North American turkeys, sitting low in the trees. I gasped at the beauty of their black-and-white feathers and the bright red knobs that decorated their yellow beaks. From the book I recognized the bird as the rare giant curassow.

Bang! I hadn't seen Lujan raise the shotgun. One bird dropped, tumbling through the undergrowth to plop onto the soft forest floor. The other bird fluttered away through the foliage. Lujan turned to me, visibly proud of his kill, and I burst into tears. I had never seen a curassow before, and now it was dead.

"How could you kill it?" I spoke in English, but the sentiment didn't need translation.

Lujan was bewildered. This bird was a big meal, why was I so upset?

"*No bueno, los animalas muertos.*" I tried to explain my philosophy.

I made Lujan promise never to bring the shotgun again when we were looking for monkeys. I could see that he thought I was a little bit crazy, so attached to these animals. But I could also see he was trying his best to understand my strange way of thinking. And I, too, tried to expand my perspective. He looked at the forest as a grocery store, and I looked at it like a living museum. Neither of us were wrong. But the two views were incompatible, because going to the grocery store could scare all the monkeys away. It was hard to get that idea across in my basic Spanish.

The next morning, Lujan arrived with a present as an apology. Suspended from a stick was a huge catfish that hung from his shoulders to the ground.

"Anoche." He'd harpooned the catfish last night in the Pichis River. He hesitated as he offered his gift. Would I burst into tears again?

I smiled. I didn't object to eating this kind of wildlife, much to his relief. But he had to tease me a bit. "Birds, no hunt. Monkeys, no hunt. But fish, no problem. *¡Claro!*"

The next week was frustrating. My nightly searches in the forest with Lujan did not result in seeing owl monkeys. The fifth evening we did hear something moving high above us, but the forest was so dark we couldn't be sure. The ease with which I had followed my monkeys on Cape Cod had been misleading. This closed canopy forest was three times as high, and much, much darker. I couldn't see my hand when I held it six inches in front of my face. And the vegetation was dense, making following anything quickly from the ground impossible. Besides, this forest covered steep slopes, and chasing monkeys up and down cliffs in the dark was a challenge. The slick red clay on the trails made falling down routine. I had found a whole skeleton of a tapir that had slipped into a ravine and perished without getting back up the cliff. Maybe Professor Kinzey was right, maybe it was impossible to follow owl monkeys in the rainforest without radio tracking equipment.

Jamie quickly lost interest in the search for monkeys and settled in to painting frogs, insects, and plants as well as playing with Amanda. Lujan also seemed to be losing interest and showed up late on the sixth night, and not at all on the seventh.

Discouraged and disgusted, at five o'clock I said to Jamie, "Lujan isn't showing up again. We saw something last night, maybe owl monkeys. I'm going back to that spot. You stay here with Amanda."

Armed with my flashlight, a compass, and a machete, I headed into the forest. Not trusting my sense of direction, I tied a strip of orange flagging tape to the vegetation about every ten yards. This Hansel-and-Gretel method made me confident I'd be able to find my way home.

It was still daylight when I left camp, and I arrived at the large tree where we had heard the monkeys the night before. Night moved in quickly. The darkness poured in like ink, filling the forest floor. With my sight switched off, I strained my ears for cues. Odors, empowered by the moist air, took on the strength of taste. I switched on my flashlight, its narrow beam making the world three inches wide.

I turned around to make sure that I could catch the orange flagging tape with my beam. Nothing. It had disappeared into the foliage. I walked back toward where I had come. No flagging tape anywhere. Panic swept over me. I had to remain calm. I extracted my compass from my vest pocket. There was a stream nearby, probably the same stream along which we were camped. I would walk along that stream and back to the tent. I set off, but after only fifteen minutes a fallen tree had closed off the stream. According to my compass I had been heading south, so I reversed direction. But as I followed the stream back, the compass read that I was going east. Oh no, I thought, I had bought this Silva compass only three weeks ago and already it was broken! Then I discovered something even worse. The compass was working just fine, but the stream had forked and in the dark I hadn't noticed. I was heading down a different branch of the stream. I was getting very lost.

Tears welled in my eyes when I realized how lost I was. How could I be so foolish as to go out into the rainforest without a guide? Visions of jaguars, poisonous snakes, and all the jungle creatures that prowl in the night surged into my consciousness. I might never make it back to camp.

I sat on the ground in despair, but biting ants sent me jumping to my feet. That sharp movement caused a rustling of leaves above me, and some red fruits dropped on my head. Monkeys?

I extricated my field notebook and started to take notes as Dr. Kinzey had instructed me: "Orange cherry-sized fruits are dropping from four places in the canopy about fifteen yards apart." I looked at the second hand of my watch. "Five fruits a minute are dropping from Site A and four fruits a minute are being dropped from Site B. Most of the orange fruit, which has an avocado consistency, is eaten, but the seed is discarded."

The rainforest was pitch black and I couldn't see into the canopy, even with my flashlight. But I continued to take notes. In a desperate way, recording notes of half-eaten fruit felt like a much better option than just being lost and panicked in the dark. I was a primatologist, wasn't I?

The animals fed for about twenty minutes, then moved to the next tree for a rest. I panicked again. What was that sound in the underbrush, a jaguar? But when I aimed my flashlight, the beam revealed a cockroach, as big as my fist. Finally, the animals in the tree continued to feed, and I went back to taking notes.

The night seemed to go on forever. I kept my flashlight on, taking notes and peering into the darkness. Light was my only defense against the unknowns of the forest. The animals in the trees only traveled a few hundred yards, and I stuck with them. But I still didn't know what they were. I only knew that they weren't scared of a lost gringa.

When I looked at my watch, it was 5:00 A.M. Almost dawn. I had made it through the night alive! I eagerly awaited the first rays of the sun.

Then behind me I heard animals heading toward me on the ground. Big animals, more than one. My brain quickly reviewed all the South American rainforest creatures I'd read about. In an instant, I decided it must be wild pigs. In South America white-lipped peccaries weigh 150 pounds each, have scissor-like tusks, and run in herds of fifty to a hundred. Because they have poor eyesight, they trample anything in their path, including humans. The only escape was to climb into a tree, I had read.

I scrambled quickly into the nearest tree, about five feet off the ground, and hung on to a nearby trunk for dear life. I shone my flashlight down on the creatures as they passed beneath me. But after a full night of constant use, the beam was very dim. I still couldn't be sure if they were wild peccaries or not.

The forest was quiet after whatever it was passed, but my heart was still pounding, and I decided to stay up in the tree in case there were stragglers. The first rays of sun were pushing through the canopy, and it would be full daylight soon.

Chuck, chuck, hmmm! Chuck, chuck, hmmm! Suddenly, there was a familiar sound. *Chuck, chuck, hmmm!*

I looked up and there, only fifteen feet directly above me, was an owl monkey. A very irritated male owl monkey. I was trespassing on his territory, and every hair on his body was erect and his back was arched. *Chuck, chuck, hmmm!* he warned me.

As I was savoring this moment—seeing my first owl monkey in the wild—my smile was punctuated by a gift from above that left me spitting and sputtering. Above me was indeed an owl monkey in the wild, and it was treating me as Herbie and Kendra had treated the skunks on Cape Cod! Next, I felt a shower of warm rain and saw the female owl monkey join her mate in defending their territory. But I didn't care. I was alive, I was with owl monkeys in the wild, and I wasn't going to let a little urine and feces bother me.

The owl monkeys scolded me for ten or fifteen minutes, by which time it was fully light. When I was properly reprimanded, they leaped off to the west, one after the other, and within a few minutes they disappeared into a thick tangle of vines in a large, dead tree. I remembered how Herbie and Kendra had returned every dawn, like clockwork, over the roof of the Cape Cod cabin to go to bed. This must be these monkeys' sleep tree.

I took my flagging tape and wrapped it around the trunk

until it looked like a birthday present, and labeled the tape with my permanent marker: AOTUS GROUP I SLEEP TREE, JULY 5. My study had begun.

Armed with the confidence provided by daylight, I looked at the Silva compass again. I knew the Pichis River was always to the west, so that was where I should head. But where was my machete? Somehow in that long night I had lost it. Bushwhacking is never easy, especially without a machete. I got tangled in vines, tumbled down ravines, and was raked by briars, but I kept going west. It was hours before I saw the forest break into a clearing. There below me was the muddy water of the Pichis River, and behind that, in the far distance, were the misty snowcapped peaks of the Andes. I breathed a sigh of relief. Looking around at the landscape, I glimpsed a thatched hut not too far away, and headed for it.

Behind the thatched house, a Campa woman was stirring a large, blackened pot over the fire. Three children of varying ages played nearby. An eight-year-old, obeying her mother, ran off to find her father when she saw me appear from the forest.

"*¡Gringa Valiente! ¡Esta Gringa Valiente!*" I could hear her shout.

I had already become known in the neighborhood. Adremildo, Julia, and Josefina had told stories about the strange family of gringos who had come to live in the forest and study musmuqui. Later, Lujan explained that everyone was amazed at my bravery, being out in the forest at night alone. Everyone in the region must have thought I was crazy or a witch. From the very beginning I was known throughout the Pichis River region as *Gringa*

Valiente, which loosely translated meant "that crazy, brave white woman who walks in the forest at night."

The man whose chacra I had stumbled upon was a friend of Lujan's, and he guided me back to our campsite. On the walk back, I worried that Jamie and Amanda would be concerned by my disappearance. "They probably think I'm killed by a jaguar, or poisoned by a fer-de-lance. Amanda must be hysterical by now," I muttered to myself as I hurried as best I could.

By the time we reached the campsite, it was almost noon. The camp was surprisingly quiet. I was eager to tell the story of my night in the forest with the owl monkeys, but the place looked deserted. Perhaps Jamie and Amanda had already gone for help to rescue me.

"Jamie! Amanda!" I called out.

Two sleepy heads popped out of the tent opening.

"I found them!" I shouted and laughed at the same time. "I followed owl monkeys in the wild! Oh, I also got lost and a herd of wild peccaries nearly trampled me to death and I had to climb a tree to escape them. That tree was right next to the owl monkey sleep tree. I can begin my study!"

Beginning that evening, I tried to follow Group I every night. Lujan joined me again, and we started at dusk at the sleep tree. There turned out to be four owl monkeys in the group. By size, we estimated there were a one-year-old and a two-year-old in addition to the pair. "The feisty four," I called them, since they continued to scold us at dawn and dusk. We followed them from the sleep tree as far as we could, marking under their path with orange flagging tape. The next day, we cleared a trail, following the markers. I knew that Herbie and Kendra followed the same pathways on Cape Cod, and I was hopeful that the wild monkeys also kept to arboreal "highways."

At first, we would lose track of the monkeys after an hour or two, but we would return to the sleep tree before dawn to track which direction they came in from, and mark that trail. Slowly, night after night, we began to have cleared trails underneath their tree-branch paths. Cleared trails meant we could move quickly and quietly below them. Within a month, I could follow them all night long. I learned that they traveled along this system of highways from 200 to 900 yards each night. They had a second sleep tree, a viney secluded tree 500 yards from the first, which I labeled Sleep Tree II.

But did any other animals use these paths? I didn't have many sightings of day-active monkeys, but one day at dawn I saw a pair of comical saki monkeys leaping along an *Aotus* arboreal route. Magnificent leapers, more than twice the size of *Aotus*, the sakis had wiry long, gray, grizzled hair, bushy tails, and big, bare, flat noses. The quizzical pair were quite surprised to see me below them on their trail and came closer for a look, growling low to each other. Their fur looked like grizzled gray lichen, making them resemble the sloths we had seen in the *Cecropia* trees in Costa Rica. But although they were cryptic and difficult to see like the sloths, the sakis were neither lazy nor slow. After their inspection of me, they leaped away down the trail, looking like Superman in flight, with their powerful back legs and front limbs outstretched.

Once, early in the morning, when I was marking a new trail from the *Aotus* Sleep Tree II, I was surprised to look up and see a single, quiet, black monkey. It took me a minute to realize it must be a *Callicebus*. Dr. Kinzey had showed me photos of *Callicebus torquatus,* a black monkey with yellow hands and yellow neck collar, from his study site at Mishana, north of the Amazon in Peru. I had also seen a *Callicebus cupreus*, with a reddish chest like Kendra, at the Bronx Zoo. I determined that this lonely, all-black *Callicebus* was a male. After that one time, I never saw him again, nor any other of his species.

On these nights, the lonely beauty of the rainforest enveloped me. Owls gave low hoots and booms sporadically. Frogs and insects kept a lively chorus in the background until after midnight. From about two until four in the morning, everything seemed to quiet down, before the mad rush to get the last bouts of feeding, territorial calling, and traveling finished before the dawn. Because of the high altitude, the rainforest was often encompassed by clouds before morning, and the air would be chilly from the heavy mist and dew.

I occasionally shone my headlamp up at the owl monkeys, hoping to get a good look at their faces, but they didn't appreciate the invasion and moved away. I could hear them call back and forth, like Herbie and Kendra had on Cape Cod, and this signaling made me confident of their location.

Often they would sit for nearly an hour in a fruit tree, dropping fruit husks or seeds as they ate their fill. It was those times, under the fruit trees, that I saw the little dramas of the rainforest. Once, I sat looking at the ground, in a sort of nighttime trance, when I saw what appeared to be a two-inch brown twig catch a cricket. The twig opened up its lower half and revealed what looked like a miniature fishing net, which it cast over the oblivious insect on the ground. In a minute, the cricket was entangled and ready for eating. It turned out that the twig was a spider in disguise. *Deinopsis,* the net-casting spider, had evolved into looking like a twig to better camouflage itself and to better catch its prey unawares. Another time, I saw a fist-sized hairy black tarantula emerge from a hole hidden by leaves on the ground. It pounced on a giant green katydid and dragged it, poisoned and immobile, into its den. These action-packed thrillers kept me awake, night after night.

Over time, I accumulated information on the fruits the owl monkeys were eating. They ate from twelve different kinds of fruit trees, and with my Macro lens I photographed each of the fruits with their leaves for later identification. But I wondered what other items they included in their diet. In the forests of Cape Cod, Herbie and Kendra ate moths, June bugs, and cicadas. But in the darkness, I couldn't see them catching insects. Surely they didn't eat just fruit.

Then one night, in the full moon, I added another item to their diet: nectar from the *Ceiba pentandra* tree.

The *Ceiba* tree is one of the most well-known trees in the South American rainforest. It's famous for producing kapok, a silky material attached to airborne seeds, that during World War II was harvested to stuff pillows and life vests. The tree is huge, with a broad trunk with no branches for the first one hundred feet. Then the broad branches spread in all directions horizontally for one hundred feet. Once a year, all the leaves

The Chapple family on the back porch in Lyndonville, NY, 1954. From left to right: my sister Diane, my brother Ted, and me with our parents, Julie and Ed. *Courtesy of the author*

On my way to the Jimi Hendrix concert, 1968. Little did I know that my whole life was about to change. *Credit: James A. Wright*

In our apartment in Park Slope, Brooklyn, 1971. Jamie attempts to feed Kendra while Herbie sits on my lap. *Credit: Michael Barros*

Amanda giving Flower a ride, Cape Cod, 1977. *Credit: James A. Wright*

Above: Jamie and
Amanda in Prospect
Park, Brooklyn, 1977.
Courtesy of the author

Left: Amanda and
me at the Bronx Zoo,
New York, 1980.
Courtesy of the author

Right: Aotus, the "monkey of the night," Manú National Park, 1981.
Credit: Charles Janson

Below: Howard the howler monkey visits the cabin at Cocha Cashu Research Station, Manú National Park, 1981.
Credit: Charles Janson

Dave Sivertson and me canoeing on Cocha Cashu (Oxbow Lake), Manú National Park, 1981. *Credit: Charles Janson*

Amanda rafting on Cocha Cashu (Oxbow Lake), Manú National Park, 1981. *Credit: Charles Janson*

John Terborgh and a
rainbow boa, Manú
National Park, 1981.
Credit: Charles Janson

Charlie Janson and
a catfish, Manú
National Park, 1981.
Credit: Scott Robinson

Above: Scott Robinson
with tiger heron, Manú
National Park, 1981.
Credit: Charles Janson

Right: Robin Foster
pressing plants, Manú
National Park, 1981.
Courtesy of Robin Foster

Me and my "Peruvian family" in Puerto Bermúdez, 1981. Adremildo is in the back row with me, and Julia is on the far right. *Credit: Robin Foster*

Kendra and me, New York, 1972. *Credit: James A. Wright*

fall from this tree, leaving the branches bare until, over the course of a night, cup-sized white flowers unfold, brimming with nectar. For nocturnal animals, this is the biggest bar in the rainforest, and all the drinks are free.

As I watched, bats and huge moths zeroed in on this tree first. The owl monkeys found it about a half hour later. They moved from flower to flower, their silhouettes illuminated by the full moon, burying their faces into the white, sweet-smelling goblets. Then I heard a long, shrill whistle call. I could barely make out the forms of two large, slinky mammals. I could tell from their silhouettes that although they were about the size of a cat, their smaller heads suggested that they weren't primates. I watched as one grasped a branch with its tail. They must be kinkajous, also called honey bears, members of the raccoon family. Although they only ate fruit and flowers—and, apparently, nectar—the owl monkeys stayed out of their way.

There didn't seem to be many dangers in the rainforest, for monkeys or humans. Most of the jaguars had been shot by hunters, and wild peccaries like the ones I had seen on my first inadvertent night in the forest were also quite rare. Thus, I felt quite safe, even though by October Lujan spent less and less time with me in the forest. A Campa Indian woman named Marga and her one-year-old baby had moved in with him, and she was occupying his evenings. I enjoyed my quiet nights alone with the owl monkeys, sitting underneath the fruit trees and following them down their pathways.

But one night, when the monkeys had scampered into their sleeping tree by 4:30 A.M., I decided to go home early. In the silent, dripping fog I turned to go back to the tent. My mind was already snuggled into my warm sleeping bag, and I hoped my legs knew their way home.

As I scrambled up one of the many steep stream banks, my brain jolted into awareness. At the top, about a foot from my head, was a big snake. The beam of my headlamp stared directly into its golden-flecked eyes. Vertical irises, arrow-shaped head, and forked black tongue. Oh my God, it must be a fer-de-lance, the deadliest snake in the rainforest. *Shush-úpe* they called it here in this rainforest. The scientific name is *Bothrops atrox*. I couldn't tell how long the snake was because it was coiled to strike, but the head looked very big.

How far down was the embankment? I had been climbing hand over hand upward, but not paying as much attention as I should have. Could I drop without shattering all my bones? I didn't dare turn my head and break the blinding lock between my headlamp and the snake's eyes.

I didn't have much time. The agitated snake pulled back its head and propelled forward with the speed of a slingshot. In an instant before it struck, I let myself drop down the bank twelve feet and rolled into the creek, and the snake missed. Adrenalin charging both brain and feet, I returned to camp by a longer but snakeless route.

Everything was going quite well by mid-November. On any bright, lazy afternoon I could be found copying and looking over my owl monkey ranging and feeding data. Jamie would be sitting at the makeshift table, engrossed in putting the finishing touches in yellow and crimson oils to his painting of butterflies. Amanda, barefoot and brown, would be by the edge of the stream, splashing and singing and trying to catch the little fishes and frogs.

During the monthly supply trip, Jamie, Amanda, and I joined Adremildo's family on the four-hour boat trip to the market in Puerto Bermúdez. Amanda wore a broad-brimmed straw hat that we had purchased in San Ramón and a green cotton tunic called a *cushma,* handmade by Adremildo's daughter Julia. As she walked through town, her hand clasped in mine, she attracted a great deal of attention, being the only blonde the people had ever seen. We filled our backpacks with cans of tuna, condensed milk, coffee, cocoa, rice, and beans—another month's provisions.

It was late in the afternoon when we arrived at our campsite with our supplies. I slipped off my backpack and started over to the fire. But something was wrong.

"Our tent's gone!"

There was a big gaping hole in the forest where our huge eight-man tent had been that morning.

"We've been robbed!" I exclaimed the obvious.

All our clothes, plates, silverware, cups, ax, machete, sleeping bags, flashlights . . . my mind raced through the list of our possessions. Fortunately, I had taken my binoculars, camera, and headlamp for the river trip, and my field notebooks were at Adremildo's house.

We began to search for clues. Jamie was optimistic that some things might have been left behind in the forest. Amanda wanted to go down to the stream to see if her rubber duck was gone, so I went with her.

"Jamie, come quick!" I called.

When he arrived, I pointed at the footprints on the ground.

"There were two robbers, one big, one small. Barefooted. They came up the stream, I bet."

Jamie crouched and squinted. "Must have been Campa or Ameushe, since colonists from the highlands don't go barefoot in the forest. Were these kids? Both prints are so small."

I glanced over at Amanda, trying to size up her feet. "Maybe they were eight or ten, even twelve years old. Indians are small."

"They couldn't have sold our stuff that fast," Jamie reasoned. "We'll find them."

As shadowy darkness engulfed the forest, we reshouldered our packs and retreated to Adremildo's house.

"Who could do such a thing? Who would steal from us?" I asked Adremildo. "All our neighbors know us."

Adremildo shook his head sadly and tried to explain the local customs.

The concept of possessions and owning things was not known among the Campa and Ameushe. Their philosophy was that what's yours is mine and what is mine is yours. For example, if a Campa was wearing a hat and you said you liked the hat, he would give it to you as a present. But then if he said he liked your hat, you would have to give it to him as a present. If they arrived at your home, and you were not there, well, what is yours is theirs. To them, it was not stealing.

"But they must have sold some of our stuff," I pointed out. "It's probably in the Puerto Bermúdez market right now. We can at least give the police a list and description of all the stolen goods. Then if it shows up in the market, they can get it back."

"Try if you want, but I doubt the police will help." Adremildo shrugged his shoulders.

The next morning, Lujan took Jamie, Amanda, and me in his boat into Puerto Bermúdez. The police station was a wooden building with a ramshackle porch and a sign that said simply POLICÍA. The chief wasn't there, and a small boy raced out to fetch him. The three of us waited outside on a narrow wooden bench for over an hour. Finally, *el jefe*, the chief of police, appeared, wearing his corpulence like a merit badge. "*¿Qué está su problema señora, señor?*" he asked us with a slight tone of annoyance.

We followed him inside to his office. His two assistants flung open the shutters and moved chairs toward the desk, which was empty of papers. I told the story slowly, trying to include all the details. I handed him a long list of all the equipment that had been stolen. I continued to explain that we had found clues, the footprints near the stream. When I had finished, the chief shook his head and stared at me directly. "Why are you gringos in the forest alone? Why haven't you registered with the local authorities? All gringos are supposed to check in with the police. Are you prospecting for gold?"

I tried to explain, but he cut me off.

"Monkeys? Research? No way. You must be looking for gold. We need to do an investigation," he proclaimed. "We will come tomorrow."

What I didn't realize was that "doing an investigation"

meant we had to pay. We had to pay per diem and gas for the chief of police and his two assistants and we had to pay for the gas and driver for the police motorboat. Lujan explained all this to us outside the office, and Jamie and he went back with the right amount of Peruvian soles.

The next morning after breakfast at Adremildo's chacra, the motorboat arrived with the investigation party. Lujan and Adremildo went down to greet them and lead them up to the house. The chief of police huffed up the hill. Perhaps he spent more time in his office, or likely the nearby bar, than on missions like this. He settled comfortably on a bench next to Julia while his two assistants stood by. He demanded some coffee and began to roll a cigarette. He had no intention of going into *el bosque*.

The two assistants followed us to the scene of the crime, less than half a mile. They looked around for five minutes, checking to make sure the tent wasn't behind the bushes. We showed them the footprints we had found by the stream. One man got down on his knees to look closer at the prints.

"Two thieves," he proclaimed. "Man and boy." He got up, brushed off his knees, and we returned to Adremildo's house.

There, the chief of police was still drinking coffee and pontificating at Julia. He talked to his two assistants in private, and in ten minutes the Puerto Bermúdez investigation team was ready with the verdict.

The chief of police spoke with absolute conviction. *"El caso está simple."* The case is simple.

"Lujan, la guía, robó la tienda y todos los cosas." Lujan had stolen the tent and all our possessions.

Before I could comprehend this meaning, they took out handcuffs and put them on our guide.

I blinked, stunned. I knew Lujan hadn't stolen our things. He never went barefoot in the forest, and he didn't have a small son. My eyes flashed fury and my face flushed. I was about to explode when I caught the warning in Adremildo's eyes. Silently, I watched the police take Lujan down to the motorboat and back to Puerto Bermúdez to jail.

The next day, we went to Puerto Bermúdez, and after much conversation and persuasion, paid off the police with twenty-five bucks and returned with a grateful Lujan. Our first brush with frontier justice.

With our tent gone for good, we needed a place to stay. Adremildo and his family very graciously let us live with them for our last month. Including us, their house was bursting with six children, five adults, and many visiting cousins and neighbors that arrived by boat for a day or two's visit on their way to town. There was only one hammock in the household for Adremildo and Josefina, and Julia and the rest of the family slept on one side of the house on the wooden platform and our family slept together six feet away with only one blanket among us. Privacy didn't seem to be important in this frontier family. More important were the vampire bats and their razor-like teeth. They usually feasted on the blood of the cattle, but Jamie's long legs stuck out of the blanket and he found pools of blood and incisor marks on his legs several mornings. Amanda slept snugly under the blanket, which protected her.

Amanda was thrilled to be back with the children and to be the center of attention. The ten- and twelve-year-old sons took her out poling in their tiny dugout canoe. The canoe sometimes tipped over and the children would tumble into the water, laughing and sputtering and hanging on to the floating canoe. Amanda soon learned to keep her balance and paddle a dugout canoe herself.

She also joined in the daily chores of the farm. She helped Julia milk the four cows, and she doted on a brown cow with white spots that she named "Brownie." She tossed out rice and corn for the chicks and enjoyed watching as they scrambled for every grain. She would sit with Julia and her cousins and watch them embroider and sew. I was surprised when they taught her, at three and a half years old, to sew a little pouch. She also, as her mother before her, decided to adopt a kitten, a gray one, and named her Frisky. Frisky became her constant companion.

Jamie was also happy with our new lifestyle. Here he had a better table on which to spread his canvas and paints, as well as an audience. The neighborhood children would come to watch as insects and plants emerged on his canvasses. Many of these children had never seen pictures on paper before, as painting was restricted to their faces and bodies, and occasionally cloth. Most of them would never go to school.

I loved being close to Adremildo's family. As I scrubbed clothes on the rocks and peeled cassava by the fire with Josefina and Julia, we giggled and gossiped. I found out that Julia's biological father was a Quechua who had come down from the highlands for timber and then abandoned Josefina when he found out she was pregnant. That Adremildo had arrived a few months later and fallen in love with her, even though she was visibly showing. I found out that Lujan and Julia had been lovers, but Julia had decided that he had no ambition and dumped him. Lujan had sung about his broken heart as he walked alone in the rainforest. Then he had taken up with Marga, whose Campa husband had left her and her baby to go downriver to find a job. Julia now had a crush on a shop owner in town, but no one in town knew about it. I felt linked to these women by their stories and secrets. It was another kind of "understanding primate behavior."

The only negative about our new situation was that my research was suffering. I had to walk an extra half a mile to the rainforest. Heavy rains, signaling the start of the rainy season, often prevented me from going out at all. There were only a few weeks left for me to finish my study.

Three weeks before our departure date, a boat arrived with the news that a cousin from a village downstream was to be married. As is the custom, the messenger was invited to stay for the night. He told stories by the fire until after midnight, and everyone stayed up late, eager to hear all the news and gossip. The next day, preparations for the wedding began. Adremildo asked Lujan to kill a capybara for the feast. That would be our neighborhood's contribution. Lujan would do the hunting,

Jamie and I would pay for the shotgun shells, and Josefina and Julia would cook the meat.

The capybara is the world's largest rodent; a big one can weigh seventy pounds. The species is widespread along rivers throughout most of South America. They come in large groups, and each female has litters of two to four offspring each year. Aquatic like a hippopotamus, they come out on the banks of rivers and lakes after dark to graze. Although they're rarely seen during the day, a good hunter can locate them. Lujan was able to bring back an adult male for the feast. I was more understanding of hunting now, and hunting a big rodent for food was acceptable.

Dressed in our finest, we slid into canoes that would take us downriver. Since walking through the forest or even on cleared land was considered dangerous, most people in this area traveled by canoe. Our trip was fast and pleasant. As we poled along, I nudged Amanda to look at a group of small, twittering black tamarins in the trees. Although the bigger monkeys could only be found far into the interior, where hunters couldn't find them, tamarins were fairly common along the river's edge.

We arrived at the village, called Cahuapanas. After introductions to the family members of the Campa tribe, we were taken to a thatched hut to see a monkey. Everyone knew that Gringa Valiente loved monkeys, so people showed me theirs wherever I went. This one was a small squirrel monkey, tethered by a rag strip around its waist and accompanied by a large green parrot on a perch. Both animals had been pets for over two years and seemed to be in good condition. The monkey was friendly and jumped on Amanda's head, blending into her blonde hair. It was obvious that the family thought of them as we thought of Herbie and Kendra and our monkey family.

Next, we joined the family members near the familiar canoe filled with masato. As in the rite-of-passage ceremony we'd seen before, the sisters, mother, and grandmother of the bride had been chewing and spitting cassava into this dugout canoe for a week so it could ferment. Everyone was dressed in their finery, with all their jewels from the forest. The mother of the bride had earrings made of shells and the father sported a string of peccary teeth around his neck. The hand-painted garments of the bride and groom were adorned with necklaces of seeds, shells, and wild peccary and jaguar teeth. Their faces were painted red and black, and their heads were crowned with feather headpieces. There was chanting and singing as the bride and groom stood in the center of the circle.

After everyone drank a gourd full of masato, family members and friends brought the young couple gifts one by one. First was a dead toucan, then two scarlet macaws. An old man humbly gave them a curassow. We presented our capybara meat elegantly wrapped in banana leaves. According to Ameushe custom, the groom was supposed to kill a jaguar for his bride, but jaguars were quite scarce now. Instead, the groom gave his bride a jaguar tooth necklace handed down by his father to him. Six men started thumping on drums made of animal skins, and all fifty people assembled, chanting together as the masato gourd made another round. As night fell, we feasted on roasted meat and cassava and drank more masato. Then the drums again filled the air with pounding and the night was alive with singing and dancing. Unlike our earlier experience in the Amazon, we were not tourists anymore, and this was our party too. Guitars appeared and the band played "La Bamba" and salsa. I didn't have a chance to sit down before I was invited to dance again. Everyone seemed to know how to do modern dances: salsa, the cha-cha, and the Twist, only they called it *el Twist*. Amanda was dancing too.

Then a commotion broke out. One of the voices sounded familiar—Lujan and a Campa man were fighting. Julia rushed to my side and whispered, "Marga's husband has just come home from Pacaya. He found a good job downriver and has come to take her back with him. He's accusing Lujan of stealing his wife. Lujan is saying he was taking care of the family that the Campa had abandoned. There might be a fight."

About ten minutes later, Lujan came over to Jamie and me and asked if we wanted to go home. During the argument with Marga's husband, he had realized that the whole Campa nation would turn against him if he stayed much longer. Lujan had settled without a fight and Marga and her baby returned to her Campa husband that night.

As we poled upriver, the bright half-crescent moon made a rippling silvery reflection on the water. The owls hooted mournfully and the paddle splashed rhythmically in the river. An evening mist surrounded us. Then Lujan broke the stillness with a plaintive, haunting *huanno,* a highland song from the Quechua Indians. It was a song of sadness and departure, of leaving your homeland for faraway places. His strong, deep voice, wavering in the moonlight, echoed over the river.

As Christmas approached, the final week at Adremildo's chacra was occupied with packing and saying farewell. By the time of our departure, Amanda's hair was very long and bleached by the sun, her skin tanned, and she'd grown taller and thinner. But more important, she had learned a lot. She could speak Spanish. She could pole a dugout canoe, shoot with a child-sized bow and arrow, peel the bark off a cassava with a machete, and fan a fire. She knew how to milk cows and feed chickens, wash clothes on rocks in the stream, and sew. As for Jamie, he came away with two large and many smaller oil paintings of the rainforest. Although I hadn't gotten close enough to the owl monkeys to observe father care, I had three full data books on them and photos of the fruits they ate. I had also tried to take some flash photos of the monkeys, but I would see if they had turned out later.

The saddest part was leaving our friends, who now felt like family, and Amanda's cat, Frisky. Amanda, Julia, Josefina, and I were in tears at the parting. We boarded the six-seater Cessna plane for San Ramón, promising that we would return. When we had arrived in Puerto Bermúdez we had been weighed down with fifteen bags, including our big canvas tent. But now the tent was long gone, and we had given away most of our clothes. We were leaving lighter on possessions but heavy with memories of friends and an understanding of monkeys.

It was snowing when we arrived at JFK. This time the reality of the bitter cold, the noisy crowds, and the honking traffic sent a shiver down my spine. After five months away, New York seemed like a new place. The quiet of the Pichis River, those nights of moonlit solitude in the rainforest, and the hospitality and kindness of the Peruvians seemed from another world.

Our friends Mia and Floyd returned our monkeys that weekend, and it was a grand reunion. Herbie and Kendra were healthy and content, and Mango and Flower had grown. Amanda was especially happy to have Flower riding on her head once again. Then I saw the tiny monkey face peeking out from Herbie's back and heard Mia's tale of watching Kendra give birth. Even while we had been away, our monkey family had increased!

Almost unable to contain myself, I called Professor Kinzey's office Monday morning to tell him that I was back from Peru with three full data books. He didn't say much on the phone, except that he would be at our apartment in Brooklyn in two hours. He was in a very good mood when he arrived and cheerfully met the monkeys, Jamie, and Amanda. But what he had really come to see were my data books. We poured over those books for hours, as Professor Kinzey explained to me how to set up and analyze the data.

"You organized them into five-minute samples, good," he said. "You had four individuals in your group, but wrote down intergroup encounters. . . . You used local names for the fruit. . . . You measured the nightly path lengths just as I said. . . . Three full notebooks, four months. . . ." He turned to me and said, "This is the first data for a group of *Aotus* in the wild. I have to call Dick Thorington and tell him. You've done a splendid job, Pat. You have to write this up!"

Motivated by his enthusiasm, I set immediately to work.

Within a month, I had calculated the numbers and drafted a paper. Professor Kinzey helped me make revisions and I sent the paper off to the only journal outside of Japan that was dedicated to primates, *Folia Primatologica,* which was published in Switzerland.

Four months later, I received a thin airmail envelope postmarked from Switzerland. I closed my eyes, praying it wouldn't be a rejection notice.

> *Dear Ms. Wright:*
>
> *I am pleased to inform you that your paper, "Activity, Diet, and Home Range of the Night Monkey,* Aotus trivirgatus, *in the Peruvian Rainforest" has been accepted for publication in* Folia Primatologica. *You will be receiving your galleys within a few months and the paper will be out in the January 1978 issue.*
>
> *Thank you for submitting this excellent paper.*

I closed my eyes and took a deep, joyful breath. I picked up Amanda and hugged her and twirled her around until she squealed for relief. I read the letter again. Yes, my paper had been accepted. There was no mistake. I ran to the phone to tell Professor Kinzey the good news.

"Well, Pat, that settles it," he said. "You've just jump-started your career. Now you have to go to graduate school."

"No, I don't," I said, thinking that Professor Kinzey had gone out of his mind. "I'll work nine months out of the year and go to South America every summer to study the owl monkeys."

"Pat, nobody will take you or your results seriously unless you have a PhD," Professor Kinzey said earnestly.

Visions of the form letter from the National Geographic Society floated through my mind, and I winced. It had said, "We only give grants to those with a PhD."

This made me worried. I had all those questions that would need time, and more funds than I could muster up by working. I still didn't know why there was father care in owl monkeys. In fact, I really didn't know much about why this one kind of monkey was nocturnal. But graduate school, at my age? Beginning graduate school at thirty-four just seemed impractical.

"I won't get in to graduate school," I told Professor Kinzey. "I've been out of school for nearly ten years. I don't know how to study anymore."

"Take your Graduate Record Exams, Pat. Fill out those applications. Let the university departments decide if they want to accept you or not. You will have a published paper, you know. Some graduate school might just take you."

Unlike when he had told me it was a waste of time and money to go to the Amazon and study monkeys, Professor Kinzey was right.

CHAPTER SIX

INTO THE AMAZON

(New York and Peru, 1977–80)

THE SUMMER OF 1977 was exceptionally hot and
sunny on Cape Cod. Our New York friends drifted in
and out of the bayside cabin in the woods. But underneath all the bliss, a forboding lurked. Jamie was drinking
more and Mike Barros, our best friend, mentioned it to me.
Mike was drinking more, too. The two of them would stay up
late taking recreational drugs and playing screeching electric
guitar. Their band was dubbed The Feeble Flute, but even with
all the practice, their sound wasn't coming together.

My transition from hippie housewife to ardent graduate student was beginning. This summer on Cape Cod, I followed our
monkey family with a more scholarly eye, and I read papers
that no one else, certainly not my husband and friends, was
the least bit interested in. Amanda was four now, and swam
in the sea with her cousin Damian. Our friends Mike, Susan,
Norman, and Sarah were perplexed by my interest in scientific
publications. There was a divide happening, as I obliviously
sat on the deck, typing notes about monkey behavior. I didn't

seem to notice that Jamie was spending more and more time with Susan, my best friend from Brighton Beach, who liked to laugh and toss her long blonde hair in the wind. Amanda felt the tension, whining and clinging to me. Mike pulled me aside and said I should be spending more time with my husband. I looked up from my typewriter and told him that I would be there in a minute. I was not reading the signals, ignoring what was obvious to our closest friends.

In September, back in New York, I began graduate school at the City University of New York with Professor Kinzey as my advisor. I'd be armed with classes on statistics, evolution, plant taxonomy, primate behavior, and cultural anthropology on my next journey to the Amazon. While I washed dishes and ironed clothes, I thought out problem sets in my head. Meanwhile, Jamie worked at the photography laboratory, Amanda entered daycare, and Herbie, Kendra, and their family slept all day as usual.

I wasn't prepared for the costs of the changed focus of my life. At the end of the first week of classes, I came home from picking Amanda up at daycare to an empty apartment. Jamie had stripped it of his paintings, the stereo, and our record collection. I stood in the middle of the living room, stunned. Jamie had left me, Amanda, and the monkeys. He had moved in with my best friend, Susan. I was doubly betrayed. I felt my very self drowning. I loved Jamie, and I didn't think I could live without him. While I recognized that following my dream of studying the monkeys of the night was part of the reason for our break up, it didn't matter. Our marriage of ten years was over. I had to pull myself together and move on. As Amanda said, "Mom, please quit crying, I'm hungry."

Two weeks after Jamie moved out, the electricity was turned off. According to the uninterested voice on the other end of the phone, the bill was in the name of James Wright, and James Wright had said he wanted the electricity turned off. There was nothing I could do, even though I had been the one paying the bills on time. I had no money saved to put down the deposit to change the electricity account to my name. Amanda and I had to eat by candlelight each night. I tried to pretend it was a game, that we were out in the forest again around the campfire, but she didn't buy it.

I spiraled into depression. Amanda and the monkeys tried to console me, but our future looked bleak. I wasn't close enough to any of my graduate school classmates to tell them about my divorce. And all our shocked friends were avoiding both Jamie and me. I couldn't tell my parents; I was too ashamed. I didn't even know anyone who had been divorced. It seemed like I couldn't continue to live. Taking care of Amanda kept me going through the motions of living. I couldn't abandon her.

One afternoon, when I couldn't lift myself from the bed, I heard the telephone ring. It was Sandra Castleton, from La Jolla, California. We had met through letters, since she also had an owl monkey as a pet, and we exchanged photos of our pets. Sandra had visited me once in New York to meet me and the monkeys. As soon as I answered she knew there was trouble. "What's wrong? Are you sick?" she asked, and I just fell apart from all my pent-up bitterness and grief. I sobbed my story of despair. Sandra listened for nearly an hour and then she said firmly, "Call your parents and tell them Amanda is visiting them for Thanksgiving. I'm sending you a ticket to California." I obeyed.

The California sun can cure many ills. Sandra picked me up at the airport in her white Thunderbird convertible and graciously hosted me in her spacious high-rise apartment overlooking the Pacific Ocean. Her male owl monkey, Diego (named after Diego Rivera), had been red-chested like Kendra. Sandra had found him in a Los Angeles pet store and cherished him until he died after fifteen years. Now she owned a white poodle, but Diego was still first in her heart.

Sandra and I briskly walked every morning along the beach, talking and talking. Her British husband, Richard, had divorced Sandra for his young secretary soon after Diego had passed. I hadn't been able to tell anyone my story, and now I had someone who understood. Sandra reassured me that I was not a failure, and that Jamie was a fool. She explained gently that that chapter in my life was over, and I needed to put it behind me. And then one morning after breakfast, she said, "You have to take off your wedding ring. Go down to the beach and throw it into the sea. Jamie is out of your life and you are your own self now."

The words were shocking to me. I had been in denial. I had been sure that Jamie would come back to me. As I stood on the beach in front of the sea, my body heaved with tears. Then I became angry. How dare Jamie leave his beautiful little daughter and his hardworking wife? I took off my wedding ring and threw it into the Pacific, where it disappeared in a second beneath the waves.

Back in Brooklyn, I realized I had to take charge. I found a rent-controlled sublet from anthropologists who would be away for a year in New Guinea. Amanda, the monkeys, and I moved into this sixth-floor, walk-up, two-room studio in Hell's Kitchen on the west side of Manhattan, eight blocks from my graduate school. I slept on the living room couch while Amanda slept on a small bed in the other room, which was the size of a closet. My monkeys lived in the kitchen. Amanda continued to go to daycare at the CUNY Graduate Center on Forty-Second Street. We had begun a new chapter in our lives.

Dr. Kinzey provided me with a teaching assistant position at Hunter College, which covered the rent and food, but it wasn't enough for babysitters or subway fare. Many of my classes were in the late afternoon or early evening. Amanda and I would walk from our apartment on Ninth Avenue to Third Avenue and Sixty-Sixth Street, about thirty blocks. If we were late, we would run or skip, and Amanda made up a little song, "Someday we will have a house, a horse, monkeys, and chocolate, of course. A house, a horse, monkeys, and chocolate, of course." In each graduate class, Amanda would sit on my lap and draw for two hours—a very long time for a child—while the professor gave his lecture.

Despite myself, I found that I was able to enjoy my classes once again and the semesters sped by. I welcomed the long walk to the graduate school across from Bryant Park, wedged between the businesses of Fifth Avenue to the east and the Theater District and porn shops to the west. Around the corner was the New York Public Library, whose imposing lion statues at the entrance reminded me of the link between wildlife and knowledge whenever I passed by.

The City University of New York was a wonderful place to learn about primates, and I was lucky to take classes from some of the best in the world. Professor Kinzey taught both human and primate anatomy, and I learned that bones and teeth can tell graphic stories about behavior. He was a patient and clear teacher, and he loved primates passionately and conveyed that in each lecture. He taught me to look at the big picture, to study not just their behavior, but their ecology, their adaptations, their competitors.

Professor John Oates, a young ecologist from London, brought his expertise in leaf-eating Indian and African primates to his classes on primate behavior and ecology. A natural historian raised on Gerald Durrell, John had a keen knowledge of biology coupled with a critical view of science that would come to have a big influence on my career. Tall and thin, with a craggy face, he reminded me of Abraham Lincoln, and his parties that lasted until dawn were legendary.

Once a week, I went uptown to the American Museum of Natural History for my course on mammals, both extinct and extant. Our professor, and the museum's mammal curator, Dr. Sydney Anderson, recounted stories of natural history that completed the elaborate collections held on the fifth floor. He told about the Arctic-dwelling narwhal, a relative of the beluga whale, whose males have a ten-foot-long tusk, which is really an elongated left canine. He also told us about the Bornean moonrat, a nocturnal hedgehog from Borneo which is white as the moon. We learned about tenrecs from Madagascar that have more infants in a litter than any other mammal—twenty-four. For my final paper, to broaden my understanding, I didn't choose to write about primates, but pandas instead—both the giant Chinese bamboo crunchers and the little, red, fox-like relative. Our last day of class was held at the Bronx Zoo, where we could see the animals we'd studied feeding, copulating, ranging, and grooming.

Located next to the Bronx Zoo was the New York Botanical Garden, the site of a class on tropical botany taught by Dr. Ghillean Prance from Oxford. Using the plant collections at the herbarium and gardens, he illustrated the worlds of pollination, dispersal, and distribution of plants. He held the final class at his home, which was north of the New York Botanical Garden in White Plains, and filled with artifacts collected in the Amazon—hand-carved jaguar callers, a wooden horn that gave a low roar, shaman snakeskin pouches with toxic potions and fired-mud whistles, as well as carefully crafted bows and arrows and harpoons. His stories from his expeditions made me very nostalgic for the rainforest.

My favorite class wasn't even a class exactly, but an informal meeting on primates that occurred on the third Thursday of every month. It seemed like every primatologist in the New York area converged on the Forty-Third Street bar for jungle conversation and beers. The discussions would often linger into the morning hours.

It was at one of these meetings that I met Professor John Terborgh and his student Charlie Janson.

John was an ecology professor from Princeton. He had short brown hair, horn-rimmed eyeglasses, and a strong jawline that made him look like a forty-five-year-old Clark Kent. He'd graduated from Harvard with a degree in plant physiology and had fallen in love with the rainforest while birding in New Guinea. After a trip to the Peruvian Andes to figure out why different bird species were located at different altitudes, he abandoned his laboratory research for the field. In his most recent project he had followed a community of monkeys in a remote Peruvian rainforest called Manú National Park, south of Puerto Bermúdez.

"*Aotus* are the most beautiful of South American monkeys," John said after I'd told him about my own experiences in Peru watching owl monkeys. "I've seen an *Aotus* over my tent at night, but we could never study them. Your paper in *Folia* was excellent, the first published information on those *monos de la noche*." I was encouraged by these words from one of the world's experts on South American monkeys.

Just before he left that evening to return to Princeton, John introduced me to Charlie Janson, an energetic, stocky young man with curly brown hair and a bushy beard. After graduating from Princeton the year before, Charlie had joined John's monkey-watching team in Peru.

Charlie's obsession was capuchins. Unlike the cozy family life of owl monkeys, capuchins formed large groups with a dominant male and many adult females. The male led and protected the group, especially the infants. Long into the night, Charlie and I chatted about father care in South American primates, and the adventures of living in the rainforest.

At a later primate group meeting, John and I earnestly discussed the ecology of South American monkey communities and my dissertation research project. I explained to him in detail that I wanted to understand what this monkey taxon, the only one with a night-active lifestyle, did differently than all the other monkey species. Basically, I wanted to understand why this monkey switched from the sunshine back into living in the dark.

John became very earnest. "Patricia, you need a comparison. If you study a group of owl monkeys, like you did in Puerto Bermúdez, again, you won't learn anything new. You want to know how and why these behaviors evolved. You need to know what would happen if the same monkey was day-active. Would it do the same things, eat the same fruits, follow the same routes?"

"You mean, what is the difference between the lifestyle of *Callicebus* and the lifestyle of *Aotus*? Both species have the same body weight and live in couples with offspring." I was following his line of thought.

"But you'd really have to follow both species in the same forest, almost at the same time," John continued.

I interrupted him. "I saw a lone *Callicebus* once at Puerto Bermúdez. I can't be sure to find a family group."

John nodded. "And it's risky to do your research there anyway. The forest there isn't a national park, and your study site could be cut down."

I shuddered at that possibility. "So where should I do my

research?" I'd always planned on returning to Puerto Bermúdez, and this conversation had taken an upsetting turn.

"Manú National Park has twelve primate species living
together," John replied. "*Callicebus* and *Aotus* are abundant.
And the park has thousands of square miles of untouched rainforest. It's the largest rainforest tract of national park in South
America, maybe the world. It's so pristine that there aren't
even any wild Indian tribes within a four-day canoe ride. It's a
perfect place to answer your questions."

I sat back and sighed. "Yes, you're absolutely right. The
Manú is the best place to study *Aotus*. But there's a problem.
You said that it takes eight to twelve days from Lima just to
get to the research station. It's one of the most isolated places
in the world. That's wonderful for my research, but I have a
daughter, you know. I can't leave Amanda for a year."

"Patricia." John became very serious. "Come to Manú
National Park. It's the best place to find out about the owl
monkey lifestyle, the best place to do your research. And I
can't think of a better place to raise a child."

I can't think of a better place to raise a child. The words
echoed in my head. I looked up, amazed. That certainly wasn't
how Amanda's grandparents would see it, I thought to myself.
I had full custody of Amanda, and if it was okay with John, the
Director of the Manú Biological Research Station, then this
research was a possibility.

John continued, "Klaus, my Peruvian assistant, has been
insisting on bringing his wife, Rosa, to the rainforest. They
have a two-year-old daughter, Lisbet. Rosa can bring Lisbet
and help take care of Amanda. It'll be perfect."

My mind was reeling from the possibilities. Manú did seem the ideal place for my research, but was it truly the best place for Amanda? John thought it was a great idea, but he was a bachelor. Should I really take my seven-year-old child to the most remote rainforest in the world where there were piranhas, jaguars, and caimans? Amanda's grandparents weren't going to be thrilled with the dangers or the long absence. But what about me? Could I live without my only daughter for a year? Would it be better for Amanda to stay in school, or could I teach her literature, math, and history, as well as the habits of the butterflies and birds in the rainforest? She had really felt at home in Puerto Bermúdez. What was the right thing to do?

I began to apply for grants to go to Manú National Park.

It was early in 1980 and my living situation was getting complicated. The cultural anthropologists returned from New Guinea and reclaimed their Hell's Kitchen apartment. Amanda and I had nowhere to live during the four months before we went to the Manú for my dissertation year. My friend Fran Frummer, who had so kindly maneuvered my meeting with the dean of the New School to process my first grant, agreed to take us in. Fran, her husband, and their two daughters lived in the Bronx. Amanda enjoyed playing with Meredith and Megan. The monkeys were kept in large cages at City College, thanks to Dr. Kinzey's help, and it was a close commute to care for them from the Bronx.

After two months with six people in a two-bedroom apartment in the Bronx, Amanda and I moved out of the Bronx and to Hoboken, New Jersey, to live in the basement of my friend Lisa Forman's four-story brownstone. We slept in sleeping bags on blown-up air mattresses. Tossed from friend to friend, living on couches and in basements, was not the best living situation for a child, but I felt that I had no choice.

"Are we really going to have our own house someday?" Amanda would ask.

I would laugh and repeat her song, "A house, a horse, monkeys, and chocolate, of course. Yes, Amanda, as soon as I finish my dissertation, I will find a job and we'll settle down."

I desperately hoped my optimistic prediction would come true. I hoped deep in my heart that I was not lying to my child.

Amanda and I survived our vagabond existence, and in June 1980, we left for Cuzco, Peru, to join John Terborgh's team. From this city, perched at 11,000 feet, we'd descend the Andes and travel to the park together.

Although my head was reeling and my stomach queasy from the altitude, Amanda skipped up the steps of the Hotel Conchita to meet Nina Pierrepont, John's graduate student.

"I've ordered up some coca leaf tea. That's the best cure for altitude sickness," Nina said reassuringly.

Tall, thin, and graceful, Nina, an ornithologist, was studying the foraging behavior of woodcreepers at Manú National Park. In our room, she began to brush Amanda's long, straight blonde hair and chat with her about our arrival the day before. She noticed Amanda was clutching a paperback copy of *The Secret Garden* by Frances Hodgson Burnett.

"We're going to a very special garden, Amanda," Nina said. "It has secrets that no one knows the answers to yet. It's full of beautiful flowers and tasty fruits. And the gardeners . . ." Nina tossed back her own long blonde hair, as full as a lion's mane, and laughed. ". . . the gardeners are little monkeys, and birds, and bats that work in the night. A full gardening crew."

Amanda's eyes grew round when she heard this.

Because the field site was so isolated and therefore expensive to reach, the research crew would enter the park together. There would be eleven of us, from five different universities, along with John's assistant Klaus and Klaus's wife Rosa and daughter Lisbet, and of course Amanda. This was quite a big team. Nina had already seen Robin Foster, a botanist from the University of Chicago, and Charlie Janson shopping for supplies in Cuzco. We went to go find them after our stomachs settled with the tea.

Now that I was feeling better, I was able to take in the sights of Cuzco, which had once been the capital of the Incan empire. The architectural marvels of the buildings—hand-hewn rocks that fit perfectly together without mortar—were still very much in evidence. Its beige-and-brown tile roofs and stone buildings stood out against the white-capped Andean peaks. The narrow cobbled streets were lined with buildings whose balconies were draped with potted plants. There were small restaurants everywhere that sold tasty Peruvian cuisine for less than a dollar a plate. You could always hear the clear tones of panpipes from somewhere in the street. There was a highland energy in Cuzco, encouraged by the brisk, thin air and brightened by sunshine.

We found Charlie Janson near the central square, where four hundred years ago the all-mighty Incan emperor orchestrated sun-worshiping ceremonies. Charlie had been delegated to be in charge of the trip's logistics and had things worked out to the last detail.

"I located a truck for the day after tomorrow—and all of us can ride in the back," he told us. "We've bought most of the supplies and are storing them at my hotel. JT should be flying in tomorrow. Have you seen Louise Emmons yet? She's studying jaguars this year. Robin Foster's at my hotel already. Let's try to get together at five tonight to discuss the trip." I remembered that John Terborgh was called JT by his students and I nodded.

Nina, Amanda, and I headed out to do some last-minute shopping, since it would be our last chance in many months. I was still somewhat dizzy from the altitude, but Amanda was full of energy.

"Let's go down to the market where they're playing the panpipes," said Nina, whom I found out later played the flute herself. "And Amanda, you must be cold, we should find you a warm sweater." So off we went down the cobblestone streets.

Even the toughest Quechua market lady was no match for Amanda. After much laughing, and nearly an hour of tough bargaining, Amanda settled on a handmade sweater of alpaca wool covered with images of chocolate-brown llamas. Then her eye landed on a bright red knitted chullo topped with a red yarn tassel and decorated with monkeys. When she put it on her head, with her hair hidden and her cheeks burnished from the sun, she looked like a little Indian boy. I couldn't resist her pleading eyes and scrambled into my purse to get the right number of Peruvian soles.

A little way down the street, Nina picked out a handmade wooden flute that she could play along the journey. Just as we were about to duck into a restaurant for a *café con leche,* Amanda spotted a pair of red plastic sandals on a little Indian girl. Amanda couldn't take her eyes off them. As the little girl turned the corner, I thought that would be the end of it. But after we finished our coffee and started back to the hotel, Amanda stopped at a pile of shoes in front of a seated Quechua woman.

"Amanda, why do you like those shoes?" I asked. "They're plastic and won't be very comfortable, don't you think? Anyway, I'm sure they won't have your size."

Amanda picked out a pair that looked about right, and the Quechua lady motioned for her to try them on.

"See, Mom, they're a perfect fit." Amanda smiled. "They bend fine, and they have treads. I won't slip in the mud. Can I have them?"

"I'm sorry, Amanda," I said as I looked into my purse. "I don't have any money left. I need to change more money in the morning. It's getting late, and we need to meet the others for supper." Amanda's smile disappeared, and I felt guilty. What was I doing, dragging my daughter halfway around the world and I couldn't even buy her a pair of shoes she liked? But we were late and we left the red shoes behind.

Charlie Janson was waiting at the restaurant with Louise

Emmons, a mammalogist from the Smithsonian Institution. Louise, intense and fit, had tied back her long blonde hair. As a hardcore tropical biologist, she had studied bats and squirrels in West Africa, and bamboo rats in Bolivia. She had been to the Manú before, studying populations of squirrels and rodents. Her question this trip was about bigger beasts, specifically what jaguars did in the rainforest. Although jaguars had been studied in the savannahs and more open areas, nobody knew what they did in this habitat. In addition to looking at footprints and scat, Louise had radio collars with her and planned to capture the jaguars and follow them. This was the first time anyone had followed jaguars in a rainforest.

Ten minutes later, Robin Foster, the botanist from the University of Chicago, arrived. Robin smiled shyly, said hello, and brushed his brown hair aside. The shortest of the men, he had a twinkle in his hazel eyes, dimples, and a keen sense of humor.

He was followed by Anne Wilson, a Princeton undergraduate, who had come to help JT with the tamarin study. Behind Anne were two people holding hands. Martha Brecht, a grade school teacher, looked preppy and fashionably well groomed. Charlie Munn, whose research was forest birds, was tall and classically good-looking, as if he had walked out of F. Scott Fitzgerald's *The Great Gatsby*. I later learned that Nina and Charlie Munn had previously dated. In environments like these, it was easy for couples to form and just as easily break apart.

After the introductions, we settled into a hearty Peruvian meal of spicy onions, garlic, rice, and diced meat. Amanda quietly picked at her food, watching each of these strangers. She had heard them muttering negatively about bringing a child to the rainforest, and it seemed to her that no one was in favor of her being in the Manú except her mom and Nina.

JT and his girlfriend Harriot Smith, who studied tamarins in captivity, would arrive on a flight later that night.

In the chilly dawn of the next day, the team for the Cocha Cashu Biological Station gathered at the truck. JT introduced everyone to Harriot, who had long curly brown hair and a pleasant smile. Then his attention turned to the loading of the truck. Loading up our expedition gear and supplies was no minor task, since we'd purchased supplies for fifteen people for five months. JT and Charlie Janson stood inside the back of the truck, taking the twenty gunnysacks of rice, eight sacks of beans, plus twenty-three gunnysacks of canned goods that we hoisted up to them. The few cases of Chilean wine for celebrating special occasions were placed near the cab of the truck, but the cases of beer were tucked in at the sides toward the rear for easy access. "We have a few friends who'll be happy to see these cases," was JT's explanation, implying that the park guards had put in a special order.

In addition to these and other beverages, the truck was loaded with personal backpacks and fifty-gallon drums that would be filled in Shintuya with gasoline for the motorboats. When the truck was loaded, Harriot and JT climbed into the cabin of the truck and the rest of us piled into the back and tried to make ourselves as comfortable as we could. We nestled into the mountain of gunnysacks. Along the sides of the truck were sacks of perishable vegetables, including carrots, potatoes, onions, garlic, and manioc, that would only last the first month in the rainforest. Afterward, we would eat from the sacks filled with cans of tuna fish, tomato paste, jam, and sweetened condensed milk. There were also sacks with more fragile items: salt, pepper, cinnamon, raisins, baking powder, tea, pasta, cooking oil, and candles. The day before at the hotel, Charlie had encased each of these items in two layers of Ziploc plastic bags brought from the States, protection against the wetness of rain and the river. Charlie Janson sat next to two large sacks labeled "C, C & C," as if guarding a treasure chest. When I asked, he would only say that the sacks contained special items that needed to be rationed to researchers and protected from pillaging jungle creatures.

It would be at least twenty-four hours in the back of this truck before we reached the end of the road at Shintuya. We headed east, and ascended to the pass at 12,000 feet, one of the highest passes over the Andes Mountains. The altiplano tundra was cold, especially on winter mornings like this one. The world sparkled with frost and the sun reflected on ice patches. JT was particularly susceptible to altitude sickness. Every hour or so we had to stop as he vomited. Harriot sat in the middle, wiping his brow with a cloth. Nestled between Nina and me was Amanda, bundled up in her new alpaca sweater, chullo, and winter boots with thick socks. She slept, snug under a blanket. It was dark and bumpy in the back of the truck, and the exhaust fumes drugged us into drowsiness.

After the pass, we descended along the hairpin curves of the Andes. The road was so narrow that the traffic was only one-way. On Monday, Wednesday, and Friday all vehicles went down, while on Tuesday, Thursday, and Saturday they traveled back up to Cuzco. On Sunday, legal traffic went both ways, but only the foolhardy attempted the journey. People who hadn't been to church in decades were inspired to pray after looking off the side of the road at the hundred-foot drops. Most of us inside the truck were too uncomfortable and sick to care.

I began to perk up after the tundra gave way to bushy vegetation. Soon, we were traveling through cloudforest, lush with ferns and lichen. Scott Robinson, a burly birder from Princeton University, made his way to the edge of the back of the truck in hopes of seeing a cock-of-the-rock, a crested neon orange bird the size of a quail that was only found in the cloudforest. Scott had won the world's record for "ticking" the year before. "Ticking" is a sport, especially popular in England and Australia, which involves scrambling around woods and fields all over the world trying to spot as many bird species as possible. If you become obsessed with this sport, as Scott had, it meant you had to do a good bit of traveling to tick off thousands of species.

I fell asleep again, and when I woke it was 7:00 P.M. and dark. The truck had stopped, and Charlie had already jumped out the back. Roused from our slumbers, we left behind our beds of gunnysacks and snoring pigs. Snoring pigs?! I realized there were more of us in the back of the truck than when we'd started. While I'd been asleep, the driver had picked up some hitchhiking Peruvians taking their chickens and pigs to lowland markets. Since we'd paid for an "express" service, and picking up extra passengers extended the trip even longer, Charlie went up to the cab to discuss these extra passengers with John, Klaus, and the driver. Then Charlie returned to count our team to be sure we'd all survived the tortuous twelve hours.

We had arrived in the mountain village of Pilcopata. As Amanda and I emerged into the night, we were engulfed by the sounds of the tropics. It was chilly, and the moon was high in the sky and nearly full. We could see the dark outline of forest away from the road and hear lively crickets and frogs and the low hooting of an owl. I looked for Scott in the darkness to ask him which species of owl. But Scott, famished after the long trip, had already moved inside the restaurant for dinner.

The Pilcopata Hotel was a truckstop with simple food and simple beds. We sat on benches around a wooden-plank table lit by candles. Dazed and stupefied by the trip, we responded automatically as big plates of rice and beans were put before us. We ordered beers and ate and drank without speaking. I was jolted into awareness by high-pitched squeals coming from one corner of the restaurant. I felt furry animals brush by my feet, and I recoiled at the thought of rats.

"They're guinea pigs," Charlie reassured us. "They let them loose in this restaurant. There's maybe forty of them here. Guinea pig is a delicacy in these parts. They call them *cuy cuy,* like the sound they make."

"It's a rodent native to the Andes and people have been eating them for centuries," Louise added her expertise.

Amanda had reached down to pick up a furry brown guinea pig. "They eat them? I thought guinea pigs were just for pets." She wrinkled her nose.

"Yes, people around here love to eat guinea pigs more than

chicken. And sometimes they cut them up for roast shish kebab," Louise Emmons went on.

It was obvious from the look on Amanda's face that she didn't approve of this culinary habit.

"Here's a plate of guinea pig meat, Amanda." Charlie Munn teasingly pushed over a plate of brown strips in sauce.

Amanda just shook her head, sipped her *café con leche*, and petted the guinea pig in her lap.

Meanwhile, Klaus had moved away to chat with the truckers to find out about the weather. "It's been raining in the headwaters," he reported to us, "and there could be more rain tonight. We have to leave early tomorrow to get through the river while it's still low enough."

Charlie, JT, and Klaus were clearly alarmed at this news, but there was nothing we could do now. After dinner, we all bedded down on straw mattresses in the flimsy wooden rooms, happy to be out of that truck.

At daybreak, we were up and ready. Packed into the back of the truck once again, we continued our descent of the Andes. Within an hour, we came to a river with no bridge. At this hour, the water was barely up to the middle of the tires, so the truck began forging across. What had Klaus been so worried about? However, it had indeed rained that night in the highlands, and the water level was rising fast. In the middle of the river, the truck stalled. The driver turned the key, nothing. He pumped the gas pedal and tried again. Nothing. The truck wasn't going to start. The rushing water was covering the truck's wheels.

We were in trouble. JT barked commands. All the supplies and goods had to be moved from the truck to high ground on the shore in case the vehicle was washed downstream. A huge rope was cast and tied to a tree on the high ground as a guideline for people to hang on to. With each passing minute, the churning water swelled. Amanda and Lisbet left the truck first, riding high on the shoulders of Klaus and Charlie, who came back once they'd taken the children to safety. Then they and Robin, Nina, Scott, Anne, Louise, Harriot, Martha, and Charlie Munn carried the first loads across the strong current.

JT and I stood inside the truck handing out sacks from the back of the truck to the others, who resembled a line of leaf-cutter ants. After the first few loads, only the tallest and strongest people were able to withstand the power of the rising water for return trips.

Within an hour, most of the goods had been ferried across, but the force of the water was too strong for anyone to walk in the river anymore. I'd been so busy handing out sacks that I hadn't thought of the danger JT and I were in. Suddenly, I felt the truck move underneath me. The river rushed inside, sending swirls of water around our feet. The vehicle began to rock back and forth like a toy. I looked out to see Amanda waving at me from the high ground, and tears sprang into my eyes.

Then I heard a motor start. Unbeknownst to me, another truck had arrived behind us and had attached a chain to the front of our truck to pull us out of the river. Within a few minutes, our truck was safe on the side of the river opposite to the goods and the other people. I jumped out onto the firm, high ground, fighting back tears of relief.

Amanda and I were still separated by the river, but at least we were both safe. I sat on the shore and waved to her, trying to reassure her that her mother was close, while the drivers and JT played cards, waiting for the river to retreat. Amanda began rustling through her small yellow daypack that her grandmother had packed for her. Inside was a jar of chunky peanut butter, crackers, and chocolate bars. I watched from a distance as Robin, Charlie, Nina, and the other researchers clustered around Amanda as she shared her treats. Our side of the river made do with a case of beer. The team on the other side of the river had all the equipment. I watched them put up two tents and pile inside as defense against the mosquitoes. The reality of being split from my daughter was tough, and my mind whirled with how close we had both come to disaster. I stayed up all night, wrapped in a blanket by the river, watching Amanda's tent. My little girl meant more to me than anything, and I hoped that she was safe.

Miraculously, by morning the river had lowered enough for us to drive across, load up the supplies and crew, and continue on down the foothills of the Andes. The next twelve hours were much like the day before, with the droning truck and soporific exhaust fumes. Visions of owl monkeys drifted through my hazy mind. That night, we reached Shintuya, the end of the road.

The end of the road. The reality was lost on me in my trance-like state. I just wanted to be out of that truck and breathe fresh air. Once we'd unloaded our supplies and personal gear from the truck, we were freed from wheeled vehicles for months. Our only means of transport would be dugout canoe. What freedom! The end of the road was the boundary between the "civilized world" and a world beyond human control. We were journeying into the heart of wildness.

Everyone hates Shintuya. This port on the Alto Madre de Dios ("High Mother of God") River is the entrance to the Madre de Dios Province, one of the most remote places on earth. Shintuya, at an elevation of 1,400 feet, is the port where boats are negotiated and gas is purchased before the voyage down to the rainforest. To foreign researchers, it's a cement warehouse, where the rats run over our feet at night, roosters start to crow at four in the morning, and bats in the roof smell like acrid dung. At Shintuya we are prisoners. Our truck loads up with timber planks brought here by river and disappears back on the road up to Cuzco the next morning. We sit marooned at Shintuya, a place with the charm of an abandoned lot in New York City. The only escape is by boat, and we hope the negotiations to hire one won't take too many days. There are no market stalls, only thatched roof houses where Indians live and trade. In the distance, the hills are covered with beautiful rainforest, but in Shintuya only weeds and scruffy vegetation exist, a true purgatory.

All morning, Klaus and JT negotiated with the Piro Indians by the port, and we waited. First we chatted, sitting on the cement steps of the warehouse, then we explored the road, looking for birds with Scott. By the time we returned to the warehouse, the tropical sun was beating down on us. We weren't used to hot weather, and our Cuzco sweaters and heavy hiking boots were too warm.

"Mom, I'm really hot." Amanda had removed her sweater, but she still had on her thick pants and rubber boots.

"Let's find some lighter shoes," I said. When I searched

through her belongings, no canvas shoes were to be found. "Amanda, is that all you have, just those rubber boots?" As I rummaged around in the bag looking for the shoes, it began to dawn on me why Amanda had been so fascinated by shoes in Cuzco. In New York she hadn't wanted to pack her canvas shoes. She said she didn't like them anymore.

Amanda said, "Mom, I'm sorry, but I threw those old shoes out before we left home. I guess . . . I guess that was a mistake." Her face trembled as she tried to hold back tears.

"Amanda, that means you have no shoes." I collapsed on the cement steps. The repercussions of this small act of a child overwhelmed me. This would have never happened if she had stayed in New York City. Why had I been so foolish as to bring my only child out here—out here to the ends of the earth? What was I thinking? Despair was creeping into my mind, but I had to be brave in front of Amanda.

I started again. "We won't be near a store that sells children's shoes for a long time. I'm not sure what we are going to do, Amanda."

Tears began to roll down Amanda's face, and I felt even worse.

Just then, Nina appeared with a smile; she'd been eavesdropping. Bringing them out from behind her back she said, "Amanda, here's a present. I went back and bought them in Cuzco!" And there were the little red plastic shoes.

Amanda gasped. "Oh, Nina, those are my favorite shoes in the whole world. Thank you, thank you!" And she quickly put them on. A perfect fit. She smiled up at me, and I hugged her and then Nina, whom I now thought of as Amanda's honorary godmother. For the next three months, Amanda rarely took off those shoes, except for sleeping.

Robin offered to take Amanda for a walk down the path to look at some flowers while Louise joined Nina and me to chat.

By the time Robin and Amanda returned, Klaus had come up from the port with news. "There's a Piro Indian with a boat who says he will go to Cashu. His boat's small, so we'll have to split the group into two boats. The price would be two hundred dollars for the four of you plus the child. Okay?" Robin, Nina, Louise, and I agreed to share the cost of the boat. "We'll load up in an hour," said Klaus, and he returned to the river.

We would be safe; the Piro tribe lived along the large rivers and were good *motoristas*. Charlie had explained to us earlier that motoristas usually owned their boats and earned extra money for motor parts and gas from trips such as this. The Piro heartland was to the north along the lower Urubamba and upper Ucayali rivers, closer to Puerto Bermúdez.

During the growth of the rubber trade in the late 1800s, the Piro were forced into the service of various rubber barons, especially Fitzcarraldo. The Piro showed Señor Fitzcarraldo the rubber-rich Manú River basin by marching across a mountain pass, which was only a few miles in width. Fitzcarraldo then conceived a grand scheme to enslave the Piro and Campa to haul launches, heavily laden with rubber, over this pass, now called the Isthmus of Fitzcarraldo, and move the rubber down to the Urubamba River and out the Amazon River to market. However, the Manú, Madre de Dios, and Alto Madre de Dios rivers were inhabited by Mashco Indians in the times preceding the rubber boom.

The story went that the Mashco were exterminated by death squads hired by the rubber barons to clear the area for rubber extraction. Many Mashco fled into the remote headwaters. The Indians that remained, mostly the Piro, did so as slaves in the service of the barons. The Piro who were working for the rubber collectors at this time settled at Diamante, at the headwaters of the Manú River, which we would pass through on our way to Cocha Cashu. Some of the descendants of these slaves still lived there.

An hour later, we began loading the two boats with the cargo. I looked at our Piro Indian motorista as he helped arrange our gear in his boat. He had a bow and arrows with him, one arrow fashioned at the end like a harpoon for fish. He also carried a handmade net bag patterned with fish designs that Klaus told us were painted on using dyes made from forest berries. Klaus also told us that the motorista intended to fish in the Manú River. He never went up the Manú River except when he took researchers because the Manú was Machiguenga and Yaminahua territory. The Machiguenga and Yaminahua were uncontacted Indian groups who were hostile to any intruders. We were instructed by the park service that for our own safety we could not trespass outside the Cocha Cashu trail system into their territory.

As we stood by the shore, Klaus waded into the river, carefully carrying the heavy motor for John's boat on his shoulders. JT kept his boat stored at Shintuya, but the motor was new from Cuzco. The long shaft with a propeller at the end of the motor could be raised and lowered at will depending on the depth of the water. Normal outboard motors didn't work here, where rivers swelled and diminished rapidly depending on the rainfall in the mountains. They had to be specially designed so that when the water became shallow, the propeller on the tail could be lifted up and extended out back, rather than touch bottom and run aground. The motor was called a *pecky-pecky,* named for its rhythmic sound.

This was a particularly difficult time of year, with the river low and rocks lurking under the swirling waters. A boat arrived from downstream, and Klaus and its driver chatted about the conditions we were soon to face.

"Klaus, I don't think our boat is loaded very evenly," Louise said, calling his attention to the overburdened prow.

Klaus waded over to take a look at our boat. *"No hay problema,"* he responded.

"Klaus, there'll be six of us on this boat," Nina pointed out.

"No hay problema," Klaus repeated. "No problem!"

Seeing the camel-like hump of the boat, I turned to Amanda and acted like we were going out on a boat in Cape Cod. "You have to wear this life vest, just like Grampa said." Amanda, accustomed to Cape Cod rules, obeyed.

Anxious to leave Shintuya, Robin, Nina, Louise, Amanda, and I took our places on the crude plank benches in the canoe. Klaus and JT were conversing earnestly with another boatman who had just arrived from Madre de Dios, downstream. Klaus came down to shore to see us off.

"Maybe you *are* loaded too high," he eventually agreed, seeming to have changed his mind when he saw the boat with its passengers aboard.

JT came over for a second opinion. "It's full, but I think

it's okay. That Piro knows his boat's capacity. You'll make it."
With the clearance to take off, we nodded to the driver and
the small Piro boat left first, while Klaus and JT continued
conversing with the local boatmen. Their boat was sturdy and
their motor was three times bigger than ours, and we realized
they would eventually catch up with us.

We looked out to the river, the Alto Madre de Dios, with its
clear water and breathed the fresh river air. No more roosters
at dawn, Norwegian rats, or tangles of imported weeds. No
more riding in the back of a truck, drugged by exhaust fumes.
The sun glistened on the water and the hills covered by rainforest were blue in the distance. A single kestrel flew overhead,
peering down for prey smaller than us. Was that a group of
black skimmers, with their orange bills and matching legs, flying in formation just over the water, ready to grab a fish? They
swerved right over our boat. The river's breeze ruffled our hair
and the whitewater splashed our faces. The boat began to rock
and we looked at our motorista. The Alto Madre had many
rocks and rapids and was always considered treacherous.
Having a Piro at the helm gave us confidence, since he'd been
raised on this river. He slowed down and the boat recovered
its balance. Then, again, we felt the scrape of the pecky-pecky
propeller on hidden rocks. After the experience with our truck
nearly overturning in the headwaters, we were tense. The boat
started to lurch. We'd hit a rock in the rapids. Being loaded so
high, the boat leaned left and flipped.

The next moments were a blur of splashing water, jagged
rocks, and strong current. As I grabbed on to the overturned
boat, I looked desperately for Amanda. She was being swept

downstream along with all of our gear. She bobbed in the midst of backpacks and boxes, her arms flailing to grasp onto something. I couldn't reach her. I was going to lose her. Then Nina, a stronger swimmer, caught her up and hauled her to shore.

"Amanda, Amanda!" I cried, scrambling to the beach. I hugged her shivering body inside her life vest. "Are you okay? Are you okay? You almost drowned."

Amanda's teeth were chattering and her heart was racing. She coughed to clear her throat and said, "I think I'm fine. The water was really cold."

The five of us spent the next few hours trying to recover our supplies and equipment from the river. Everything was scattered hundreds of yards downstream, where the rapids ended. We hauled item after item onto the beach and laid them on a blue tarp to dry. I inspected my case on shore. During the first meeting with Professor Kinzey, he'd advised me to put all my camera equipment and binoculars in an aluminum case to protect against the rain. Would it still be waterproof? I sat on the sand and carefully opened the case. It was dry as a bone inside.

Louise, however, never recovered her binoculars and she lost rolls of unexposed film. Robin's stacks of Cuzco newspapers, essential packaging for herbarium plant collections, had been turned into a mushy porridge. Amanda had lost her grandmother's yellow daypack with its nearly empty jar of peanut butter and one candy bar that she was saving. Our clothes, sleeping bags, and mattress pads were soaked. Shocked, chilled, and wet, we were scared of what would happen. The

Piro Indian began to tinker with the motor as we spread out our wet things in the sun to dry.

Almost two hours later, JT's big boat appeared. Klaus took over from our Piro Indian and adjusted the motor until we heard the pecky-pecky sound. We repacked the boat—with a lighter load—and solemnly followed the other boat. For the rest of the trip, with Klaus leading, the boats easily negotiated the rocks, rapids, and whirlpools. It was dusk when we reached the Piro Indian village of Diamante, the home of our motorista, at the entrance to the mouth of the meandering, muddy Manú River.

We pulled both boats up to the steep bank and staked them. JT greeted the head of the village and asked if we could camp for the night. After dinner by the fire, we listened to the nightly news, the last word from the outside world that we would hear for months. We didn't get the news from TV broadcasters, or even shortwave radio, but three Piro men who spoke Spanish, sitting around the roaring fire.

"Three villagers, a woman and two of her children, died of the white man's disease last month," said an old man who leaned on his heels before the fire.

Chicken pox, a common childhood disease in the States, routinely kills Indians in South America even today. Their lack of immunity is a frightening reality that extends back to conquistador times, when millions of Indians died with the arrival of the Spaniards and their diseases. On this trip, we would be so far removed from that white man's world that most Indians were still as immunologically naïve as before the "conquest." It was like we were traveling five hundred years back in time. I was grateful that Amanda had already suffered through chicken pox and had her vaccinations.

When JT explained that Louise had come to study jaguars, the old man sighed. "Juan, my grandson, killed a jaguar last month. It had attacked his pig. Juan tracked that jaguar down with his bow and arrow."

We looked over at Juan, who was grinning and wearing his jaguar's teeth around his neck. Jaguars were rarely seen near villages these days.

Louise asked, "Was it an adult? Male or female?"

"Big male," Juan responded, pride in his voice.

The fire was getting low, the major stories had been told, and two cases of beer had disappeared by the time we stood up, ready to retire to our tents. But as the last of us were leaving the fire, the village headman said under his breath, "There are rumors of three wild, naked women from the forest who have been sighted on the beach. Talk to the park guards at the station. No one knows who they are."

The next morning, we ate rice and fried fish for breakfast and left the Alto Madre de Dios River. That broad whitewater river would continue down to the Madre de Dios River and then to the largest tributary of the lower Amazon, the Madeira. The Madeira rapids in Brazil are formidable and prevent any transport of goods from Peru to Brazil via that path. But the water would eventually join the Amazon in Brazil and reach the Atlantic Ocean.

Quite a contrast after the dangerous, rapids-filled Alto Madre, the slow, plodding, and brown Manú River curved methodically all the way to Brazil. The Alto Madre, the Madre de Dios, and the Madeira rivers had settlers all along them, but the Manú River was uninhabited. As we turned toward the interior, we were truly leaving any trace of modern life behind.

"Look, Mom, monkeys!"

Amanda pointed to tiny golden squirrel monkeys, twittering like birds and splashing in the trees next to the bank of the river. A toucan with a giant beak flew over the river in front of us. All of us were spellbound by the beauty, by the peacefulness.

Late that afternoon, we landed our boats to camp on the beach for the night. I had never seen white beaches along a river before, but broad expanses of perfect pale sand accented every turn of these meandering Amazon headwater rivers. As if she were back on Cape Cod, Amanda set to work building a sandcastle, pleased that no tide would destroy it, while we set up the tents. Then, Louise checked the beach for tracks since jaguars often hunted along beaches. Klaus, Charlie, and JT left with the ax and machetes to collect firewood. Scott drifted off after a flock of black and yellow birds. Robin found some flowers at the edge of the forest. Nina, Martha, Rosa, and I were trying to sort out dinner. As our rice finished cooking, the sun set, turning the river red as blood and the sky as vivid as an oil painting. And then the darkness fell, and we lit candles for dinner. JT broke out a bottle of fine Chilean wine to celebrate our passage. After our long, tedious, dangerous journey, we were feeling alive again.

After dinner, we walked along the beach in silence, looking at the brilliant stars. The Southern Cross shone clear and halogen-bright. Fireflies sparkled at the edge of the dark forest.

I was always listening for owl monkeys, but all I heard were the lonely hoots of owls. The moon rose, its pale light casting a mysterious pall over the beach. Yes, we were closing in on paradise. But we still had three days to go before we reached our destination.

It took two more days before we reached the Manú National Park guard station at Pakitza. High on the bank of the river, it consisted of two buildings, a shed-like office and a meeting room, both in need of repairs. The five park guards ran out to greet us, glad to see Professor Terborgh and his team again. The park guards were from Lima and Arequipa and of Spanish descent. They led an isolated life, days from any village, and were treated like newcomers in the region, separate from the world of settlers or Indians. This park had few visitors, and only researchers had authorization to enter.

Created in 1971, at 1,881,000 acres Manú National Park is the largest protected area of rainforest in the world. Its goal is to safeguard not only its nonhuman population, but also its human population against invaders. The park guards reiterated that our permits said that we weren't to associate with the Indians inside the park. We were allowed to research the wildlife at Cocha Cashu Biological Station, but we couldn't go farther into the park than that.

The park guards talked rapidly and loudly with Klaus and JT about the year's events. They pointed to a shed containing five hulks of boats, remnants from a decade ago, when the World Wildlife Fund had helped pay for setting up the park. Now only one small boat was intact, but the motor had been dead for over a month. Had Professor Terborgh and Klaus received the message to bring motorboat parts? The park guards were eager to know since this boat was their only mode of transport, their only lifeline to the outside world.

Yes, we'd brought Evinrude motor parts, and a case of beer for them. In addition, JT offered a few small presents, like Swiss Army knives the guards had requested the previous year. The guards were overjoyed, and they and JT and Klaus set to tinkering with boat motors while the rest of us set up tents and prepared the fire and dinner.

Over dinner, the park guards told us about the three mysterious women.

"I saw shadowy figures in the forest about three months ago, when I was patrolling up to Tayakome, the Machiguenga village," one of them, named Jorge, said. "When I stopped on the beach, three Indian women peered out of the forest. They weren't wearing any clothes, no cushmas or anything, completely naked. Before we could get on shore, the three women ran back into the forest, and I continued on patrolling upriver." Jorge drank some of his beer, the first he'd had for months, and then continued with his story.

"When I came back, I stopped at the same beach and saw the women's footprints. Three sets of small feet. This time, the women peeked out from the forest, then timidly came out onto the beach and approached me. The older woman talked to me, but I didn't understand. She didn't speak Machiguenga or Piro. I couldn't understand any of the women when they spoke. The older one was talking very loudly. The younger ones were quiet and scared. The older one was frustrated that I couldn't understand her. She became aggressive and ran at me and grabbed my cap. Then she ran away into the forest with the others. I tried to chase after them, but they were gone.

"I came back to the station and got Carlos, here. The next day, we went back to get my hat. The women were there, still naked. They came out of the forest, but Carlos couldn't understand them either. It was amazing that these women were alone, without men. We asked in sign language what they ate, and they indicated that they ate turtle eggs buried on the beaches.

"Carlos and I suddenly realized they had no fire. Machiguenga and Piro Indians keep their fires burning continually in the villages. Where were these women's villages, we asked? The women shook their head to all our questions, not understanding. Carlos brought out his matches. He lit a match and the women screamed and ran into the forest and we couldn't find them. They were afraid of fire. Can you imagine that they might not know about fire? They were naked, no fire, eating raw turtle eggs. There are no villages near there. We know that. Where are these women from? They can't speak anybody's language. What are they doing living there on the beach?"

Who were these women? Where did they come from? They must have lived far into the interior before.

"Well, we went back a third time," Carlos responded, "but they weren't on the same beach. They had moved half a day's boat ride from here. They were braver this time and climbed into our boat and stole our jackets, but we caught the women before they got away and took the jackets back. On that trip back to the station, the motor broke down, and we had to paddle here. We've been marooned here at the station ever since."

The next morning, we loaded up for the final journey to our destination at Cocha Cashu. JT graciously gave the guards several weeks' supply of rice and beans, since their basic food had run out and they were relying on boiled plantains and manioc harvested from their garden. Klaus included some gas for the motorboat so they could make a supply run to Cuzco.

"Be careful of those women. They'll come on board and steal all your supplies. They are very wild and crazy. We don't think they are normal in their heads. If you see them on the beach, don't stop," Jorge warned as he pushed off our boat.

This time, our eyes were glued to the shoreline, not just to see glimpses of monkeys or birds, but to see wild humans as well. JT's boat led, with our motorista about twenty-five yards behind. I had both my camera and tape deck handy, just in case.

Up ahead, Charlie Janson signaled for us to look to the left. There they were in plain view, standing on the shore. The three women were indeed naked, almost—one woman was wearing a park guard's cap. The three women ran down to the edge of the shore when they heard the motors and waved frantically at the first boat, like sirens from ancient Greece luring sailors to their ruin.

JT's boat had slowed down so we could catch up with it. The women were wailing and singing and crying. I turned on the tape deck. They swayed rhythmically and paced along the shoreline as they sang. There was an older one who looked like a grandmother; the middle one, about thirty; and then the youngest, who was perhaps sixteen years old. Perhaps three generations. Were they crying for their lost husbands, their lost tribe? Had the rest of their community been killed? Had they been banished from their families, or just lost their way in the forest while gathering food? Questions raced through our minds.

Then the women saw Amanda. A child—a very blonde child with red skin from the powerful sun. The three wild women started to laugh and clap and sing, beckoning Amanda to join them. Amanda smiled and waved, and looked to me for reassurance. The women pleaded with all of us to come ashore, chanting loudly in a language no one could understand. Finally, frustrated by our reticence, they began to walk into the water toward us, beckoning with outstretched arms and shouting loudly. JT gave the command to start the motors at full speed and the woman's chants were lost in the drone of the motors.

"Mom, why didn't those women wear any clothes?" Amanda asked. "Why did they want us to stop? Did they want our clothes? . . . There really aren't shops here, are there, Mom?"

"Amanda, I wish I knew. The park guards say that they are from a lost tribe, and no one can understand their language, so it's a real mystery. But don't be scared. They're a long way from where we will be living. They're moving toward the park office, not toward our research station. We'll be safe at Cocha Cashu." I wondered what other surprises lay ahead of us.

That afternoon at about three, JT's boat turned toward the bank of the river. Shaded by a gigantic tree was a tall stake and chain to tie up our boats. We'd traveled nearly a dozen days from Lima, in trucks, in boats, always staying on the outskirts of the forest. Now we stood at the entrance to what the park guards called the Green Cathedral, the grand portal to Trail One, the double-lane path that led straight east like a tunnel into the rainforest and to the lake called Cocha Cashu. We had reached the most remote rainforest in the world, and we were about to enter what would be our home for the next year.

CHAPTER SEVEN

GREEN CATHEDRAL

(Cocha Cashu, 1980)

I CLIMBED OUT of the boat, and picked up Amanda and put her on solid ground. It was wonderful to have reached our destination. Our first task was to unload the boats and carry our supplies down Trail One to the research station half a mile away. I had never seen a forest so high, the canopy so dense, like a layered umbrella. "Amanda, this is our new home!" I told her, and she smiled.

Amanda and I put on our backpacks and followed Charlie Janson and Louise down the wide Trail One to the research station, which was a large, wooden house painted green and raised up three feet on stilts. It overlooked the large oxbow lake, Cocha Cashu, from which the station got its name. The clearing which contained the station was big. There were two or three *Scheelea* palm trees in the clearing, and the rainforest bordered it on three sides. A big tree in front of the research house had blown down into the water, making a pier out into the lake. We could see twenty side-necked turtles sunning themselves on top of this log. "The butterflies are kissing the turtles!" Amanda said.

We walked to the edge of the water of Cocha Cashu. *Cocha* means "lake" in Quechua, and *Cashu* refers to the cashew nut it's shaped like. The lake used to be part of the Manú River. Over time, maybe fifty to a hundred years, the river sediments filled parts of the river and this lake remained. Now it was rimmed with trees and vines that dripped into the glass-like water. We watched a purple jaçana with its long toes and sharp beak peck for insects near the shore. Statuesque black cormorants spread large wings over the water like scarves on a clothesline.

"Can we swim in this lake?" asked Amanda.

"Yes, Amanda, every afternoon. This is our bathtub," I replied.

Next, we walked into the green wooden station house, which had been built by the Frankfurt Zoological Society a decade ago. The windows had screens, and there was a dining area with a table and two long benches, a storage area, and a kitchen with a fireplace. Overlooking the lake was a library room accessed by stairs. The outhouse was at the eastern forest edge of the clearing, and clotheslines for laundry were strung between the palm trees. An outdoor campfire, where most of the cooking took place, was on the forest side of the building. All researchers slept in tents pitched further from the clearing and inside the forest. Amanda and I couldn't linger longer because we had to choose a campsite before dark. But before that, we helped carry another round of supplies from the boat.

I noticed that Charlie Janson himself carried the sack labeled "C, C & C," the secret sack we had spied earlier. At the cabin, Charlie heaved the sack off his back into the corner of the storeroom. Amanda, who had just arrived with a sack filled with toilet paper, set it down and gazed curiously at the "C, C & C" sack.

"Look inside, Amanda." Charlie untied the twine and beckoned to her.

Amanda was a bit apprehensive as she peered in.

"Wow, it's chocolate!" she exclaimed.

"Chocolate, cheese, and coffee: the three most precious things on earth. But you can only have one bar of chocolate a day. Each of us will get our ration at dinner. This chocolate has to last a long time, since we won't be going back to Cuzco for supplies for another five months. Peruvian chocolate is really good," Charlie added and winked.

"Come on, Amanda," I called from outside. "We have to set up our tent."

Amanda and I chose a lakeside location with a waterview on Trail Seven, not too far from the research house for safety. Above our tent site arched an ancient *Ceiba pentandra* tree more than a hundred feet high. This tree would be good for shade against the hot sun, especially important if I was going to be sleeping during the day. With a machete we cleared the underbrush. Robin stopped by and asked if we needed help. He wanted to pitch his tent near ours and Amanda said, "Sure." They had bonded along the trip.

By the time our tents were up and we returned to the cabin, it was late in the afternoon. JT had begun to swim across the lake, which he did at the beginning of every field season as a kind of baptism. After each researcher finished setting up his or her tent, he or she jumped into the lake to join him.

Amanda and I were just stripping for our first dip when a loud "Help!" echoed across the lake. Nina rushed to get her binoculars. With the naked eye we could see JT's head in the water, but bobbing next to him was another head, about the same size, with whiskers even bigger than the professor's. Then that head disappeared under the water, and a third head popped up, again with whiskers. Soon there were six heads in the water, and only one of them was human.

"Are they seals?" Amanda asked.

Finally, Nina arrived with her binoculars. "They're giant otters," she said. "They can be six feet long and weigh over 170 pounds. JT could be in big trouble!"

"Help!" JT yelled again. "Bring the boat!"

Scott, closest to the water, jumped into the small handmade dugout canoe that was tied to the bank in front of the cabin and began to paddle fiercely to JT's rescue. But because he was only paddling on one side, he spun in circles, creating his own special kind of whirlpool. It dawned on us that Scott probably had very little experience in paddling. Charlie Janson managed to climb aboard and started paddling from the other side.

The rest of us watched with our breaths held as the five giant otters turned their whiskered heads from JT to the approaching canoe. Louise muttered that even jaguars avoided giant otters. When the canoe was twenty yards away, the otters retreated, barking loudly, while Scott and Charlie rescued JT. Back on shore, JT, visibly shaken, hypothesized that he had swum too close to the otters' dens and their babies. Underwater the otters had rammed him with their heads, but with their mouths closed.

"Mercy," said Louise, who knew the abilities and habits of large mammals well. "One of those otters could have ripped you to shreds. But they must have decided you were harmless, and they were just playing."

A new station rule was decreed. There was to be no swimming near the north side of the lake—at least until the baby otters grew out of that den.

Amanda and I set up our routines the next day. After breakfast at the house, we would go back to the tent for homeschooling. I had brought second-grade textbooks and workbooks with me and we would labor on these tasks until noon. Then we would go back to the house to cook our rice and beans. Amanda continued not to like rice and beans, and thrived on *café con leche,* occasionally with rations of peanuts, cheese, and canned tuna fish.

In the afternoons, Amanda would join the other researchers while I searched for my monkeys. Nina and Charlie Munn taught her how to pluck a bird out of a net and hold it in her hands, its feet between her fingers. Charlie also taught her how to draw birds in her notebook, and how to burp loudly. The two of them had burping contests that more often than not ended in laughter. Robin taught her how to identify the flowers and JT took her fishing in the dugout canoe. Amanda avoided Scott and Louise. She could sense that they were against having children in the rainforest on principle.

In the afternoons, Amanda also would play with Lisbet,

Klaus and Rosa's daughter, who was now three. Amanda often carried Lisbet on her back, like Campa girls carry their sisters. Then she would join the rest of us for a swim in the lake to cool off after a long day in the forest. The sun set at 6:00 P.M. and dinner was ready shortly afterward. Dinners at the research station were lively candlelit events, with each researcher reporting on animals they had seen in the forest that day, and of course there was the joy of a Sublime (a well-named brand) chocolate bar for dessert. Everyone was in bed by 8:00 P.M.

Every researcher at Cocha Cashu was studying the secrets of the rainforest, but each had a specialty. The two largest interest groups were those that studied monkeys and those that studied birds. The "monkey watchers" were detectives, shadowing individuals from dawn to dusk, gathering evidence. Working beneath the canopy like undercover agents, monkey watchers dutifully recorded every association, every vocalization, even every copulation, for each monkey. Monkey watching was not for the dilettante. Dawn to dusk, every day (and for me, dusk to dawn, every night), week after week, month after month, all year long, the monkey watchers worked. We worked six days a week and on the seventh day we did our laundry. Charlie Janson, Anne Wilson, and I were the monkey watchers.

Birders were different. They certainly rose at dawn, but because their targets could fly, they didn't doggedly follow individuals. The birders were more like the opinion pollsters that send out questionnaires or take random samples from people at shopping malls. Birders relied on inventory data or looking at large samples of groups at periodic intervals, usually a few hours at dawn and dusk. After these few hours of work, birders could indulge in other activities, such as swimming in the lake, writing letters back home, doing laundry, or taking a siesta, activities that monkey watchers were only able to observe in their monkeys. John Terborgh and his three Princeton graduate students Scott Robinson, Nina Pierrepont, and Charlie Munn were the bird watchers that year.

Unlike the other birders, Scott didn't appreciate monkeys, especially howler monkeys. He pitched his tent to the north of the cabin on Trail Six, and as luck would have it, a howler monkey group often slept in that neighborhood. At dinner, Scott would give us details from the exciting soap-opera dramas of his blackbirds, the melodious caciques that lived in hundreds of basket nests suspended over the lake. Then at the end, Scott would mention disgustedly, mumbling into his beard, that he'd seen a clump of howler monkeys on Trail Six again. As Nina pointed out, Scott looked a little bit like a howler monkey himself.

Howler monkeys were the second largest monkey in this forest, weighing in at about twenty pounds. In the Manú, howler monkeys are Irish-setter russet in the rainforest shadows, turning brilliant orange in the sun's spotlight. They feed at the "salad bar," selecting from greens, while other South American monkeys have a more diverse menu that includes fruits and insects. It may not be difficult to find a "salad" in the rainforest, but there is a tax to easy access. In order to squeeze enough energy from greens, nearly a bucketful has to be eaten each day. That requires a bigger storage container, and leaf-eating monkeys like the howler often have prominent bulging bellies. Extracting the energy from those bellies takes four times longer than the digestion of other foods. Howler monkeys quietly rest while digesting, and even monkey watchers acknowledge that howler monkeys can be a bit indolent. Three quarters of their day can be spent immobile, sitting together on a large branch. When howler monkeys do move, it's in a slow, deliberate way, clumsy compared to other primates.

Their lazy lifestyle means there is no available energy for social graces or activities; no grooming, no playing, no chit-chat. The only enthusiastic action that howler monkeys have is roaring together like lions, especially before dawn. During these sessions, the whole group roars ferociously, but the big males are particularly loud, having come equipped with a built-in bass tuba in their throats. This expanded hollow bone (hyoid bone), near the Adam's apple, is four times the size of any other primate's, including that of humans, and acts as a resonating chamber that causes sound to boom out like a fog-horn from the extended lips of the howler. It can reverberate for a mile in the forest. We monkey watchers assumed that these roaring sessions were to warn other howler groups to stay away from their property, a sort of a verbal "no trespassing" sign, but Scott had a theory that the roars were meant to wake him up before dawn or during his afternoon siestas.

There was another reason Scott hated howler monkeys. On the fourth night after our arrival at Cocha Cashu, it rained hard, and Scott decided he should cover his tent with a tarp.

Most of us had rigged over our tents tarps of forest green or deep blue, colors that blended into the surroundings while protecting us from both sun and rain. After the first rain, Scott discovered that while he'd been in the States, he'd been so intent on packing two pairs of binoculars, his spotting scope, and other birdwatching gear that he'd neglected to bring a tarp with him. The only one that he could find in the cabin storeroom was old, abandoned the previous year by a researcher. It was without holes or tears, but it had one drawback: it was fluorescent orange. With no other choice, Scott rigged the orange tarp over his tent on Trail Six.

The next day, perched like gargoyles above the brilliant orange tarp covering Scott's tent, was a group of howler monkeys. The five animals, swaying together like a barbershop quintet, began to produce a deep, rich, bass roar. It was mid-afternoon, an unusual time for howlers to call, but they were quite serious about this afternoon serenade. The bright orange howlers regarded the bright orange tarp as an intrusion. As the sound began to crescendo, they stopped. However, the performance was not over. Each of the five animals simultaneously emptied their bowels in tribute to the splendid orange tarp, leaving an intense odor of monkey manure that radiated throughout the forest along Trail Six.

And then Scott emerged from the tent. Roaring like a bull, his face turning the color of his tarp, he picked up a stick and waved it at the monkeys. The monkeys slowly climbed into the canopy, but Scott could not chase away the overpowering smell they left behind. Even washing the orange tarp in the river didn't help. After days of suffering, Scott moved his tent but not the orange tarp, which remained on Trail Six as evidence of who had won that battle.

I was eager to begin studying the behavior of my monkeys, but first I had to find my study groups. Searching for monkeys is like the game children play of "find the missing animals in this picture." But this game was real, in a three-dimensional, very tall maze. A closer look into the depths of the forest rendered the picture ever more complex: shiny green scarab beetles, bright yellow and red walking sticks, tiny green frogs with yellow dots that turn red when you pick them up. Sprays of tiny white orchids cascading from a tree trunk. A pair of playful tayras, cat-sized carnivores, romping through the forest. A tumbling, frenetic, chattering group of olive-yellow squirrel monkeys, maybe thirty-five of them, busily searching under leaves for insects and splashing from branch to branch. Yes, there were lots of animals, including monkeys, but my *Aotus* and *Callicebus* monkeys remained hidden in the picture.

I had spent weeks searching for monkeys when one day I returned tired and discouraged after nine hours of walking the trails, peering intensely into the foliage, hoping for a glimpse of the monkeys, listening attentively for a monkey call. And, for all my efforts, I'd seen only squirrel monkeys. Exhausted, I threw down my daypack in front of the tent and called to Amanda, thinking she was inside. Amanda answered, but she was about ten feet further down the trail, her eyes focused on a tree.

"Shhh," is how she greeted me.

I slowly and quietly walked down the trail, and there they were on a branch eight yards up. Fudge brown in the sunlight, black in the shadows, they were just sitting there. They looked like Angora cats with intense eyes and monkey faces. They didn't seem concerned by Amanda's stare, but as soon as I arrived, they scowled and disappeared.

Amanda had found the *Callicebus* that I'd been searching for all day! *Callicebus Group I, 15:35. Trail 7.125,* I wrote in my field book.

The next morning, I emerged from the tent, armed with notebook and binoculars. The dawn chorus of birds had already begun. When it started to diminish, I spotted the family of four *Callicebus* monkeys twenty-five yards away, huddled together on a branch about fifteen yards up. The way they opened their eyes, yawned, and stretched together, reminded me of a litter of kittens after a nap. The *Callicebus* stretched again and each jumped in turn from the sleep branch for their morning urination and defecation. Once these necessities were completed, they moved together again to look out over the lake.

As the sun began to beam down on their fluffy brown fur, both mother and father leaned together and started their dawn duet. Looking like a plush toy, the subadult joined his parents in the call, as the yearling sat nearby. The sound began—a bubbling, gurgling, low rumble increasing in tempo and loudness until it became an ear-splitting turkey gobble. The female hit some high notes, the male rattled a few whines. The youngster joined in. The delivery was earnest, and above all, loud.

"Yikes, Mom, what's happening?" came Amanda's sleepy

and anxious voice from the tent nearby. "Are you okay? What's that sound?"

By the time Amanda emerged from the tent, I was laughing. The duet was ridiculously modern in its dissonance, yet the monkeys were so serious about it. Amanda couldn't help but laugh too at the outrageous sound. Then we heard a *Callicebus* group across the lake answering with the same call. Then to the south, another group began calling, and then another far across the lake near the otters' den, as if the lake were a sounding board. Then the broadcast was over, and the monkeys moved on to breakfast. This was the first time since we'd arrived that we had heard that call.

After eating some fruit in a nearby tree, the *Callicebus* family disappeared into the forest. It was like they had just vanished. *Callicebus* Group I was very good at losing their detective when they wanted to.

But all monkeys are difficult to follow at the beginning of a study. The "habituation" procedure is a contest to see who gets bored first: the monkey, trying to escape, hide, or outpace the researcher; or the researcher, trying to outwit the monkey. Whether this habituation takes weeks or years usually depends upon the leader of the monkey group. A leader that has been shot at, or is just shy, can make habituation impossible.

Callicebus Group I was accustomed to the presence of the researchers, who arrived in their neighborhood like migrating birds every year, so it took only two weeks until I could follow them all day easily.

After this group was habituated, *Callicebus* life became my life for six straight days at a time. Each morning, I would rise before dawn, eat a quick breakfast of leftover rice, gulp a hot cup of coffee, and then rush to the sleep tree of my *Callicebus*. From the moment the group woke up, I followed them until they retired to their sleep tree, perhaps twelve hours later. Every month for a week they would be followed this intensively for a full year. Their schedule was routine. First, get up out of the vine tangle and stretch and yawn. Then rest a few moments, thinking. Maybe fifteen minutes. Then begin the synchronized dawn duet. After a half hour of calling and listening, ascertaining the whereabouts of all the other groups, it's time for breakfast and, literally, coffee.

The mother leads the group from the calling branch to a tree she knows has ripe fruit. Her two-year-old and one-year-old follow her with the father trailing the family. *Callicebus* often eat in short, small trees in the understory and many of these trees are from the Rubiaceae, the plant family that gives us coffee. I often wondered as I stood in the cold dawn mist, clinging to my field book and binoculars, tired and hungry and in very desperate need of coffee, if these plants contained any caffeine. The peaceable *Callicebus* family certainly didn't seem to be showing any effects.

The group feeds twenty minutes to an hour, then finds a hidden shadowy spot, and rests for more than half the day. Then they get up for a leisurely walk for five to fifteen minutes, find another good eating spot, feed for half an hour, travel five minutes to a shaded spot, and rest an hour. That was the rhythm. A quiet, calm life. Definitely the "slow lane" of monkey lifestyles.

In the afternoons, after a two-hour siesta, the family has "foraging outings." After moving about thirty yards apart they sit, searching for insects and new leaves. The father might grab a leaf, turn it over, and find a spider in the web on the other side to munch. Then half an hour later he might find a line of ants marching up a trunk. He'll begin to eat them, and the one-year-old will join him in the snack. Foraging sessions last about an hour or two, before a dash for the last fruit tree.

After that, it's bedtime for the monkeys. About four in the afternoon, they ascend to a broad comfortable tree branch for the night. *Callicebus* don't go to sleep right away; the family twines its tails together for balance, and then the whole family will groom each other for lice, lint, ticks, sap, and clinging pollen. Ears are inspected, eyes are inspected. Underarms are cleaned. The process takes from one to two hours, until they nod off to sleep.

And then I would be free until morning!

Charlie Janson's life was quite different. He chased brown capuchin monkeys. These monkeys are known from children's books such as *Curious George* or as cute little organ grinder monkeys dressed in jackets. Charlie's monkeys weren't cute. They looked like bulldogs. If they could have worn jackets they would have worn black leather jackets with metal studs. When my *Callicebus* monkeys heard capuchin monkeys in the distance, they would shudder, look frantically in that direction, and run for their lives. A gang of looters, capuchin monkeys can form a phalanx fifty yards across and gallop steadily through the forest, ripping it apart and eating anything they want. Females will linger in palm trees, pulling apart the long fronds in their search for insects, lizards, and frogs. Males will eat birds' eggs, large fruits, and geckos. Weighing about eight pounds, these monkeys nevertheless can take on just about anything in their path.

Out of Charlie's monkeys, Big Male was the godfather. He had a bald blotchy face with bulging jowls and broad canines that instilled fear, especially when he smiled. He was so powerful, he never had to fight. Everyone stayed clear of him, except the baby capuchins. Big Male had a soft spot for all capuchins under two years old and often got saddled with the babysitting. He had four female mates, so there were usually a lot of youngsters around. If a teenage male found a good feeding spot, Big Male would come along and the young male would quickly leave. Big Male would then share the fruits with the playful, cheerful youngsters. If Female A arrived, Big Male would share with her, because she was his favorite. About the same age as Big Male (over thirty-five years old), Female A was a serious, diligent forager, a responsible mother, and they'd seen a lot of jungle together. Female B adored Big Male and groomed him as much as possible. Female C was more of a loner and ignored Big Male most of the time. Female D was neurotic. She cowered when Big Male strolled by, chittering and acting subordinate. Big Male ignored this faint-hearted female, but she never lost her fear of him.

The richest food in the rainforest is the *Scheelea* palm nut. Filled with delicious, nutritious nutmeats that look somewhat like peach-sized coconuts, these palms ripen in clumps at the center of a palm tree. No monkeys other than capuchins eat these palm nuts, and I once asked Charlie why.

"See the big, broad fangs on Big Male?" he replied. "They're nutcrackers. Big Male carries around some mean tools. He's the only one who can open those nuts, all the other group members are just too weak."

The next week, I saw Big Male in action. After ripping open the nut cluster with his powerful forearms, he put the first nut into his mouth. It filled his entire mouth, and his cheek muscles bulged as he cracked it open. As soon as he was finished, several youngsters grabbed it from him and started to bite the nutmeats inside, squabbling over the biggest chunks. Meanwhile, Big Male went on to open the next nut. He ate some himself, of course, but he obviously loved to share this treat with the kids. And Female A, if she happened by.

By the beginning of September, Louise was not having luck finding jaguar tracks, and I could see she was anxious for data. But I was a little alarmed to enter the station house one day after supper and see her polishing the blowgun.

"Want to go hunting?" she asked me.

"Sure, but isn't that a little small for jaguars?" I answered.

Not responding to my joke, Louise looked into the distance. "Hear that?"

I heard an ascending call, ending in a *caw, caw, caw*. "That loud bird?"

"That's not a bird." Louise was now checking her darts to

make sure they were filled with anesthetic. "It's a bamboo rat. It lives in bamboo and is half as big as a housecat. Like your *Callicebus*, the male and female pairs give duets to protect their territory. Nobody's studied them. I need to put radio collars on them tonight and get their home range. So do you want to come?"

It was a privilege to go out at night with Louise. Agile as an antelope and as quiet in the forest as a native, Louise, considered in her field to be the world's expert on jungle mammals, was a keen hunter who rarely missed her mark.

We walked swiftly and silently in the forest, listening to the calls and the silences. The moon was beginning to rise, and frogs and insects livened up the blackness with their constant din. I started to identify a pattern of four notes and then silence.

"What's that low-pitched hooting?" I whispered to Louise.

"An owl, I think, but I don't know which species. We should ask Scott, he's the owl expert. We have to be quiet now, we're almost there."

Just then, the bamboo rats burst into song, loud and ratcheting. Louise acted quickly, shining her headlamp on the furry form, taking careful aim with the blowgun and hitting her mark before I could glimpse what she was aiming at. Then Louise shot the other rat, which fell to the ground as if in a coma.

"We'll weigh, measure, and collar them back at the station," Louise said.

We put each of the chunky, brown, anesthetized animals into separate gunnysacks.

I went out with Louise every chance I could. Nobody else

knew the secrets of the night, and I had a lot to learn. She taught me how to trap, inventory mammals at night, and walk without making noise.

"You're quiet when you walk," she noted, and I thought of my dad's early training to walk like a Chippewa. "Have you ever noticed how heavy Charlie and JT walk? You can hear them coming like a train! Fortunately, they study noisy monkeys and birds. They could never make it in the night." I beamed in the darkness at her praise.

Studying nightlife is a lonely affair. Even when Louise and I were together, we rarely spoke. She walked ahead slowly, beaming her headlamp first to the right, low to high, center, and then to the left, low to high. I walked twenty-five yards behind her with my headlamp, only moving toward her if she sighted something. The narrow flashlight beam seemed pathetically inadequate against the vast darkness.

The rewards didn't come often, about one exciting thing an hour. It could be a sleeping bird with an iridescent turquoise eyebrow, or the red eyes of a tree frog. My favorites were the raccoon-like kinkajous, the same species that I had seen eating nectar in the trees at Puerto Bermúdez. Their yellow eyes, bright as car headlights when reflecting our beams, made them easy to identify in the darkness. Unlike kinkajous, monkeys don't have a *tapetum lucidum*, that reflective aluminum foil–like material in the eye that enables most nocturnal mammals to see in the dark. Maybe that was why I hadn't seen an *Aotus* yet—they were invisible to our headlamps. But I knew this wasn't true. Louise and I were good at night work. If owl monkeys were there, we would have seen them.

There were some animals we weren't happy to see, like the fer-de-lance, which I had come eye-to-eye with in Puerto Bermúdez. It was not the largest of the poisonous snakes, but it was the most aggressive. Louise and I were always on the look-out for them.

One time when we were doing a night census, at about midnight, Louise stopped ahead of me.

"Big snake," was all she said.

I froze and could see in her flashlight beam a ten-foot-long snake that was a rich mahogany brown with black diamonds. Its body was as thick as a football. And it was coiled on the trail, its triangular head glaring at Louise.

My first thought was to bolt back down the trail away from the snake, but if it were a fer-de-lance it would give chase, and they moved faster than humans. I remained still, heart pounding, waiting for a signal from Louise.

After what seemed like an hour but might have been a minute, Louise spoke again. "It's a bushmaster. It's as poisonous as a fer-de-lance but not as aggressive. If you step on it, it'll attack and inject its poison into you. Within five to ten hours you'll die. But look at that bulge in its middle. This one's just eaten and seems pretty lethargic." Louise hesitated for a minute, watching the snake.

"The bushmaster is the longest pit viper in the world, as long as twelve feet. Females lay about twelve eggs and then guard them. This could be a female. Let's move off the trail and go around it."

With adrenaline still pounding in our veins, we continued our census. But the rest of the night was quiet, with only an owl hooting plaintively by the river. And alas, we finished another night without seeing any owl monkeys.

As we began the second week of September at Cocha Cashu, I was becoming irritable. First of all, my research plan had been crafted to include two groups of *Callicebus*, and a second group was nowhere to be found. But worse than that, the main reason for being in this isolated forest, for me dragging my daughter out of second grade, for eating rice and beans nearly every day, for facing the fer-de-lance, buzzing mosquitoes, and slippery mud on lonely night walks, was to study owl monkeys. And I hadn't even *seen* an owl monkey yet. Charlie's capuchins were ugly, but at least he was able to follow them.

Then one day my luck started to change. Nina and Amanda had been down by the river mist-netting for birds. As dusk approached, they hurried to roll up the nets before the bats swooped in. Mist nets are like a fine black fishing net, as fine as a waitress' hair net, strung vertically between poles across an open place. The bird can't see the fine threads and flies into the net and becomes entangled. Birders dread bats because their wings get entangled in the nets easily, and bat teeth are more vicious than bird beaks during removal from nets.

After they closed the nets, Nina and Amanda started up Trail One. And out of a hole in a tree came a monkey. Having been raised with them, Amanda immediately said, "Nina, it's an owl monkey! Look, there's three—no, four."

By this time, Nina had her binoculars on the monkeys.

"White faces, black eyebrows, bright orange chests. Long black tails, orange at the base." She called out the identification marks just as I arrived from Trail Two.

"Do you hear those owl monkeys?" I was breathless from hurrying the last hundred yards.

"Mom, they're above your head."

I raised my binoculars up to the monkeys in the trees. My hands were trembling so much with excitement that the monkeys were going in and out of my field of vision. Amanda was turning out to be the best field assistant ever. Not only had she seen the *Callicebus* first, but now she had found the owl monkeys, too.

"Look at those faces, Mom. They're so white compared to Herbie and Kendra. But that one has a pumpkin-orange chest like Kendra's. Darker and redder, maybe."

"It doesn't look like there are any babies. Maybe they didn't have one this year," I said just before the monkeys leaped into the ever-increasing darkness.

I took off after them into the underbrush, but they were gone. I was elated that night at supper, talking about my first sighting of *Aotus*.

But contrary to my expectations, the *Aotus* group did not return to that sleep tree. The next dusk and dawn I waited, but nothing appeared out of that hole in the tree.

However, the following day my luck held, when Robin found a second group of *Callicebus* by the Manú River. Robin was a very quiet observer. As researchers often adjust their behavior to resemble their study subjects, Robin moved very slowly to study his plants. Often, it turned out to be Robin who was most successful at finding animals. That morning, he had been watching hummingbirds pollinate lily-like yellow and orange flowers by the river when the *Callicebus* group had moved up from the water's edge into the tall forest. Robin counted a mated pair and a yearling. No babies. The male of this group was dark brown like the others, but with a distinctive white tip on his tail.

But by the time I reached the river that day, the group was gone. The River Group of *Callicebus* monkeys continued to be trouble. Like the House Group (Group I), the River Group had observed researchers for years, but they didn't like them. When I caught a glimpse of the River Group, the three monkeys would look at me with suspicious eyes, raise their fur like a cat, chuck rude noises down at me, and vanish silently into the forest. And I wouldn't be able to find them again for weeks. While my detective work faltered, I turned to other parts of my jungle education.

Primatologists have to know the plants. After all, juicy fruits and tender leafy greens are the "bread and butter" of our monkeys. So I tagged along with Robin to learn a Latin dictionary full of names. Gradually, I also learned more about his personal life. Robin and his two brothers had been raised on a remote Vermont farm by his dad. His mother had died when he was seven years old, which was one of the reasons he liked Amanda, who was that age. As a child, since his dad didn't talk much as he was growing up, he'd had a lot of time to study plants. After graduating from Dartmouth he had gone straight to graduate school at Duke to work with Professor William Billings, and he now had a job at the University of Chicago with a research focus on tropical plants of the Americas. One of Robin's goals was to collect and identify all the thousands of unknown plants in Manú National Park. He was also interested in the seasonal behaviors of the plants and their relationships with the animals.

With such an immense agenda, he really didn't have time to be teaching me. Trying to be useful, I carried the large black plastic Hefty bag into which he put his specimens, such as a tiny orange-colored spray of orchids gathered from a giant tree that had fallen in the last storm, and a fleshy-leafed bromeliad perched in a tree crotch. Each specimen would be pressed and identified that evening and labeled with a number, date, and location.

Other times, I carried the "pikka-planta." This was a hedge clipper on a series of aluminum rods that acted like a giraffe's neck, to allow a botanist to snip off greens and flowers yards out of reach. Robin had tree grippers too, metal claws worn on the feet to grip and scale tree trunks up to canopy levels. When he wore them Robin looked like King Kong scaling the Empire State Building, collecting a delicate orchid instead of Fay Wray. The tree-trunk grippers terrified me, and I stayed firmly on the ground while Robin threw down the clipped branches for me to put into the Hefty bag.

At work, Robin was thorough and almost mystical. He smelled and tasted leaves, rubbing them between his fingers to capture their character and distinguish one species from another. For example, he explained that families of trees could be identified by making a small cut in the bark, smelling the inside, and watching for sap.

"Smell this tree trunk," he'd instruct me. "Doesn't it smell like bay leaves?"

I nodded.

"And there's no obvious sap flow, which indicates a tree from Lauraceae, the laurel and bay leaf family. See how light-colored the bark is inside? Another sign of the laurel family. You've eaten avocados, right? Avocados are laurels too, but no one is sure from which wild species the first avocado came." He instructed me to look at another trunk. "This one has clear red sap, like blood. The Indians never cut vines from this family because it's bad luck. This tree has a special spicy smell, a sign of the Myristicaceae family."

And then a third. "This tree has thick, white sap, like milk. Don't lick it though, it's poisonous. The shamans sometimes recommend a dose of that milky sap as medicine. It makes you sick, but then you pass out all your intestinal parasites. This is in the Moraceae family, the fig family, just like the figs in the supermarket." I must have looked hungry, because Robin cautioned me, "Remember, figs are smaller in the rainforest than those you're used to, and they're not very sweet."

Then his words slowed. "These fig trees are some of the biggest in the forest, over fifty yards in canopy diameter—that's half the size of a football field—and every branch has hundreds of figs. Monkeys come long distances to eat them." He paused. "Patricia, I'm leaving before these huge fig trees come into fruit, but you should watch them carefully. I'm not sure exactly what they will tell you, but they may explain some monkey secrets to you."

After an afternoon with Robin in the rainforest, I could see why Amanda liked being around him so much.

Every once in a while, somebody new would walk up Trail One to the Cocha Cashu research station. One day at the end of September, a sturdy twenty-five-year-old German named Brigitta arrived. She had trunks and trunks of equipment, all packed efficiently in aluminum boxes, which the motorista and Charlie very kindly helped her transport to the station. JT had known of her plans to come to Cocha Cashu to study the lake and its productivity, but he had forgotten to tell us. She set up her two-room tent, and we all marveled at this luxurious palace. She spoke English but not Spanish, and she had been sitting in Lima for a month waiting to get her boxes out of customs.

Brigitta had also brought a large inflatable rubber boat to collect lake samples. Every day, she'd go out and take samples of lake water in ten different places. As a limnologist, she was studying the lake's temperature, acidity, and algae viscosity. Aside from Charlie, who was looking to brush up on his German language skills, the American researchers ignored Brigitta. However, Amanda chatted with her, and one afternoon Brigitta asked Amanda if she would like to go out in the boat to help her collect samples. This was the offer Amanda was waiting for. They became good friends, and after a month, Brigitta allowed Amanda to paddle out on the lake by herself. On these solo trips Amanda would paddle out across the lake to the opposite shore where butterflies sipped nectar from bright

orange flowers. She would move quietly past the lazy caimans, sleeping submerged near the logs. She would sneak up
on the hoatzins, who have disheveled orange feathery hairdos,
and sharp spurs on their yellow legs. She would watch these
strange birds, the only bird species that eats leaves, dine on
trees at the edge of the lake. One day, she reported the hoatzins
were building stick nests near the water's edge. And another
day, she had paddled close to the giant otters, and watched the
now-grown infants wrestling and diving from a log.

One morning, my *Callicebus* House Group had a surprise for
me. None of the family had moved from their sleeping spot,
and I didn't understand their laziness. The mother seemed to
be licking herself continually, and the father looked worried.
Then I saw the tiny wet tail and realized a baby had been born.
Fully furred and clinging to its mother's belly, the little monkey
looked like a wet mouse. Opening its eyes and blinking, it began
to move toward the mother's armpit. Baby's first breakfast.

The monkey family didn't move far that day, but by the next
morning the mother was hungry. After she had gorged herself
on little red fruits, she hopped out of the tree to a broad hori-
zontal branch and raised her arm, comfortably holding on to a
higher branch while the baby suckled. I could see clearly that
the baby was strong, and I felt as proud as a godmother.

I wasn't prepared for what I saw next. After only three
minutes of the baby's suckling, the mother nipped its back
and the baby screamed. It wasn't an accident, because the

mother nipped it again and it squealed uncomfortably. The father was there in a flash, looking alarmed and rubbing his back toward the baby. The baby moved away from the annoyed mother and crawled onto the father's back. As soon as the baby was securely on him, the mother leaped away to another tree.

My heart raced at this sight. I was seeing the same behavior I had seen in *Aotus* families: the father was taking on child-care duties! It seemed that like owl monkey mothers, *Callicebus* mothers only nursed, and that was where her duties ended. I had already resigned myself to the fact that I could never observe owl monkey infants because it was just too dark in the forest. But now I could watch how this system worked in the wild after all, in the day monkeys! And sure enough, like owl monkey babies, the baby *Callicebus* returned to the mother every two hours for milk, but after three minutes the meal was over. If the infant lingered too long, the mother nipped. It didn't take long for the baby to know when to dash off to dad. I eagerly wrote down every detail.

It wasn't until after the baby was a month old that the older brother joined the father in the babysitting chores. The two-year-old would carry the baby on his back for half an hour before the father returned to take the baby again. By the third month, the baby only nursed four times a day and was becoming heavy for the father to carry. For hours in the afternoon, the three offspring and the father would play wrestle. But the mother never played, she just ate or rested.

In the afternoons, the mother would search for luscious grasshoppers or tasty spiders. For small monkeys, their prey is mainly insects, filled proportionally with more fats and proteins than an antelope. The mother could spot them, leap on the unsuspecting prey, then quickly move ahead in her search. When it came to hunting, the *Callicebus* father had a handicap. Since the baby now weighed nearly half of what he did, he had to carefully judge distances and land on branches that could hold that weight. A miss and father and baby would plunge to the forest floor. So during the afternoons, while the mother and juveniles hunted, the father usually opted to sit on a thick branch while the baby reached out to taste twigs and learn to climb. As hyperactive as a human child, the baby moved constantly and scared away any insects in the vicinity, so hunting and babysitting were not compatible activities.

By the fourth month, even the father was tired of carrying the baby. He would reach back and try to dislodge it, much as Herbie had done with Mango. But the *Callicebus* baby would scrunch its face and hold on tight. The father would try to buck it off, and then, totally annoyed, race up to a trunk and rub his back against it. The baby would lose his grip and the father would bolt into the next tree. The baby would just sit there and begin to play by itself. I had never expected to see the very same behavior that I had seen in our Brooklyn apartment here in the rainforest.

Nina Pierrepont studied woodcreepers, brown birds that climbed up and down trunks like woodpeckers to glean insects. But one day after lunch, Nina burst into the research station, out of breath. "My birds are following a line of army ants. The army ants are coming!"

We had all read about the long lines of carnivorous ants that march through the forest, eating everything in their path. They are one of the most feared dangers in the Amazon, and we rushed out with Nina to see them. We heard them first, a rumbling, almost like the drone of a machine. The moving mass of ants was only a yard and a half wide, but behind the front lines were nearly 200 yards of soldiers. Insects and lizards ran ahead of them trying to escape. Taking advantage of the easy prey, Nina's birds were swooping down on the cloud of flushed insects. This army had no generals or lieutenants; those in front caught the prey, and as the ants piled on to eat, others moved to take their place in front. We watched this flood of death from a distance, the leaf litter boiling with the fierce mass of ants, the river of blackness scouring the forest.

Suddenly, we heard the squeals of a forest mouse. Ant jaws clamped down on the hind legs, stinging the victim, and more ants piled on as the mouse faltered. Its entire body was covered with writhing black ants, with not one bit of fur visible. For the next fifteen minutes we watched the throbbing ball of ants in horror, and then the death squeals were silent. The death parade continued, leaving the glistening white bones of the mouse behind.

I watched as they continued south and realized that direction was toward our clearing where Amanda was. Amanda was a little big for prey, but remembering how quickly the forest mouse had been reduced to a pile of gleaming white bones, I rushed to find her.

JT was at the station telling Louise and Amanda about the habits of army ants. "They're nomadic and spend their whole life marching in file across the forest floor. They eat everything in their path—spiders, lizards, rodents—nothing is safe. Some people say they eat scorpions and tarantulas. The army ants are a mobile death machine that no one can escape."

"Don't they sleep?" asked Amanda.

"They must sleep at some point. I don't really know. Most other ants have nests or burrows."

This conversation seemed oddly academic after what I'd just witnessed. After I told them about the forest mouse, Louise rushed off to collect the bones for a proper identification.

She returned to say, "They're definitely getting closer. Anyone with tents on Trail Six had better be on alert." When Louise was worried, we knew it was serious. Scott and JT rushed off to move their tents.

After twenty minutes, Scott returned, breathless. "They missed my tent but it looks like they'll be at the station clearing in half an hour."

"Let's make a fire line out of kerosene," Charlie Munn suggested. "Even ants are afraid of fire, and that would force them to move to the east."

"The fire could get out of control and burn the cabin down," Nina pointed out. Plus, if it doesn't work, the ants will be even angrier."

"We don't have enough kerosene to make an effective fire line anyway, so forget that idea," Charlie Janson interceded.

"What about insecticide?" suggested Scott. "We can just spray them like they're cockroaches."

"Scott, we're talking about millions of ants, not a few cock-roaches. It would take a warehouse full of insecticide!" Nina was beginning to pace.

JT arrived. "They'll be here in a few minutes. There's nothing we can do but stay out of their way. Nobody get too close. Hear that, Amanda?" Amanda nodded. "Let's get away from the cabin. Worse comes to worst, we head for the lake and swim away from them."

At four-thirty in the afternoon, we could see the undulating black death parade enter the clearing from the north. We exited the station house and moved to the forest at the east of the clearing where we could have a good view. The line was marching straight through the center of the clearing. Would it turn to avoid our wooden house? The line did not turn. We were silent as black ripples moved up the stairs and into the house. All of us were outside, but we rushed over to see in through the screened windows. The ants went into the storeroom and we could hear the death squeals of the forest mice we had been trying to trap. The ants engulfed the gun-nysack labeled "C, C & C" and all we could see was a writhing black mass for twenty minutes. As quickly as they had attacked the sack, they left it and invaded the dining room. A platoon moved up the walls, behind the calendar with the photo of snowcapped peaks in Japan and the World Wildlife Fund poster of elephants in the Serengeti. About ten giant cockroaches scuttled out, only to be engulfed by the writhing ants, stung to death, and ripped into little pieces. The jaws of the ants clamped on to giant spiders, and the silverfish and earwigs that had been eating our books. The walls were completely black with the moving mass.

What was going to happen next? They couldn't get out the windows—would they just turn around and go back out the door?

Suddenly, the front line of ants turned around, and I thought they were going to eat each other. They formed a writhing mass but nothing was at the core. More and more of them piled together until there was an oven-sized mass of ants in the corner of our dining room. They appeared to be bivouacking for the night.

When they had stopped moving, JT decided it was okay for us to go back into the house. He didn't want to eat outside with the hordes of mosquitoes. We even went into the dining room, but the ants didn't move. We watched them apprehensively that night, thinking that they would awaken and attack us while we ate dinner on the opposite side of the room. But they slept on.

In the morning, Scott, Charlie, Louise, and I went back to the house and watched the black ball of ants unravel, spread out like a river of oil, and spill out the door. As the last ants disappeared south of the clearing, we entered the cabin.

"Great, now we don't have to do our fall cleaning," Louise said. "The ants got all the cockroaches!"

"They just gave the entire forest floor a vacuuming!" Charlie chuckled.

We were still laughing when Scott returned, angry, from the storeroom.

"Goddamn, they took it all. They ate all the cheese and the chocolate. I hate rice and beans. Chocolate was all I had to look forward to every day. I can't believe they ate the chocolate. They left the coffee, but they ate every bit of chocolate. I hate this place." He stalked out of the house and slammed the door.

All of us just stood there as the realization sunk in. We had lost our only luxury for the rest of the year.

CHAPTER EIGHT

JUNGLE TALES

(Cocha Cashu, 1980)

"ANNE, WHAT'S THE problem?"

Anne Wilson and I were sitting at the research station in mid-October, and her pen had stopped on paper as we looked out at the kingfishers flying over the lake.

"I'm trying to write to my parents without worrying them," Anne replied. "They didn't want me to come to Peru. They think it's too dangerous—I'll catch a tropical disease or get eaten by a jaguar."

Anne was only twenty years old and a junior at Princeton University. Six months ago, she had decided to work with Professor Terborgh on her senior honors paper. Her parents didn't know that meant going to the farthest jungle in the world for almost a full year. Although both scientists, her parents had only worked in laboratories and only knew about the tropics from vacationing in the Caribbean. Anne had never told her parents about the bushmaster hidden in the leaf litter or about the jaguar footprints that we saw once on Trail One.

And she certainly didn't want to mention that the beginning of her tamarin study wasn't going well.

Tamarins are in a totally different classification from any of the other monkeys in the rainforest. Like fashion models, each species has a different decorative feature—ear tassels, or well-manicured mustaches, or fan-like white hair sprouting from the top of their heads like a white-plumed hat. Lion tamarins have fur of spun sunlight. King Midas monkeys have gold-colored hands. Crested tamarins have Mohawks. Pygmy marmosets have tiger-striped tails.

There are dozens of species of tamarins, and two of them could be found in the Manú. The saddle-back had a black head and tail, a white muzzle, and a speckled yellow "saddle" on its back. The other species, the Emperor tamarin, was the fanciest of all, with a velvet black body adorned with a spectacular long white mustache and a russet-red tail.

The high-energy lifestyle of these tamarins is primarily fueled with fruit and nectar. But they're also alert hunters, and feed on katydids, moths, crickets, ants, snails, frogs, and beetles. They never sit still and are very noisy, communicating with whistles, chirps, and piercing calls among the whole troop, which can be as large as nine individuals.

Anne's project wasn't an easy one. The tamarins were so small they were difficult to see or tell apart in the trees. Anne needed to tag them with plastic color-coded bead collars so she could distinguish individuals. The plan was to trick them into coming down out of the trees and into metal mesh live traps. She carefully distributed her ten tamarin traps in the forest at twenty-five-yard intervals, nestled on branches or

fallen logs about a yard off the ground. Each trap was baited
with a tiny slice of banana. We had brought bananas in to
Cocha Cashu on the boat, since they're not naturally found
in the rainforest. Charlie Janson said the tamarins wouldn't
recognize them as food, and for a week it looked like he was
right.

Then one day, Anne found an Emperor tamarin male sitting
in the trap, quite furious. She carried the cage back to the station to put him under anesthesia, weigh and measure him, and
put on his bead collar. He weighed 450 grams and could fit
in the palm of Anne's hand. He woke up after an hour, just as
insulted and outraged as before.

It was Cocha Cashu policy to always return an animal
exactly to the site where it was captured so the animal could
get its bearings quickly. Once at the site, Anne opened the door
to the trap, but the Emperor tamarin continued to sit inside,
scolding her for ten minutes until Anne, an animal lover, wondered if she had truly done something unforgiveable to him.
Finally, he finished his lecture and disappeared into the canopy. In the eight years that Anne continued to trap tamarins
at Cocha Cashu, she never caught another Emperor tamarin.

Anne soon figured out that using live traps to catch monkeys
was not a good procedure. Live trapping is designed to catch
raccoons and squirrels, rabbits and guinea pigs. If rodents
see their capturer, it doesn't affect their future behavior—at
least not for very long. But monkeys are different. They have
complex brains and long memories and can recognize their
captors. Anne had planned to follow individuals to document
their behavior and trap them to check their weights, health,

and reproductive conditions. She couldn't do that if the monkeys remembered what she had done to them.

Anne decided to continue to trap, but she had to devise a system whereby the monkeys wouldn't recognize her afterward. She moved on to trapping her second species of tamarins, the saddle-back, who did not have bad memories of her yet. With them, she checked the traps in disguise. She painted her face black with charcoal and put white dots of flour on her eyebrows. Then, she took out of the cabin storage closet a rejected bright yellow raincoat, the color that school crossing guards wear. She even found a special pair of boots, only worn to check traps. She made sure to cover the cage with a gunnysack during the trip back to camp, and she never said a word during the whole process, even when the monkey was under anesthetic. She couldn't take a chance that it would recognize her voice later.

Charlie and Scott made jokes about her ridiculous outfit, but Anne was successful. It took only a week before the Yellow Raincoat Demon, as Charlie and Scott called her, had captured her first saddle-back tamarin. Anne had six groups—twenty-four individuals—collared. We were all amazed at her good luck. And even after release, the research strategy worked. The tamarins with their colorful bead necklaces were terrified of the Yellow Raincoat Demon, but they never noticed Anne Wilson when she followed them.

Then, after a few more weeks, Anne arrived at the cabin, looking discouraged.

"My monkeys have a problem," she confessed to me. I felt like I was back to being a social worker as Anne told me about "the addiction."

At first, Charlie was right, the monkeys had never seen or smelled bananas before and ignored the traps. Then the first individual, the mother, ventured into the trap and ate the quarter-sized slice of banana. The next time Anne arrived, one tamarin would be inside the trap, and the other group members would be outside the trap, squabbling to get inside. The banana was eaten, but the smell remained. So Anne set out four traps at a site. When she came back one hour later, all four traps were full, but with tamarins she had caught before. The dominant tamarins wouldn't let the subordinates get to the bananas. It became a nightmare. The same tamarins were "trap-happy," searching the forest for traps with bananas.

"The traps are like banana-candy vending machines, set out especially for their pleasure," Anne said.

"Vending machines in the forest?" Scott, who was sitting nearby, had overheard us. "Mars Bars would be good, and Snickers and Hersheys, and remember those little bags of potato chips and pizza-flavored ripples and cheese crackers with peanut butter inside?"

Anne and I ignored Scott and continued to discuss her monkeys. Then JT joined the discussion. "Anne, stop trapping. You've collared enough monkeys. They'll return to their normal routine in a few days, and you can begin to follow them."

Our last remaining problem was Scott, who continued to walk around the cabin muttering about Almond Joys, Reese's Peanut Butter Cups, Mounds, and Heath bars.

Meanwhile, I was following *Callicebus* and learning new things about them and their interactions with other monkeys. One morning, when they were giving their territorial dawn duet near my tent, a young male howler monkey appeared. He looked around and then moved up near the *Callicebus* group and started to howl along with their duet. The *Callicebus* group was startled and a bit annoyed and moved closer to the lake, away from the howler, and began their song again. The howler moved up to participate. When they moved to a fruit tree, the howler moved with them as if trying to join their group. The group kept looking at him, as if he were daft, and he moved over my head, as if to join me. So the rest of the week, I followed underneath the *Callicebus* group and the howler monkey male followed me, just above my head. I had never seen any type of interspecies relationship like that before. Charlie nicknamed him Howard (in other words, "How Weird") and joked about this odd howler at dinner.

Then one day, when I had switched to nocturnal *Aotus* studies, and was stuck with washing the dishes on the verandah of the house, I heard a sound behind me. It was Howard, in a tree near the lake. He looked down at me while hanging by his prehensile tail. A second monkey, an adult howler monkey, shimmered orange-red in the sun, but stayed higher and farther from me. I didn't know what these monkeys wanted, but I knew they wanted something to come so close and stare at me.

Howard began to slowly, clumsily, climb down the trunk of the tree until he was on the ground less than a yard away. I moved up onto the verandah so as not to be in his way. We had never seen a monkey walk up to the house before. Then Howard walked up to where I had been washing dishes and ate the dirt underneath. I could hear him wolfing down mouthfuls of the dirt, as if it were a Snickers bar. Then Howard stopped, looked up at the adult howler monkey as if to say, "Come join me, it's delicious," and I moved a bit father down the verandah to give him space. What was in that dishwashing dirt that was so appealing? When the two monkeys had eaten a big hole into the dirt, they both ambled up the tree and jumped out of the clearing with the adult male in the lead. I never saw either howler monkey again, but I analyzed the soil and found that it was high in phosphates, probably from the dishwashing soap. These leaf-eating primates must have needed these nutrients, like how cows go to a salt lick to help their digestion.

One day, I made a major breakthrough in understanding the territorial defense of the *Callicebus* monkeys. The Lake Group approached their favorite *Spondias* fruit tree to feed on the ripe plum-sized yellow fruits. The tree was on the border with East Group, and East Group had arrived at lunch first. Lake Group stopped, almost as if they couldn't believe their eyes, and they clustered together, getting ready to chorus. Although *Callicebus* is the size of a house cat, their calls are the size of lions' roars. The four of them trumpeted their turkey gobble battle cry simultaneously. The East Group looked up, startled, and saw the four roaring monkeys with their tails wagging with anger. The East Group turned to face their enemy and began to countercall.

Then the Lake Group stopped calling and burst into motion. The Lake Dad and oldest son led the charge against the enemy. The son was in the lead, attacking the lead male from the East

Group. The East Group turned tail and retreated. Lake Dad stopped attacking when he saw the enemy turn back, but not the son. The Lake Group son continued his attack, stopping only for a minute to give another roaring war whoop, then continued to chase the East family deep into the East Group's territory. Twenty minutes later, when he returned to his Lake Group family, he was out of breath and panting. He lowered his head and bellowed a long triumphant victory call. The *Spondias* tree belonged to the Lake Group. A definitive triumph! Lake Dad leaped over to his son's side, proud of the victory, and the two gave a victory duet together. Lake Mom and the juvenile joined in. I was happy to have been a witness to the event.

Aotus groups didn't like their neighbors much, either. Later that month the *Aotus* River Group met the *Aotus* North Group. In the full moon, the River Group moved first to the Myrtaceae tree for a quick breakfast of those grape-like fruits. After a half hour rest, the group moved to their northeast border where the *Clarisia racemosa* tree was now filled with ripe fruits. It was just before 8:00 P.M. and the moon was so bright I could distinguish the red color of the fruits through my binoculars. The River Group stopped outside the tree, and I sensed that something was wrong.

Then a sound I had never before heard started to reverberate through the forest: a low series of whoopings that increased in loudness and up the scale. About thirty yards high on a branch, I could see one owl monkey lower his head and expand a pouch under his chin to create a resonating chamber. The call sent a chill down my spine. The monkey began a sort of stiff-legged jumping, and I swear the monkey's hair was standing on end.

The monkey looked bigger and sounded huge as it resonated this call six times. The monkey next to it started making the same call four times, and for about three minutes there must have been four or more monkeys reverberating this sound. It was like a cross between a tuba and bagpipes. I counted eighteen reverberating calls in total.

The tree erupted in movement. Like splashing in the canopy, I could see monkeys attacking one another, wrestling, jumping, whooping, trying to bite. I saw one direct attack. Two monkeys, clutching, fell about ten yards, so engrossed in trying to kill the other that they must have lost their grips.

After nine minutes of fighting, the North Group retreated back into their territory. The River Group spent over an hour feeding in the tree, and then after resting returned for a second meal. Perhaps they wanted to be sure the North Group wouldn't come back.

I continued to see these patterns repeat themselves. Both *Callicebus* and *Aotus* had noisy battles, complete with war whoops, at their territorial borders. Fruit trees were always the bone of contention. But I had never seen actual teeth-to-teeth combat in *Callicebus*. The fights between *Aotus* groups were fiercer, with grappling and biting. *Callicebus* might fight at any time of the month, but *Aotus* always restricted battles with neighbors to when the moon was bright and overhead.

In late October, I was sitting on the steps of the house and combing Amanda's hair while Nina washed her clothes in a bucket nearby. We all looked up when a Machiguenga Indian walked into camp with his two wives. The Machiguenga women were dressed in traditional robelike brown cushmas made of handspun cotton, and the man wore a tattered beige shirt and cotton shorts and carried a long bow and arrows and a handmade net bag filled with fifteen catfish and bananas. JT welcomed the man, whose name was Zakarias, and invited him and his wives and sons to sit down for coffee.

The two women stood ten yards away from the men and the fire and looked at Nina, Amanda, and me as if we were from the moon. I tried not to stare and told Amanda to ignore them, but our eyes kept drifting their way. We all knew it was against the law for them to talk to us. All Indians that lived in the park were off limits to us. In fact, if the park guards knew about their visit, there would be trouble. But it turned out that the Machiguenga had paddled their dugout for four days down the Manú River from their village of Tayakome just for this visit, to trade fish and bananas.

When he was eighteen years old, Zakarias had spent a year with the missionaries at the Summer Institute for Linguistics in Cuzco, so he knew how to speak a little Spanish. At the end of his mission year, he had returned to Tayakome with a Bible and a machete. He had taken his first wife over fifteen years ago. He was the only person in his village who had visited the outside world, and this knowledge gave him high prestige.

The previous year, Zakarias had visited Cocha Cashu twice, and the visits were always a surprise. It had almost become a tradition now: first JT and Zakarias would tell the news of the year over coffee, and then the bargaining would start. Zakarias always wanted fishhooks and salt. Last year, JT had only one fishhook and, much to the horror of the other researchers, had given Zakarias the station's three-month supply of salt. Luckily, JT was prepared this year and had purchased extra fishhooks and salt in Cuzco. But determining how much fish and bananas these items were worth could take days to decide. This back-and-forth dialogue was the way these two men from different worlds developed their friendship.

But first the news. "I have a new son this year." Zakarias pointed to the young wife, who had a small sleeping baby wrapped snugly to her back.

The bad news came out slowly.

"My sister's son died of fever during the rains. My mother died, too.

"The Yaminahua attacked my cousin's village last month," he continued in a low voice. "It was a surprise attack in the early morning. They killed almost all the men in the village. My cousin escaped and told us this story. The Yaminahua are bad people; they burned the houses, and stole the machetes, cooking pots, and the women. We fear they will attack us next. We don't know when."

There was silence for nearly ten minutes, as both Zakarias and JT stared into the fire. The Yaminahua had never been successfully contacted by outsiders, since they were at war with all the neighboring Indian groups. It was one reason why the park prohibited Peruvians and foreigners from going farther into the interior of the park.

Then it was JT's turn to tell his news of the year.

"There are ten research projects this year. We will study the monkeys, birds, and plants. Do you remember Charlie Janson from last year? He's here to study capuchin monkeys."

Charlie, who had just arrived out of the forest for lunch, came over, shook Zakarias' hand, and joined the men at the fire.

"We have a baby woolly monkey back at camp," Zakarias said. "It has been with us for a month."

It was understood that the mother had been hunted and eaten, as was the custom all over South America, but the Indians knew foreigners didn't like to hear about monkeys as food. Zakarias knew about our strange custom of hunting monkeys without bows and arrows, and how we didn't eat any animals from the forest.

Although they were invited to stay for lunch, the Indians returned to their camp on the Manú River beach. As we ate our rice and beans, Charlie explained to us the social system of the Indians as Zakarias had explained it to him. It turned out that once a son had shown his courage and hunting skills, his father gave him a special gift, his youngest and most beautiful wife. This wife, often older than the son, could teach him sexual skills. Zakarias's first wife was, in fact, a wife of Zakarias's father. After seven more years, Zakarias chose a second wife when she was about sixteen years old. But his first wife had to approve. The younger wife then had to do all the cleaning and cooking and child care, while the older wife became her supervisor.

The next morning at dawn, while I was getting dressed in my tent, I heard anxious voices and a woman sobbing. When Amanda and I arrived at the cabin, I saw some of the researchers with Zakarias and his wives. The younger wife was carrying a limp woolly monkey in her arms. I gasped at the pathetic little body, half the size of a human child's.

"Zakarias was bringing the woolly monkey to show us," Charlie explained to me. "But the monkey jumped out of this woman's arms and onto the trail. An ocelot leaped out of the bushes and grabbed the monkey by the nape of the neck. She had to beat the ocelot off the monkey."

The unconscious monkey was breathing shallow breaths. The Indian woman gently handed it to me, and as I cradled it I saw the puncture wound at the base of the skull.

"I don't think it's going to make it," I said, and tears started down both Amanda's and my cheeks. According to Zakarias, the women hoped that we could save their pet, but they knew there was not much hope. Indeed, the woolly monkey died a few hours later.

Louise examined the monkey. "That's the way ocelots kill," she said. "A bite to the base of the skull. Jaguars kill like that too. Just remember, Amanda, that you are the same size to a jaguar as that monkey was to the ocelot. Never walk on the trails alone, Amanda."

Amanda, her eyes round from the thought, agreed.

We buried the woolly monkey in a corner of the clearing and marked its grave with a stone.

The third morning, the Indian family appeared again. The ice seemed to be broken among me and the two Machiguenga women now that we had all grieved for their pet monkey. As JT counted out fishhooks by the fire, the two women joined me on the bank by the lake. I was brushing Amanda's hair again, a morning ritual. She scowled and cried, "Ouch!" as I tried to get out the knots and tangles. But when the two Indian women approached, Amanda stopped complaining, embarrassed. We didn't know quite what to do, since we didn't understand their language. The two hesitantly sat down near us. The older wife talked while the young wife sat timidly, sometimes giggling. The older wife pointed to her own hair, and then my hair.

"I think she likes your hair," Amanda translated.

Next the woman pointed to the brush.

"I think she likes the brush," Amanda continued. I knew that Amanda didn't like that brush very much.

I looked at the older woman's hair, which was quite matted.

"Amanda, your hair would look like that if you didn't have a brush."

"Mom, she wants the brush. We have to give her the brush. . . . I don't mind."

"Hmm, but what do we want? This has to be a bartering game."

Amanda knew all about bartering from her experience in the Cuzco market. "Look at her earrings, Mom, how they shimmer different colors. What are they made out of?"

"Looks like mother of pearl. Let me ask."

After lots of gestures, it appeared that the material came from shells in the lake.

"Mom, what's that decoration in her nose? Why is she wearing an earring in her nose?"

I asked and both women burst into laughter. I asked if I could have the older woman's nose ring, and again my request was met with laughter.

But the older woman had an idea. She beckoned that I

follow her, and I walked with her to the clothesline where Amanda's and my sheets were hanging. The woman pointed to Amanda's sheet and then to herself, nodding. I was horrified at the suggestion that I give her Amanda's bedsheet, which we had brought from home.

Amanda started laughing and said, "Mom, it's all right, give her my sheet. I never liked the flying cat anyway."

It wasn't that I didn't want to part with the bedsheet, but rather my whole idea of cultural purity was on the line. I didn't mind bartering away something like a hairbrush, but I couldn't pollute the Machiguenga with this bedsheet that depicted a cartoon of a caped cat flying over the skyline of New York City.

But the older woman was adamant. The brush and the sheet or no earrings and nose ring. Amanda suggested we add to our request the younger wife's bag. It was made out of handmade rope with patterns in natural brown dyes and had a long shoulder strap. Eventually, we reached an agreement. The two women left camp that night with a hairbrush and a flying super cat bedsheet. Zakarias had his usual salt and fishhooks, but this time he had convinced JT to add fifty yards of fishing line. And Amanda and I had earrings, a nose ring that fit into my nose without piercing, and a new handbag.

The next day, we went to see Zakarias and his two wives off as they boarded their dugout canoe for Tayakome.

Amanda had started a special garden near the tent. She had cleared the spot with a machete, and Robin had helped her build a palm-thatched roof over it to protect it from too much sun. Robin had looked seriously at the garden and sighed. "It needs something more. It's not quite there yet. What about these purple leaves? Let's make a border of Calathea, and some passion fruit vines. . . . What about planting them here on a pole that leads to the roof? Vines grow fast and the flowers are great for butterflies."

Amanda was an eager student of horticulture, and the two worked closely on this project of growing jungle plants.

"It's my secret garden," Amanda said to me, referring to the only storybook we had, and by the time I saw the garden, it was indeed a masterpiece. On this particular morning, I was watching Amanda water her garden. On her way to breakfast she had seen a two-foot-long black snake pass over the trail in front of her. She had been terrified at the immense snake, but when she reached the station house Charlie had said it was a black rat snake and harmless, and she shouldn't be afraid of a snake.

Amanda was in a bit of a huff at Charlie's indifference to her story, and she had retreated to her garden, where I was inside the tent, trying to sleep. I was beginning to fall asleep again, and Amanda recognized my heavy eyelids.

"Go back to bed, Mom, I'll go find Robin," she said.

But Robin was nowhere to be found so Amanda wandered back. I got up and we went for a walk and ran into Robin looking up at a very tall tree with a thick trunk. Right away, it was obvious to Robin that Amanda was not in a good mood.

"This is a tachi tree, in the pea family. Remember when Klaus made peas with the rice? You like peas, right?"

Amanda nodded. Then she poked at the trunk of the huge tree.

"Ouch!" she said and jumped back. A furious black ant reached out with his feelers from where she had placed her finger.

Robin grabbed Amanda instinctively to protect her.

"Amanda, be careful, those ants are fierce," Robin said.

Amanda was put into an even worse mood. She grabbed a long stick and hit the tree as hard as she could. The stick broke and thousands of angry ants swarmed over the trunk, ready to take on the intruder. Amanda backed off and Robin tousled her hair, saying, "Told you they were mean."

Amanda waited a minute until the ants went back inside the tree, then she smiled up at Robin, teasing him, while she picked up another long stick and hit the trunk. Thousands of black ants swarmed out. Amanda ran into Robin's arms and she started to giggle. He picked her up on his shoulders and the two of them watched the ants disappear into the tree again.

"Okay, Amanda, time to go," I said.

On the way back, Amanda ran ahead and Robin and I lagged behind. We had been making a habit of lagging behind together, mostly learning botany, but it was more than that. I was beginning to have that "I want to be with you all the time" feeling about Robin, which some people call "love." Robin wasn't sure what to call it either, but it was pretty strong stuff.

In her tent Amanda had a calendar that her grandmother had given her. Amanda was supposed to count the days until she came home to Grandma, but she only looked at the calendar once in a while. She did, however, figure out that Halloween was coming very soon.

"Mom, about Halloween. Lisbet and I are going to dress up in costumes and go trick-or-treating," she told me. "Nina, Martha, and I have been planning the costumes. You'll see tomorrow. It's a surprise, so don't go out to find owl monkeys."

And so it was that two little wild Indians, all dressed up in toucan and macaw feathers and war paint, wrapped in sheets as cushmas, came trick-or-treating to the tents on trails Six and Seven. Some people had bubblegum and Snickers bars that they were hoarding from the States, but they gave them up so they wouldn't get tricked. It was a pretty good haul.

There were two camps at this time. JT and Harriot, as well as Martha and Charlie Munn and Klaus and his family, had moved down to the river, leaving the rest of us by the lake. By seven o'clock Lisbet had to return to her parents' tent near the river. The plan was for Amanda and I to take Lisbet back and for the girls to go trick-or-treating there, too. By the time we reached the site it was late, but the pair gained a few more candy bars and JT was amused by the costumes. We sat and chatted awhile, but the weather started to turn chilly, and a wind began to blow off the river.

It was nearly nine o'clock that night when Amanda and I started back on Trail One toward the house. The clouds were rolling in and the blackness got blacker. The wind was blowing stronger and the trees in the canopy began to creak and groan.

This was the first time that Amanda had walked in the forest at night.

"Why is it so windy, Mom?" she asked.

"It's probably going to rain. There usually isn't wind like this at night. I've never seen such a windy night, even with all my nights following the owl monkeys," I replied as the wind started howling through the top of the canopy.

"Mom, this is really spooky. I'm scared."

Amanda began to shiver under her costume. I hugged her to warm her up, and we tried to walk faster along the trail.

"Can't you make the flashlight brighter?" Amanda asked. But I couldn't. The flashlight batteries were dying. And in the bustle of the Halloween festivities, I had forgotten the cardinal rule of night work that Professor Kinzey had taught me so long ago: always, always bring two flashlights.

"Hold on to my hand tight. We can just walk slowly." I tried to sound reassuring.

"Mom, I'm scared. I can't see anything. What's that noise? Isn't this where the woolly monkey was killed? Is it a jaguar?"

Just then, there was a terrible crack. It was a sound I had heard before—a tree trunk breaking. A tree was about to fall. I strained to hear exactly where the sound was coming from. If a 130-foot tree falls, it can flatten ten trees in its wake. Nobody can run away fast enough to escape.

I kneeled down with my arm around Amanda. "It's far away. We're okay here. Now we don't have a light, so we must feel our way carefully with our feet here along the trail. Trail One is wide and straight. We'll be able to find our way home, even in the dark."

I was sounding braver than I felt. Our visibility was zilch. The house was a long way away, especially going at a snail's pace. We patted the darkness ahead of us with our hands and feet as we slowly groped forward.

We had gone about twenty yards when Amanda said softly, "Mom, I've lost my shoe. The right one. It slipped off my foot." Her voice trembled, and I could tell even in the darkness that she was on the verge of tears.

In the pitch black, we dropped to our knees and felt randomly around on the trail for her little red shoe with the plastic strap. But it was gone. We couldn't leave this shoe behind. This was Amanda's only pair of shoes, and she loved them ever since the Quechua woman had shown them to her in the market. It was a miracle we had gotten them in the first place. And now one was lost.

"Amanda, I'll carry you back to the cabin. We can find it in the morning."

"No, the jaguar might come and take it away. I have to have my shoe now."

The howling wind, the pitch dark, and now the lost shoe. Amanda was getting panicked, and I didn't blame her. She started crying, and I picked her up, turned around, and headed back to JT's camp by the river. I would borrow a flashlight and find the shoe. It started to rain, but I couldn't move quickly in the dark. And Amanda was heavy. Why was it taking so long to go such a short distance?

Then I saw lights, and I realized it was the station house. A broad inner sigh of relief welled up in me. I had gotten totally turned around in the darkness and had gone the opposite direction. But we were home. Scott was in the house, reading by candlelight, and he listened to Amanda tell him what had happened that memorable Halloween night. Meanwhile, I grabbed two flashlights and went back for the red shoe. I found it right on the trail.

After Halloween, Amanda's school lessons became shorter and shorter as my owl monkey research expanded. After a full twelve hours of following the group all night, I would fall sound asleep in the middle of a reading lesson or before Amanda finished her first math problem. But Amanda's lessons in natural history took up her time. For example, the giant otter infants were swimming after the adult otters, and Martha Brecht trailed them in the small canoe. Amanda joined in paddling, and came home eyes ablaze with stories about the playing otters: "Mom, they have playgrounds just like in New York, with slides and pools and sand boxes. Those baby otters play tag, and wrestle, and dunk each other in the water!"

Then she would go out with the bird watchers as they set up their mist nets. There are over a thousand species of birds in Manú National Park, more than in any other spot on earth. So on an average day of catching birds in the mist nets, sometimes there could be a hundred kinds in the nets.

"They're as beautiful as jewels, Mom," Amanda reported. "You can hold them in your hands. Like this, with their feet between your fingers. I helped put on the bird rings too, for identification, and then we watched them fly free. That was the best part."

But one day, I found Amanda quite upset at the station

house. In her lap, wrapped in a blanket, was a spiny, beige porcupine, a baby. Charlie Janson was warming up milk for it. Prehensile-tailed porcupines were one of his favorite animals. Rare and difficult to see in the rainforest, they're distant cousins to those in the North American woods.

"Charlie, so Big Male killed another helpless animal," I accused. "He killed a baby squirrel last week, and remember that beautiful silky anteater with fur like spun gold? One of the rarest animals in the forest, and your capuchins dropped it a hundred feet and it died."

Charlie wasn't in the mood for talking about his capuchins' latest atrocity and ignored the comments.

But the next day, the prehensile-tailed porcupine was added to the list of capuchin kills.

Louise had a different take on the mounting list. "Nature red in tooth and claw . . . that's the way the rainforest works," she said. "If it weren't for the capuchins, we never would have seen those rare mammals. Besides, most baby animals don't survive in the rainforest."

Then one day Scott came storming into the research cabin, obviously distressed about his oriole-like black and gold caciques. They lived in a complex of basket nests in a tree overlooking the lake, which I called "Scott's Tenement District," since the nests were all so close together it might as well have been in Brooklyn. A few days previously, Scott had been proud as punch to report that eggs were hatching in the nests, and the ardent parents were busily feeding the ever-open mouths of the hatchlings. But now Scott was very upset.

"What's wrong, Scott?" Nina asked.

"My study is ruined. My project is over. I've been robbed, pillaged! All my baby birds are dead! Damn Charlie's monkeys!"

Silence enveloped the station house. This was Scott's dissertation project he was talking about. His future career, his whole life, hung by a thread.

"What happened exactly?" I asked.

"You know how the tree where the birds are is coming into fruit? Well, Charlie's monkeys were feeding there when Big Male looked out toward the nests. Maybe he heard the baby birds inside. Big Male makes a food call, which sounds like a fire engine siren, and walks way out onto a branch. He reaches for the hanging nest and puts his hand in the round front door. Pulls out a fist full of baby bird and eats it head first. Before he even has a chance to burp, he reaches in for another one. The rest of the monkeys in his group see what's going on and hurry over for the feast. They watch his technique and soon the whole group is pillaging nest after nest. I still can't believe it. They gobbled down baby birds for almost an hour. My whole study is eaten up. I *hate* monkeys."

"Your caciques have hundreds of nests, Scott. There must be some of your nests left." Nina was trying to be optimistic.

"There are sixteen monkeys in that group and each ate about a bird every five minutes. It was terrible to watch. Where's Charlie?"

Of course, Charlie couldn't bring Scott's birds back to life, but there were two branches of nests that were even out of reach for the capuchins. Those baby birds survived and prospered, and the adult birds who had lost their offspring helped feed them.

We all grieved for Scott's loss, but we didn't think it could happen to us. At least, I didn't. Until one day in November, when Amanda and I were eating lunch in the station house. Suddenly, we heard Charlie's booming voice, breathing hard. "Pat, come quick, [pant, pant], Big Male [pant] is after your monkeys."

Amanda and I ran outside. Sure enough, in the trees bordering the clearing was the female owl monkey, running ahead of the juvenile and yearling who were close behind, leaping rapidly from tree to tree, all terrified for their lives. Ten yards behind them leaped the father owl monkey with the baby, nearly half his size, on his back. He was so tired he was panting. In hot pursuit was Big Male, tough as a pitbull. The chase was going on right in front of the station house, and it was easy to see.

Amanda began to cry. "Mom, he's going to catch the dad and eat the baby!"

Charlie was keeping pace behind Big Male, and Amanda and I followed him across the clearing. Shouting at the monkeys, all three of us followed them into the forest. Blinded by the darkness under the canopy, we couldn't see any monkeys. Then I saw Big Male looking around, probably as blinded as we were. The owl monkeys were gone. Able to see in the dim light, they had probably disappeared into the safety of a well-known tree hole. Even the father and baby had made it. Big Male, exhausted after the chase, moved off to find his group again.

"That was close!" Amanda exclaimed. "That father couldn't run very fast with the baby on his back."

"You know what?" I said, realizing something. "The mother wouldn't have been able to escape if she was carrying the baby. She's making milk, and that takes a lot of energy." I was making a major theoretical breakthrough.

"Small animals require more energy to travel per unit pound than large animals," Charlie pointed out. "So a two-pound owl monkey would proportionally need more calories to carry that load than a larger monkey, like a capuchin."

Amanda's eyes were beginning to glaze over.

"Well, Charlie, thanks to your capuchins, now I have one good reason for father care in owl monkeys," I said. "The baby survives if it's on the dad when chased by ugly, vicious predators."

In November, it started raining in the evenings. The spirit of the research group had changed, and the high energy of first encountering the rainforest had evolved into a more somber routine. All of us felt the heavy hand of time prodding us to work harder, to find the solutions to our detective stories fast, before the heavier rains came. JT became more and more remote, only speaking in Spanish with Klaus and Rosa. Supplies were getting thin, and that put a competitive edge on meals. The eggs, fresh fruits, onions, potatoes, and carrots had been eaten by the end of September. Then the army ants had eaten the cheese and chocolate in October. By November, our wine was running out, and the variety of six kinds of dried beans had diminished down to one. And in mid-November we discovered that the rice was being slowly eaten by an invasion of black weevils. By the third week in November, our last remaining hope for flavor, a huge bottle of barbecue salt, had been used up. Scott's conversations were dominated by talk of Big Macs with a large Coke and fries from McDonald's, or he would pretend he was calling Domino's Pizza or start describing Pizza Hut's Sicilian slices with pepperoni and sausage.

In fact, everyone was getting a little obsessed by food fantasies and food distribution. Individual cooking groups began to form. Charlie and his field assistants had their own stash of food, and they were still preparing gourmet meals with onion and garlic salt, Parmesan cheese, and freeze-dried ice cream. JT, his field assistants, and graduate students still had an occasional spaghetti with tomato sauce meal or tuna à la king to relieve the monotony of rice and beans. Robin, Louise, Amanda, and I were on a more stringent budget and our meals were basic: two portions of rice and one portion of beans. But sometimes, for variation, we cooked one portion of rice to two of beans. I really missed that cheese and tuna. Amanda didn't mind, since she had refused to eat much of anything except hot chocolate, *café con leche,* and condensed milk since September, and we had saved enough of these items so that she would survive until December. With the food situation so grim, it didn't look like Thanksgiving was going to be much to look forward to.

Thanksgiving Day was declared a Cocha Cashu holiday and no one did any research. Realizing that a turkey dinner would have required a turkey to somehow fly in from America, we had to find an alternative. Robin had an idea.

"How about a plump curassow or a trumpeter?" he suggested.

The faces of the ornithologists reflected horror. "Curassows are shot out of every other forest just for that reason!" barked Nina. I recalled Lujan shooting the colorful curassow that first trip in Puerto Bermúdez.

"Trumpeters are so rare, even I haven't seen them anywhere else," Scott said. If he, a world champion ticker, hadn't seen a bird species anywhere else, that was rare indeed. "Great idea," boomed JT, as he arrived on the porch. "Curassows are very tasty, and one is big enough to feed us all."

We all knew that JT was a crack shot and prided himself on his hunting skills. Many of his graduate students were horrified that Professor Terborgh had made his reputation as a tropical biologist by shooting birds at different altitudes in the Andes Mountains in the 1960s.

"But, it's illegal," JT concluded. "We made an agreement with the Peruvian government that we won't hunt any game animals in the national park."

Nina, Scott, Anne, Charlie, and I looked relieved. And Robin, who had been teasing all along, smiled.

JT continued, "Let's eat fish for Thanksgiving. It's not illegal for us to fish. Come on, Amanda, are you ready? Let's catch a big one."

So JT and Amanda went out on the lake in the dugout canoe to catch a fish. The rest of us continued planning the dinner. Charlie was contributing his stash of freeze-dried potatoes and onions. Robin went off foraging in the forest for some edible vine leaves for a salad. Louise, skeptical that JT would actually catch anything, volunteered to trap some forest rats for rat-trap stew.

"It's an old mammalogist's recipe," she said.

Nina and Anne exchanged less than enthusiastic looks, but no one dared negate Louise's suggestion.

"Or maybe I'll catch a opossum. Opossum pie, *mmm*." Louise seemed to be talking to herself as she gathered up her traps. The thought of a opossum for Thanksgiving dinner was even less appetizing.

By noon, the fishers returned. JT was empty-handed, but Amanda had caught seven piranhas that JT had strung on a line, each fish as big as her hand. Piranhas can be vicious predatory fish that devour big mammals that enter the water, leaving only bones as evidence of the kill. Here at Cocha Cashu, the piranha lake species had vicious teeth, but they seemed intent on eating other fish as opposed to humans.

"Piranhas are tasty, but very toothy and bony, with not much meat. Even seven of them aren't much to eat," Charlie said. "Sorry, Amanda, they might make a good appetizer but they won't make it as the main course."

Thanksgiving dinner was starting to look like rice and beans again.

In another hour or so, Louise returned, stating, much to everyone's relief, that she hadn't trapped any rats or opossums.

"Let's go out on the river," Charlie suggested. "There has to be big fish out there. Who wants to come?"

JT, Charlie, Scott, Nina, Amanda, and I grabbed the fishing gear and off we went down Trail One. Nina started singing with Amanda: "Over the river and through the woods, to Grandmother's fish we go. We all know the way, where the jaguars do play, and the waves go to and fro-oh!"

Reaching the river, we untied JT's blue motorboat and launched it into the water. We boarded and settled, waiting as Charlie pulled hard on the cord to start the Evinrude twenty-five horsepower motor. We all held our breath, worried that the motor might not work, as the boat hadn't been used for several months. But on the sixth try, the motor chugged and rumbled, indicating we were in luck. Using our last two tins of sardines as bait, we huddled in the boat, clinging on to our fishing lines as if our lives depended on it.

"Look, there's something on my hook," Charlie reported.

"Reel it in slowly," JT directed.

"Careful," Nina chimed in.

"Damn. It broke the line. Don't we have any high-caliber fishing line? My fish was huge." Charlie's fish seemed to be getting bigger in his memory.

"We don't have any," murmured Scott. Then his voice lowered even further. "Machiguenga." He motioned at JT, who was facing the other side of the river. What Scott was hinting at was the fact that we all had to use thin fishing line and safety pins as hooks because JT had bargained away all our high-caliber fishing line and fishhooks to Zakarias. But there was no use in complaining now. We had to try our best with what we had.

"Hey, I got one. It can really pull!" Scott braced himself against the boat.

"I saw it—it looks three feet long!" I tried not to rock the boat with my enthusiasm.

"Looks like a pacu," JT said.

"It's huge!" shouted Charlie. "Give it some line, Scott! Don't let the line break now!" The boat shook precariously.

"Quick, get the net," JT commanded, and Nina and I passed the net down to him. After a blur of splashing and churning action, I realized that Scott and JT had jumped overboard with the net. They somehow entangled the giant fish in it and threw it into the boat. There it was, the grand trophy, a giant bronze-green Amazon fish, bigger than a turkey. We had caught our Thanksgiving dinner. Our individual issues were forgotten in the grand collaboration to make Thanksgiving happen. We toasted and gave thanks.

CHAPTER NINE

THE RETURN OF GRINGA VALIENTE

(Cocha Cashu and Puerto Bermúdez, Dec 1980–Jan 1981)

DECEMBER, THE MONTH when snow begins to fall in New York, is the month of summer morning heat and afternoon rain in the Amazon. It was also time for some of us to leave Cocha Cashu. Unlike monkeys, birds have annual migration patterns, and so did the birders of Cocha Cashu. While all the monkey watchers were going to follow their study animals for over a year, the birders were getting ready to disappear north for the winter, and wouldn't return until the next tropical bird–breeding season.

After many discussions with my family regarding Amanda's well being, it had been previously decided that Amanda would spend half my dissertation year with me, then return to the US and attend a proper second grade. She was going to live with my brother Chris and my sister-in-law Maureen while Chris finished graduate school in Buddhist Studies at Stony Brook University on Long Island. Chris and Maureen had been married for about four years, didn't have children of their own, and were very fond of Amanda.

"They're going to practice on me," Amanda said with good humor, having overheard Maureen tell me back in the States that they wanted to have children soon. The letter we had received from them, delivered by the park guards, reconfirmed that Chris and Maureen were eagerly awaiting Amanda's arrival.

All of us would travel out to Cuzco together and resupply, so there were no sad departures at camp. The Piro Indian arrived with his dugout on the agreed-upon day, the week before Christmas. This time, our load was unlike the bulging camel-hump baggage we had arrived with. The food had been replaced by filled data books, a much lighter cargo. Our boat team consisted of Charlie Janson, Nina, Louise, Robin, Amanda, and me.

That first day on the Manú River, we decided to stop for lunch on the beach. Nina spread a blue tarp over the white sand and Charlie opened cans of tuna fish that the Piro Indian had been instructed to buy and bring with him.

Suddenly, Louise said, matter-of-factly and not very loud, "There's a jaguar on the log behind us. Don't anyone move. It's about twenty-five yards away and asleep in the sun."

None of us questioned how Louise had seen it while the rest of us had not. We all just froze. None of us were hungry anymore. In slow motion, we turned our heads to see the sleeping jaguar. Nobody said a word.

It was a very big cat. Male jaguars can be more than 300 pounds and kill prey up to its size, and this jaguar was a prime example of that. He was indeed asleep in the sun, and his sleek, velvet, chocolate-brown coat with beige spots shimmered in the light. But he must have sensed our presence, for his eyes opened, lazily. He yawned and faced the forest, not the river and not us. It seemed like an eternity before he moved again. He bounded off the log and rolled over on his back on the sand, his white belly matching the glistening white of the beach. He rolled from side to side like a cat in catnip, totally oblivious to the fact that six scientists and a child were intently watching his every move.

Standing up, he gave a majestic shake to scatter the sand off his back, then walked slowly, determinedly, toward the forest. He did not even so much as glance at us. Then he abruptly stopped, his back haunches tensed, and his tail began to flick. I wondered if he had smelled the cans of tuna we had just opened.

But no, he squatted and an overwhelming aroma filled the river air. After he had delivered his personal signature, the jaguar pawed at the sand, covering his leavings like a cat in kitty litter. He flicked his tail again and strolled straight ahead, disappearing into the rainforest.

There was a long moment of silence as all seven of us sat, entranced by his nonchalance, his grace, his style.

Then Louise jumped up. "Great! I can't believe our luck. Quick, hand me that plastic bag." And off she went to collect her treasure. "Bring me another plastic bag, this one's full!" she yelled and Charlie brought another.

"He didn't even look at me, Mom." Amanda had just spent the past six months thinking that a jaguar was going to eat her. "He knew we were here, he just wasn't going to let on." Her voice quivered.

By this time, Louise had returned with her steaming pack-ages. "He's been eating white-lipped peccary, there's hooves and hair. He must have found a herd and had a feast." I imag-ined those poor peccaries mesmerized by the jaguar just like we had been a moment ago and was relieved that they had met the jaguar first.

"He must have heard us out on the water, our motor isn't exactly quiet," Louise continued, "but a jaguar isn't much afraid of anything. We may have been the first people he's ever seen. He sure didn't care much about our picnic."

"I guess our tuna sandwiches didn't look very tasty," Amanda said.

"Nor did we," I added.

Our next stop was the national park guard station at Pakitza. During the months that we had been in the Manú, the three wild women had walked down the beach until they were living across the river from the station.

They rushed down to the shore as soon as they heard our boat coming. The last time we had seen them, they had been naked. Not anymore. Now they wore pink and yellow flow-ered dresses. The oldest woman had a straw hat and the other two wore red baseball caps. I recognized the three women's faces and their eager gestures as they waved to us, but where did they get those clothes?

"Do you remember Father Antonio, the priest from Shin-tuya?" the park guard named Carlos told us when we asked.

"When we went in for supplies after your last visit, we told him about the three wild Indian women. Father Antonio got very upset when he heard they were naked. And he came upriver to save their souls." Carlos was chuckling at the thought.

"Father Antonio had someone make him three dresses and he came up here in his boat. It's illegal for him to come into the park, but by this time the women were pretty near the boundary. When they saw him coming, they rushed out to his boat, took the dresses, and then stole his straw hat. They wouldn't give the hat back to him, no matter what he said. Did he ever get sunburned on the way back to Shintuya!" Carlos was laughing so hard that he couldn't continue.

"Did Father Antonio understand their language?" asked Charlie. The priest was an expert linguist and knew most of the Indian languages in the area.

"Nope, he couldn't understand a word! It's still a real mystery where those women came from, and no men have arrived to claim them. I wish they would. They sure are causing us a lot of trouble. What are we going to do with them? I guess we're responsible for them. We deliver food to them, but we don't want them on our side of the river. They'll just take everything. They keep us awake with their singing and laughing all night. I think they're *loca,* crazy, but who knows? Nobody can talk to them."

As we left the station, we looked across the river at the three women in their new flowered dresses, waving goodbye to us and chanting. The Piro Indian pulled the engine's cord and the hum of the motor drowned their voices out.

The Cuzco sun shone bright, the air was crisp, and Amanda and I had to do some serious shopping. Christmas was coming, and gifts from Peru would be cherished. A handmade pan flute for Aunt Maureen, a wall hanging with long-necked llamas for Uncle Chris. We bargained and bargained until we had presents for all.

Almost all. I asked Amanda what she wanted for Christmas.

"My ears pierced. Let's get our ears pierced together, now, here in Cuzco."

So we went into a shop with a sign that said EAR PIERCING 10 SOLES, and it was done. I joked about the Machiguenga women and their nose rings. But ears were enough for today. In addition to silver studs in our ears, we bought each other little turquoise llama earrings. To remember Cuzco and each other.

A phone call to the States confirmed that all was well with our family. Maureen and Chris chatted with Amanda about how they had just painted her new bedroom and bought a bedspread and curtains decorated with prancing Arabian horses. The next day, Amanda bravely boarded the plane for Lima and the States with Nina, Louise, and Scott. Clutching Nina's hand, she turned around and waved as she ducked into the cabin. Tears rolled down my face as the plane took off. Child-leaving was tougher than facing down fer-de-lances.

My next phone call to the States conveyed bad news. My advisor, Professor Kinzey, had received notification from the National Science Foundation that I had not received my dissertation improvement grant. The reviewers were doubtful that anyone could study *Aotus* in the dark, even with radio collars. Gravely disappointed, I didn't know what to do. "Resubmit," was Professor Kinzey's reply. He and I discussed ways to improve my proposal, and he reassured me that he would resubmit the revised document to the National Science Foundation before I returned.

Hanging up the phone, the reality hit me. I had been relying on getting that grant money to be able to continue at Cocha Cashu. Now I had no money, but I had to finish my dissertation research, as I had just started getting good data. In a daze, I walked back to the hotel.

In the lobby of the Pension Hotel, Charlie and Robin were in deep discussion. Charlie had a problem. His field assistant had quit a month early to go home for Christmas. His second field assistant was arriving in late January. Charlie was despairing at losing more than a month of data. Then he looked up and saw my face.

"Amanda's gone and my NSF grant didn't get funded," was all I could say before the tears took over again.

By dinnertime, one of my problems was solved. Charlie with his NSF grant money would buy enough food to include all my meals until August. It would mean a little less food at meals, but by now we were used to living without cheese and chocolate. In return, I agreed to go to Puerto Bermúdez and ask Lujan to be Charlie's capuchin watcher for December, January, and February. During the rainy season it was tough to find Peruvians who wanted to stay in the rainforest, but I hoped Lujan would welcome the challenge.

Robin and I had wanted to spend more time together because he was going to leave for Chicago soon, and if we went on this mission for Charlie, this would be a good opportunity for him to see the Pichis River area. As a side benefit, Robin could identify the fruit trees at my study site that I had marked as *Aotus* food.

Robin and I took off on a bus through the Andes towns of Ayacucho and Huancayo and then to San Ramón to take the small Cessna to the Rio Pichis. On the endless three-day bus ride I told him stories about my friends in Puerto Bermúdez and tales of my monkey studies.

As the Cessna landed at Puerto Bermúdez, I noticed that the village had changed in the four years since I had last visited. First of all, the plane had landed on tarmac, a big improvement from the previous mud run. And then there were new houses. As soon as I emerged from the plane, I asked one of the little boys to run to find Adremildo. Within five minutes Julia came racing up to us, embracing me and chattering with all the news. She was wearing a bright green dress and new black shoes, and had gained a little weight. There had been no way to alert the family before my arrival, but Robin and I were royally welcomed and brought to the new house they were constructing.

Adremildo himself had been hammering on the floor of the second story when we arrived, and he descended the ladder to greet Gringa Valiente. Josefina was just finishing lunch and dropped the cassava when she heard who the visitor was. Amanda was the first subject for discussion, and I told them about her adventures in the Manú and showed them some photos we had developed in Cuzco. They were very sad that she couldn't come this time.

After a house tour, we sat down to dinner and shared more news as well as rice and beans. Julia was engaged, with the wedding planned for June. Having moved into town, Adremildo and the family took weekly trips back to the chacra to check on the chickens and cows. Lujan was married to a distant cousin from Lima. Everyone's health was good. Adremildo told me about the new road, funded by USAID, that was planned from San Ramón to Puerto Bermúdez. Half of it had already been cut through the forest. Julia was marrying one of the road builders, and she was expecting new shops in town. She was going to open a fabric store. Adremildo explained that with the road, trucks would be able to transport goods all the way to the Rio Pichis.

The next day, we planned to visit Lujan and his new wife, Justina, at their chacra. I explained to Adremildo that I had come with a botanist to look at the trees I had marked on my trails. His brow furrowed a bit, but I didn't get a chance to ask why, as just then Julia interrupted us with yards of flowing white lace that would become her wedding dress.

In the morning, Robin and I boarded the canoe for the peace of the Pichis River. Hours later, we docked below Lujan's place and climbed up the bank. Lujan wasn't there, but his new wife, gentle and pretty, greeted us. Her face, with its high cheekbones, betrayed her Quechua ancestry. We shyly sat on the porch, enjoying the quiet atmosphere while we waited. Lujan arrived with a bundle of firewood and an ax over his shoulder. He dropped the wood in surprise and rushed over to hug me and shake Robin's hand.

Later that evening, I explained our mission to offer him an opportunity to work with Charlie Janson in Manú National Park. He smiled, pleased that we had thought of him. He spoke to his wife in Quechua and told me he would have an answer tomorrow.

Robin and I had brought tents and sleeping bags and wanted to stay in the forest, but it was late by the time we finished dinner so we stayed with Lujan. In the morning, I couldn't wait to show Robin the *Aotus* feeding trees for him to identify. After a delicious breakfast of fish head soup, Lujan looked very somber. His words came out slowly, painfully.

"Did Adremildo tell you? All your trees are gone. He needed money for his new house. He cut them months ago, when it was dry in October. He's burned one hill so far."

The words cut like a knife, and I couldn't speak. I looked at Robin. "What about my monkeys?" I gasped.

Lujan just shook his head. "I don't know where they are. I haven't seen or heard them. I'm sure they went farther into the forest."

Later, Lujan, Robin, and I walked over the hills to what used to be my trail system. Charred stumps stared back at us. Making my way to the site where the first *Aotus* sleep tree was, I felt as somber as if I were walking in a funeral cortège. It was slow going as we lifted and climbed over the charred remnants of the trees, and with the forest felled, the hot sun beat down even at this early hour. I reached down and picked up a fluorescent orange tag. It had somehow survived. I held the fragment of plastic flagging tape between my fingers. Sleep Tree I, 9/76, it said in black marker. The only memento of my first study of *Aotus* in the wild.

I remembered the iridescent blue Morpho butterflies, glinting down the crystal-clear stream rimmed by bamboo and vines. The night that two paca—giant rodents as delicate as fawns—had shared fruits thrown down by the monkeys. The funny-faced furry saki leaping like Superman through the trees, its tail spread like a flowing cape. And the bright blues of the tanagers, the jewel-like macaws, the turquoise heads of the motmot birds, and the intricate patterns of the passion flower.

It was all gone. I felt as if I were a curator at the Metropolitan Museum of Art who had come to work on Monday morning to see the whole museum burned to the ground.

"There is the new house and the upcoming wedding." Lujan was trying to make me understand.

I just walked silently, tears tumbling down my face, staring at the felled trees scattered over the landscape, remembering those harlequin monkey faces scolding me that first day.

I realized that this study site had experienced the same deforestation that had occurred twenty-five years ago in the Chanchamayo Valley, my first chosen study site. And now I hesitated thinking about the paradise at Cocha Cashu. Manú was a national park, but was it safe from the future?

Robin, understanding my deep shock and sorrow over the loss of the trees, gently suggested we walk into the beautiful rainforest at the back of Lujan's property and collect plants.

The next day, Lujan agreed to the two-month contract with Charlie, and after two more days of collecting plants, we left Puerto Bermúdez. I never went back again.

I sadly bid goodbye to Robin at the Cuzco airport as he headed for Chicago. As the plane took off, tears streamed down my face and I readied myself for the next six months without either Amanda or Robin.

CHAPTER TEN

THE LONE RANGER

(Cocha Cashu, Jan–May 1981)

T HE MORNING OF Christmas Eve I was jolted
awake in the dark by roosters crowing.

"I must be in Shintuya," I muttered, thinking that
Santa and his reindeer would have a tough time getting to this
purgatory.

The hot, damp air amplified the musty smell of the concrete
storehouse where we lay in our sleeping bags. It was made
even worse by the acrid odor of rats, bats, and cockroaches
settling down for their winter hibernation. Snoring rumbled
from the other side of the room.

"Christmas in Shintuya!" I said cheerily, hoping to inspire
Charlie and Lujan to get up. Lujan rolled over in his sleeping bag. Charlie, grudgingly facing the day, ignored me and
went down to the river to negotiate a boat. Our cargo was
light, indicating the heft of our budget, and a Piro motorista
helped us to load, impatient to embark. The water was high on
the Alto Madre in December, and every night the rains added

more to the brimming pot. We reached the villages of Boca Manú and Diamante by mid-afternoon.

The village was in high holiday mode. No pine wreaths or nativity scenes, but a lot of rum and a purple drink called *chicha,* which was made out of corn and highly alcoholic. Most of the men were already reeling from the holiday spirits, and Charlie, Lujan, and I searched for tent sites away from the action. Our Piro motorista had refused to drive us up to Cocha Cashu on Christmas Eve, but with much pleading and a bonus, he had agreed to depart from Diamante on Christmas Day.

Charlie and I were thinking about monkey behavior and worried about missing another day of our monkeys' soap opera. Lujan was eager to see Cocha Cashu for the first time. But our motorista had a Christmas Eve party to attend so we had to put our impatience on hold. We cooked our own pot of rice and canned tuna fish with tomato sauce and silently ate supper near our tents pitched in a corner of the village. I was sad, missing Amanda and Robin.

Around us, lively laughter competed with mournful highland Quechua songs mixed with Piro chants. Dancing was breaking out around the fire like an infectious rash, and the Peruvians invited us to join in. We drank one gourd full of chicha with our Peruvian hosts to show our goodwill and Christmas cheer. The Peruvians started clapping and beckoning in earnest for us to enter the makeshift dance floor. Charlie and I did a sort of waltz. After our formal bows and the subsequent cheering and clapping, Lujan and I danced a Puerto Bermúdez–style salsa. The crowds were getting more enthusiastic as the chicha flowed, and before Lujan and I could take our bows everyone was stumbling onto the dance floor. The three of us shared one more gourd of chicha and then slipped off to our tents, exhausted after our river travels, and thinking of our respective families so far away on the Christmas holiday. The rains started pelting down, and even my thoughts were dimmed by the noise. I slept.

Although Santa didn't come to Diamante on Christmas Eve, there must have been plenty of other action. As I emerged from the tent in the morning, I saw inanimate mounds scattered like trash about the village. Most of the men had collapsed before they had reached their bed, overcome by the holiday spirits, and even the rains didn't rouse them. A young Piro woman in a brown, sack-like cushma and brushing her long, black hair had tears streaming down her face. Next to her, another woman, older and plumper, sloshed dirty water around in a large cooking pot, cleaning up from last night's dinner. She spoke low and reassuringly to console the sobbing woman. I gathered from fragments of familiar words that the young woman's husband had been with a new lover that night.

About twenty-five yards away stood a short, sturdy woman with braids and a bowler hat. I was already sweating this morning from the December heat, but she was wearing the many-layered, bright-red wool petticoats of the Highland Quechua. Last night, Charlie had explained that she was a recent bride of a colonist who lived in a chacra a few miles downstream. I had noticed that she didn't talk to the others. Perhaps she didn't understand the Piro language. She appeared to be concentrating on preparing potatoes for the next meal. But as I looked closer, I realized tears were streaming down her face too, as her flutelike voice trembled in a huanno melody from the highlands. She must have been homesick. I knew how she felt, missing her highland family like I was missing Amanda and Robin.

It wasn't until two in the afternoon that we could convince our motorista to leave Diamante, and then it was another two days and three motor breakdowns before we made it to Cocha Cashu. How wonderful it was to be welcomed once again by the rainforest! I walked down Trail One, savoring the tropical blend of birdsong, mossy smells, and shades of green. I wished Amanda and Robin were there to enjoy them, too.

Once I reached the Cocha Cashu station, anxiety began to creep into my mind, as we had left the site without a guard. I was particularly anxious because I had been given some very nice gifts. Brigitta, the limnologist from Germany, had left me her two-room tent that was so spacious I could stand up in it to get dressed. She'd also left me a canvas-covered cot so that I didn't need to sleep on the ground during the rainy season. I entered the cabin storeroom and both items were still there.

The next day, Charlie and Lujan searched for the *Cebus* Lake Group, with no success. I had better luck, finding the *Callicebus* Lake Group the first morning. The subadult had disappeared in December while I was away, and I didn't know why. Had he fought with his parents? Had he just transferred into a neighboring group? Had he begun a gypsy existence, wandering until he found an eligible female? There was no way to track him down, since he had no radio collar.

Charlie found his *Cebus* two days later, and none of his group members had disappeared. He did have some capuchin gossip. Big Male was still with his favorite, Female A. The news was that Scarface, the long-legged, pockmarked subordinate male, always rejected by the four females in the group, was spending more time close to Female D, the young, very timid female. The relationship looked serious.

The camp was a different place now, with so few researchers. An immense solitude had accompanied the rains, and we sometimes didn't speak for days. The plan was that Charlie would only stay a few weeks and then the Piro and his boat would return for him. Charlie had to pick up his new field assistant, Patrick Daniels, in Cuzco by January 20.

Once Charlie was gone, Lujan and I were alone in the forest. Lujan followed *Cebus* monkeys all day long and I stayed with my routine of following *Aotus* for five nights, then *Callicebus* for five days. We met at breakfast and dinners, and talked about the monkey events of the day in Spanish. Stocked up with supplies from Cuzco, we had some good meals with fresh carrots, potatoes, onions, and cheese, luxuries that lasted two weeks.

The *Aotus* River Group was easy to follow now that I had established a trail system that followed their daily routines. At first, Lujan didn't want me to go out alone at night. He had been instructed by Charlie to "protect" me, but I reminded Lujan I had spent many nights alone following monkeys at Puerto Bermúdez, so he stuck to his day schedule.

Then the rainy season turned serious. It had been raining nearly every day and night for four days, and by my fifth night of following the *Aotus* River Group, the trails were as soggy as a sponge. It was three in the morning and the owl monkeys were nearing their sleep tree at Trail Six, very close to the river. Just one more fruit tree, I figured, and then they would be snug in their tree hole, and I could go home to hot coffee and my palatial tent and my new cot. Even in the hot, rainy season, it gets cold at three in the morning, and I rubbed my hands together to keep them warm. For the first time in five days, the rain had let up. With no moon, it was one of those pitch-black, "I can't see my hand in front of my face" nights. I heard a rushing noise, like waves sloshing against the shore. I switched my headlamp back on and found that my boots were covered by water. Shining my headlamp around, I saw that water was everywhere. The Manú River had come to pay an unexpected visit. Panicked, I kept swirling the light, seeing that pools of muddy, turbid water had engulfed the whole terrain. And the water was rising quickly. It was already up to my ankles. I'd better get out of here fast.

Being near the river, Trail Six was several feet lower than the rest of the forest. I started walking quickly toward the high ground and Trail One. The water was almost to my knees, filling my rubber boots. I swung my flashlight beam around and it picked up bright eyeshine in the water. A long, scaly mountain ridge of backbone stretching behind red, ember-like eyes. I realized I was staring straight into the eyes of a caiman. I shuddered as it dawned on me that all the river creatures—giant electric eels, anacondas, piranhas—were lurking below the water. I felt very vulnerable as I moved away from the caiman. The Manú River was eddying left, right, and center. I could only progress in slow motion, as my feet were weighted down by the water and my thighs had to push against the powerful current. The water was very deep now; I was beginning to lose touch with the ground. I slipped off my boots to be able to swim. Flailing in a dog paddle, trying to hold my head up, eventually I hit land, grasped some vegetation, and hauled myself up above the water line. My headlamp was still on, and when I reached solid ground at Trail One, I sped to the cabin.

Lujan, sleeping in the house's one bed, was awoken by my shouting that the Manú River was rising. Not waiting for him, I ran down to my tent to grab all my field notebooks to carry them up to the house for safekeeping. I had no idea how high the river would come, but I carefully sealed each book in a watertight plastic bag. Then Lujan and I sloshed down Trail Seven and disassembled my tent. It was a race against time.

The dawn's early light disclosed what I was afraid of: the Manú River was still advancing inland. The trails had all become streams, rippling in the sunlight. But the streams were spreading, rushing to join Lake Cocha Cashu. Now the only refuge was the Cocha Cashu station house. It had been built on the highest ground in the area, and we wondered how deep the foundation beams, which raised the station house three feet above the ground, had been driven. Lujan began to load tins of tuna, tomato sauce, and condensed milk, as well as gunnysacks of rice and beans, into the canoe in case the research station went down.

By late afternoon, Lujan and I were marooned as the Manú River reached within feet of the station house. I reflected for a moment that we might be the only non-Indian people in this three and a half million–acre rainforest! Nobody to call on for help. By this time, most of Trail Seven was covered and had joined the lake as one body of water. Our firewood was waterlogged and lighting a fire was impossible. We dined on tinned tuna and chocolate bars. Worried that the cabin might be swept away during the night by the current, we traded off napping and guarding.

I woke Lujan up in the middle of the night. "I feel like the foundation is moving."

Lujan shone his light out on the surging water outside. "No, I don't think so," he said and went back to sleep.

An hour later, I woke him up again. "Lujan, listen to that sound. It's like a low rumbling." It was starting to get light outside. "There's a kind of clacking. Do you hear it? It's getting louder!"

Lujan was instantly alert. Even in his drowsy state, he knew that sound. He was a hunter. *"Wanganas!"*

In the dim light I could make out the shaggy outlines of giant white-lipped peccaries. Each must have weighed 200 pounds. They were menacingly clacking their dagger-like tusks together. There were hundreds of them clacking all around the cabin. As the light brightened, they began grunting and the strong smell of pig wafted through the house.

"They clack their tusks together when they are nervous. The cabin must be located on the only high ground for miles. They don't care about us. They are just trying to stay dry." Lujan was trying to reassure me that we weren't doomed.

The peccaries gathered in small groups, nuzzling and grunting. "Looks like they are doing a bit of gardening," I observed. The earth that wasn't underwater was looking churned. The peccaries were hungry and scouring the area for roots and seeds. A brown-gray mammal color, they could be almost invisible, especially when lying down. But each of them had different patterns of white marking their faces. I began to scribble notes as I sat safely inside the house, looking out the screened window.

My binoculars revealed that the vegetation above the water was wiggly, alive with ants, millipedes, centipedes, lizards—everything that lived in the leaf litter was clinging on to the last refuge available. Most would perish before the waters receded. Where was Noah and his ark? I wondered.

The next day, the wanganas stayed and we were prisoners at the house. By late afternoon the waters began to retreat, and the wanganas vanished like mist. We never saw them again.

"*Está buen,*" said Lujan ominously. "*Los wanganas, pues el tigre.*" Just as well they are gone, because the jaguar follows the peccaries!

In the aftermath of the flood, the trails were like chocolate pudding. I walked through a maze littered with the bloated bodies of dead rodents like agoutis and forest rats, which were beginning to smell. Even lizards had drowned in the waters. The flood had had a devastating impact on the terrestrial wildlife. But there were islands of high ground that had been refuges, and within a year or two the populations would return to normal numbers again. This was the worst flood in twenty years or more, we found out later from the park rangers. Nature has a built-in resilience that ensures species' survival against these natural disasters. The floods had had little effect on the arboreal wildlife. However, the monkeys didn't get off scot-free—a half hectare of *Aotus* and *Callicebus* property on the Manú River, including their favorite sleep trees, was swept downriver.

Life returned to the normal routine. Lujan and I continued to eat together and share gossip about the monkeys, but otherwise we were silent all day long. Every day, I wrote long letters to first Amanda and then Robin detailing all the monkey events, but there was nowhere to post the letters. The routine of monkey observations gave me comfort and security. I was infinitely happy, and drank up the gentle peacefulness that permeates the rainforest, especially when you are alone.

One night, I was following the *Aotus* River Group, which had been feeding on fruit from a large fig tree located at the junction of Trail One and Trail Five, when I realized the monkeys had slipped out of the tree. I assumed that they were going north to the next big fruit tree, as they had the night before.

The forest was wet, and I walked quickly and noiselessly down the riverbank trail toward the tree. I was concentrating on estimating how much of a head start the monkeys had on me. The trail ahead had a bend in it to avoid a fallen tree, and my gaze was focused on the wet leaves of the trail ahead. As I rounded the curve, my light illuminated a very large, squarish head with glowing eyes. It further revealed plush yellow-black spots, and cat ears that were laid back against its head. A jaguar. A big jaguar. He was a yard away.

We both stood dead still, like reflections frozen in a mirror. Frogs peeped. A distant nightjar called. The pungent smell of cat was overtaking the smell of wet leaves. Then, the jaguar's tail twitched back and forth, like a cat ready to pounce on a mouse in the grass. Or was he just agitated by the light? The jaguar blinked, shook his mighty head, and blinked again. Was he deciding on whether I was choice enough meat to have for supper, or was he just upset that I was blocking his path? The forest was silent in my mind, and the sound of his breathing was all I could hear. At the mercy of the predator, I waited for his decision. Then I took one step off the trail, still facing the jaguar. Although seemingly blinded by the light, he heard the leaves under my feet. He shook his giant head, annoyed, and hesitated. I could sense his tail again swaying slowly back and forth. He mustered up power in his haunches, as if he were about to spring. I didn't breathe.

The jaguar turned and bounded into the forest away from me. Three major bounds into the undergrowth. My heart was pounding, adrenaline surging through me. What a magnificent animal! What a beautiful beast! Then a chill went down my spine, and a wave of nauseating fear engulfed me. "The jaguar kills with one bite to the base of the skull," Louise had told us.

I beamed the flashlight nervously into the undergrowth all the way back to camp. In the morning, Lujan was impressed with the size of the footprints. "*¡El tigre grande!*" he said. He told me that jaguars hunt in an area a few days, then move on. To avoid the jaguar, I took a three-day break tabulating my data books in the station house and then started the day shift, following *Callicebus* Group I. I watched the *Callicebus* with a new awareness. Being prey is a once-in-a lifetime event, and it can happen at any moment.

When Charlie Janson returned, he brought two strange men, both tall and blond. One was wearing orange, pink, and lime-green flowered shorts and Vietnam canvas jungle boots with purple shoelaces and matching socks. I greeted Charlie with enthusiasm and he mentioned that he had some letters for me from Robin, Amanda, and Professor John Allman from CalTech. I nodded to the strangers, then returned to watching the monkeys eat *Cecropia* fruit, thinking to myself that it was fortunate that one of the strangers was wearing purple shoe-laces so I could tell the two apart.

Privately, I felt hostile toward them. They were foreigners, invaders. I didn't want to share the forest with them. They didn't belong here. During dinner, I avoided the newcomers, talked only to Charlie and Lujan, and retired early. Luckily, the strangers were too weary from the six days in a motorboat to notice my indifference.

The next day, Lujan left on the boat that Charlie and his team had come in on. I would miss Lujan and his good company. I gave him a stack of letters to mail to my parents, Amanda, and Robin, and to hand carry to the Adremildo family.

I had received a very short letter from Robin, saying that he had arrived back in Chicago and was getting back into the routine. He said he missed me and Amanda, but his passion was not equal to my stack of long love letters. I worried about this.

Then I opened the letter from my brother Chris, and inside was a short "I love you and miss you, Mom" from Amanda with several of her drawings of monkeys. The letter from Chris was devastating. He described how difficult Amanda had been, and that he and Maureen just didn't know what to do. There had been a series of problems; for example, Amanda not wanting to put on a hat in the cold. She asked to go to McDonald's all the time, which Chris and Maureen objected to as vegetarians. I felt horribly guilty and started to sob. Charlie stopped by the tent and I showed him the letter.

"Pat, look at the date," he said. "That letter was written a long time ago. The three of them have probably worked out all their problems by now. Chris and Maureen haven't had their own kids yet. Amanda will teach them a lot. Don't worry. You know Amanda is strong and adaptable. There's nothing you can do now, but take my word for it, the problems have been solved."

I was grateful for Charlie's good, practical sense. And indeed, as I found out later, Maureen, Chris, and Amanda enjoyed their time together after a bumpy beginning.

Now I had to face the strangers again. My weeks of being nearly alone were showing. I was suffering from a state known among field biologists as "being out there too long," an antisocial state where all perspective, good manners, and sharing behavior have disappeared.

Patrick Daniels, the tall blond from Seattle with glasses, dutifully joined Charlie watching the brown capuchins. The other blond, even taller, the one with the purple shoelaces, had come from the California Institute of Technology in Pasadena, and asked to talk to me. I was distant, almost rude, in explaining that I couldn't discuss anything with him until after my *Callicebus* sample was over. He made an appointment for three days in the future.

Three days later, our discussion took place after breakfast, in the library overlooking the lake.

"My name is Dave Sivertson," he said earnestly. "I've come to work with you on owl monkey vocalizations. I brought a Sony 5000 tape deck and two Sennheiser directional microphones. And I have very acute hearing. Didn't you receive Professor Allman's letter?"

The first time I had known about this student was when I saw him walking down Trail One. I had received no letter in advance. But then again, this was the first mail delivery. I knew and respected Sivertson's advisor, Professor John Allman of CalTech, the world's expert on the owl monkey visual system. His articles had been published in *Science* and *Scientific American,* and I had discussed my field studies of *Aotus* with him once. But I had just received the letter from Professor Allman about this student, and the letter didn't mention the purple shoelaces.

"I start an *Aotus* sample in a few days," I said. "I'm following the River Group from dusk until dawn for five nights. Let's see how well you can do in the dark." My voice carried all the formality of a job interview.

That night after dinner, I summarized my owl monkey findings for Dave. "*Aotus* families sleep in protected vine tangles or tree holes and are very prompt about exiting after sunset and being snug in their shelters before dawn. They have small territories and seem to stick to certain highways night after night, month after month. Mated pairs attack intruders when they find them at borders. Fathers are responsible for caretaking, including carrying and food sharing, and mothers just provide milk."

Dave listened attentively. "I've been getting ready for this field expedition for a long time. I've brought lots of toys you'll like. See this watch? It's waterproof to a hundred feet and even has an altimeter. And I'm very good at fixing things. Any technology breaks down, I'll fix it, no problem."

I looked around, trying to think of any technology that had broken down, or even any technology that we had. Cocha Cashu wasn't exactly a technology-driven place.

"My tape deck is top of the line. Brought a great camera too, and macro lenses and zoom telephotos, and a super flash for night shots. I have an image intensifier to see in the dark. It uses infrared light. And if there's something I forgot to bring, I can probably invent it. My grandfather invented the automatic washing machine, and my family says I take after him."

Now that was interesting, the inventor of the washing machine. My biceps were bulging from carrying water up from the lake to wash clothes. I kind of wished Dave had brought one of his grandfather's inventions with him.

When I saw Charlie shaking his head the next morning, I asked him what the problem was.

"Dave set his tent up on Trail Six. Have you seen it?"

I shook my head.

"It's the smallest tent I've ever seen. He says it's great for backpacking, but you know how tall he is. . . . Well, he's too tall to fit in his tent, so his feet stick out the end. He's going to live in that tent for five months? With all that gear? And without a tarp over it, the rain will just pour right in. I really don't think he's even camped out before in his backyard."

Three days after that, Dave arrived at the house all geared

up for his first night of monkey watching. I stared in disbelief at his field outfit. A purple bandanna was wrapped around his forehead with his headlight below that. A camera with a telephoto lens, binoculars, an infrared nightscope, and a compass hung from his neck. He wore a *Star Wars* T-shirt, and a belt with a Swiss Army knife and hunting knife in a nylon sheath. His short pants left his long legs a treat for mosquitoes and thorns, and his jungle boots had purple socks tufting above the ankles. Quite a contrast to the rest of us, attired in drab green long-sleeved shirts with drab green field pants.

"These army boots are great, built for the rainforest," he assured me. "I can walk in the water and they have holes in them so the water runs right out. And they dry quickly. I bought them at an army-navy store."

"Right. Let's go to the forest," I said, thinking about all the wormy things that would happily swim into those boots and not come out. I turned on my headlight and started down the trail.

Less than two minutes later, I heard a thud and a "Darn!" behind me. Dave had slammed his head into an overhanging branch. I am five feet six inches tall and I had cut my trails to fit my height. Dave was a foot and many branches taller. He hit his head sixteen times that night and the next day had huge black-and-blue bumps on his forehead and a cut eyebrow. He couldn't see much in the night, and was totally distracted by the bites and buzzing of thousands of mosquitoes.

"How can we tape-record with mosquitoes humming that loud in the background?" he asked.

"The buzzing dies down in the dry season. Maybe by May or June."

I tried to be reassuring, but the mosquitoes were abundant. Even I lathered myself with Deet every two hours to keep the insects away. My Leitz binoculars had my fingerprints permanently imprinted on the metal from being held night after night by mosquito repellent–coated fingers.

The second night out, Dave only hit his head twelve times. But he stumbled, fell a lot, and he talked too much, distracting me and causing me several times to lose the monkeys.

"This darkness is like slipping into the black hole of the universe," he commented once. "There's no way to get your bearings. No landmarks, just the intangible darkness everywhere. Being out here is like being an astronaut lost in space."

I looked back at him, all entangled in wires from his headlamp, with his antennae and earphones perched on his head, camera with telephoto lens around his neck, and tape deck at his hip. "Yes, an astronaut or an alien," I said solemnly, thinking that was exactly what he looked like.

At the end of the five-night sample, I was frustrated by my inability to follow the monkeys with Dave. I had an idea. Mustering all my past abilities to be charming, I sat Dave down for a chat.

"Dave, you're enthusiastic and cheerful, but I just don't think that you should start with nocturnal work." I hesitated, trying to be diplomatic about this restructuring. "Let's talk with Charlie about the possibilities of tabulating fruit-trap data."

Dave looked down and began to tinker with our broken

shortwave radio. I felt sorry that he had taken the news so hard.

I had switched to the *Callicebus* day shift and was enjoying rice and beans for dinner with Charlie, Patrick, and Dave. It was a beautiful night with a half moon rising above the canopy, and in the center of the clearing, a palm tree cast a moon shadow toward the house. In the middle of our chocolate bar for dessert, Dave cocked his head like an owl monkey and said, "What's that sound?"

"An owl," Charlie responded.

"Great, I want to record the owls here." And Dave began to set up his tape deck. Always ready for a night walk, I joined him in the search for the owl.

Hoo, hoo, hoo, [pause], hoo, hoo. The owl must be close and overhead.

Hoo, hoo, hoo, [pause], hoo, hoo. It seemed to be moving to the north.

Hoo, hoo, hoo, [pause], hoo, hoo.

"Look there with your binoculars," I instructed Dave. "Over there, where my light is. Wait a second. That's not an owl! That's a monkey in that tree!"

It was an owl monkey in the moonlight, lowering his head, getting the low hoot just right. I stopped for a minute, realizing the meaning of what we had just found out. It was not only Charlie who thought this call had come from an owl. It was the same call that Louise and I had heard, and even Louise had misidentified the origin of this hoot. We had been hearing owl monkeys for months and had not realized what they were.

"Dave." I moved closer to him so he could hear my whisper. "Dave, I never heard my monkeys in New York give that hooting call. I have no idea what it means. I know all the owl monkey calls. Well, I thought I did, but I never heard this one on Cape Cod."

My opinion of this CalTech techno-head was beginning to improve. Without him, I wouldn't know about this new calling behavior.

For the next hour and a half, we followed this owl monkey, which we named the House Hooter, as it moved slowly, hooted, moved ten yards, then hooted again.

We had been following the House Hooter for about fifteen minutes when Dave stopped and cocked his head again. "Listen. There. An answer from the east. *Hoo, hoo, [pause], hoo, hoo.* Different pitch, different number of hootlets per call. And there." Dave closed his eyes in full concentration. "Now one from the north, farther, maybe more than a quarter of a mile away. *Hoo, hoo, [pause], hoo.* That north voice is gruffer. I think I can distinguish different individuals. The Gruff Hooter will be easy to tell on tape. But, Patricia, what are they saying to one another?"

I didn't know. But from that point on, Dave and I spent at least two weeks each month trying to solve that mystery. Dave's ears were as keen as a rabbit's, and he could hear and record single individuals from six different groups simultaneously, while I could hear half of those groups. Slowly, the patterns emerged. As we tracked down each animal by sound, we realized that it was always a solitary individual hooting, with no other family members within over a hundred yards. The hoot was given only during bright moonlight, when the moon was directly overhead. This vocalization did not accompany territorial battles. I had observed families pitted against neighboring families at borders during the full moon. All family group members participated in this feuding; a male from one group attacked the male from the other, but females fought opposing females with the same fury, physically grappling, biting, and slashing their opponents. Fighting was interspersed with threatening vocalizations, but the "war whoop" vocalizations were produced by the owl monkey's throat pouch inflating like a balloon and resonating a tuba-like crescendo of bellows. This resounding "war whoop" was nothing like the short staccato notes of "the hoot."

The hooter may not have been transmitting hostile messages, but it was definitely broadcasting to neighbors, across territorial frontiers. The hooter would move slowly, hooting continually to territorial boundaries, to meet another hooting individual. Then the hooter would stop at the top of the trees in the bright moon about twenty yards from its neighbor. When the hooter stopped, it didn't fight, and it didn't mate. It hooted louder and faster and waited for the other to respond, also hooting louder and faster. Each monkey must have been able to see the other, since we could see them plainly, but they didn't have physical contact. Mysteriously, each turned his back on the other, retreating slowly, still hooting. Sometimes Dave followed one individual while I followed the other. We discovered that after visual contact at the border, each hooter hooted for about a hundred yards toward the heart of its territory. Then they rejoined the rest of their group. Why were these individuals wasting three or four hours each month with this moonlight ritual? What was the purpose of all this hooting? What was the sexual identity of a hooter? Father? Mother? Was it a seasonal ritual?

Then one April night in the full moon, we began to put the pieces of the puzzle together. That evening at sunset, Dave and I had counted the five individuals from the *Aotus* River Group as they scampered at full speed out of the sleep tree: the mother first, then the subadult, juvenile, and the father with the infant on his back. Even at twilight the variations in size of the monkeys could be distinguished. They cocked their heads at us and gave us a rather nonchalant *chuck, chuck, hmmm* call. The impressionist light of twilight melted into brightness as the full moon ascended above the treeline. And the family disappeared into the leafy canopy of the first fruit tree, and began to throw down half-eaten pieces of grape-sized orange fruits with one large central seed.

It was only ten minutes after sunset when we heard the first hoots from the east.

"Dave, that's quite a rapid set of hoots. It's coming into our eastern border. These *Aotus* have stopped eating, but they aren't rushing to defend their border. They're just sitting there in the tree. Are you taping tonight?"

"Yes, I have a new tape in the deck. Should we follow the hooter? It's early in the evening. The monkey is traveling quite quickly."

"Drop the River Group?" The ritual of the five-day sample

was as sacred to me as Sunday morning mass to a Catholic priest.

"This is one determined monkey." Dave was pleading.

My curiosity won the argument. "Okay, let's follow this stranger!"

The hooting monkey was plainly visible in the treetops, silhouetted against the moonlit sky. It was definitely alone and, focused in its mission of traveling north, seemed unaware of our presence below. The solitary hooting monkey continued to travel, continuously hooting. It had bisected the River Group territory, and was still headed north. This was a change of procedure from the usual pattern of "hit a border and retreat back to home base." What was on this hooter's mind?

We stumbled behind through the North Group's territory. I kept the monkey in sight while Dave struggled to follow me and tape-record the hoots, keeping the three-foot-long directional mike pointed to the sky. Within an hour, we had reached the northern boundary of the North Group and crossed into the Far North Group's territory. The trails were fairly well cleared, and I could follow the monkey, watching its outline against the illuminated sky, as it jumped, stopped, hooted, ran along a branch, hooted. It was harder to keep track of Dave because he would fall behind, especially when changing tapes. We were silent, not wanting to miss recordings of any of the hoots, or lose track of the monkey.

"I'm labeling these tapes The Lone Ranger, April 16, 1981," Dave whispered when the hooting monkey stopped for a minute. I nodded.

No one answered the monkey calling in the high moon.

We crossed through territory after territory, The Lone Ranger insistently calling ten times a minute with no answering hoots from any direction. The Lone Ranger traveled fast along the river, and we desperately followed on, or actually under, its heels.

"Dave?" It was now 10:00 P.M. and we had been following The Lone Ranger for four hours. Dave took off his headphones to concentrate on what I was saying. "We're about to leave the trail system. This is the end of Trail Fourteen that follows the river north. After this we're on our own. Should we stop?"

"What do you think? The monkey isn't stopping."

"Once we're off this trail system, we could get permanently lost. I've seen a map and there's another oxbow lake up here eventually, but not for another three miles. Can I see your compass for a second?"

Dave shook his head. This evening he had forgotten his compass, and so had I. I quickly reeled off a piece of fluorescent orange flagging tape and labeled it "Pat and Dave, 10:05, April 16, going north along Manú" and tied it to a tree next to the end of the north trail. I hoped Charlie and Patrick would find it in the morning.

The monkey started to hoot again, ahead of us. I knew how risky leaving the trail system was. There was nothing for us to eat in this forest, and without a compass we could wander forever without getting back to this tiny trail system. The Amazon basin is immense, millions and millions of acres of unbroken rainforest. The Manú alone is almost 6,000 square miles, and the trail system is 32 miles squared out of that. Once disoriented, we could be hopelessly lost.

But we were along the Manú River, and as long as The Lone Ranger stayed within earshot of the river, we could find our way back to the trail system. I decided to take that risk. We started to bushwhack without a machete.

"Ouch, ouch, damn! Help!" Dave had run into a wasp's nest. The buzzing was almost as loud as his cries.

I shouted back advice. "Move quickly out of their range. Wasps can't see in the dark, and they won't follow you."

Dave moved as quickly as he could, encumbered by his gear. Once out of harm's way, I shone my flashlight at Dave. Red welts were rising on his face, making him look even more like an alien from outer space. He was exhausted from bushwhacking, dealing with equipment, and concentrating on the location of The Lone Ranger, but we couldn't stop now.

It was three in the morning and we had been chasing this hooting monkey for nine hours. The monkey had stopped to feed on fruit only twice for ten-minute intervals all night. We had used these opportunities to change batteries in the tape deck.

Suddenly, we were stymied. We had reached another river that flowed into the Manú. This river had a very fast current and was too big to swim across. The monkey raced up and down the bank for about ten minutes. Then it took a major leap—maybe five yards—and made it over to the other side. And it kept hooting and moving. We stood there, helpless. We couldn't follow. There was no way we could get across that river.

Exhausted by our trek, we sat down. My stomach started to growl.

"We're lost, Dave," I said. "No trails, no food. Lost."

Dave snapped out the last tape in the tape deck and said, "We recorded nine tapes of hoots. Nine hour-long tapes! We got the goods on that monkey." Then he reached into his tape equipment and pulled out two Sublime chocolate bars.

"You told me to bring extra chocolate at all times." And he smiled, offering me one.

Our flashlights were getting dim, and we sat down on the riverbank, waiting for the dawn. Knowing we were in serious trouble, we distracted each other by puzzling over the meaning of this weird monkey's behavior. I knew what we had just witnessed was important to unlocking the owl monkey's secrets.

"*Aotus* live in little family groups," I said. "A young monkey has to leave home to seek his fortune as soon as he is a teenager. Emigrating is highly encouraged by his parents, who turn aggressive. But the juvenile owl monkey has a real dilemma. It has to find a great mate. They mate for life, and choosing the wrong partner can be disastrous."

Dave piped up. "And there are no singles bars."

"Right, how can you meet eligible prospects if you are a teenage owl monkey? There's a lot standing in your way. First, it's dark out there. You're only following your parents around every night. And if your parents run into another family at the border, they give a war whoop and viciously chase the group off before you can say *hi* to your peers.

"But there's good visibility during the full moon. That's the time to make a break for it. The easiest thing is to check the neighborhood out first. Call all the singles in, one at a time, to check them out. But if they're all unacceptable, for example they're all males and you're a male too, drastic decisions have to be made."

"Maybe our Lone Ranger was desperately sending out the personal ad 'YSFOM (young single female owl monkey) seeks YSMOM (young single male owl monkey) to form permanent pair bond and raise decades of children. Likes bananas and romantic moonlight nights.'" Dave was going over the top now.

"But, Dave, why didn't an eligible bachelor answer? Nine hours of calling and no responses?"

At dawn, we began the arduous trek home. We were able to follow the river and reached the cabin by afternoon. We recounted our night's events to Charlie and Patrick, who had just finished eating lunch and were going to take a siesta.

As we sat alone at the dining table, gorging on Charlie's leftover tuna noodle dish, I complimented Dave on how far he had come in becoming a field worker. No longer just a California techie, he had earned his stripes. "Dave, I'm sorry I was so discouraging at the beginning. I misjudged you. We've learned a lot of new information, thanks to you."

Then I noticed Dave's shoes—or what was left of them. The sole of one was attached only at the heel, like a wide-mouthed alligator swallowing his foot, and the other one was getting that way. The canvas tops had been ripped in several places, which wasn't a surprise since he tripped often—especially in last night's hours of bushwhacking.

"Looks like it's time for you to get out your second pair of boots," I mentioned.

Dave looked up, puzzled. "Second pair of boots? I don't have a second pair of boots. This pair of army boots was supposed to last a lifetime. All weather, no matter how wet. They were built for the Vietnam War. They sure do look ruined though. I have a pair of flip-flops, I can wear them."

I gulped, almost choking on the pasta. "It's not possible to wear sandals off trail. Only the Machiguenga go barefoot, but they have thick calluses. Dave, your feet are California-sand sort of feet, not rainforest proof. Maybe you can borrow boots from the other guys."

I walked down to Charlie's tent, awakening him from his siesta.

"Charlie, I have to talk to you about Dave. First there was the tent that was so small his feet stuck out when he slept. And he had to use my old tent. Then there was the raincoat poncho thing that he bought for five dollars that got that Swiss cheese look after a couple of nights in the rainforest. And the short-shorts and the purple shoelaces."

Charlie was nodding his "yes, yes, get to the point" nod.

"Well, now his jungle boots have fallen apart. Completely. He can't walk in them anymore. He can't walk in the forest without boots, and he brought only one pair. Do you have boots that he can borrow?"

"Common sense just doesn't come easily to Dave." Charlie sort of chuckled and sighed simultaneously. "I don't think he can borrow my boots. His feet are size thirteen, mine are ten.

No way he can fit into any boots I have. And Patrick wears size ten and a half. But Dave will think of something, don't worry."

And indeed, the next morning Dave did his grandfather proud. Mustering up his inventiveness, he had solved the boot crisis. He was wearing what appeared to be "moon boots." Silver and puffy, they resembled what the astronauts wore for their walk on the moon. At close inspection, I realized Dave had constructed boots out of duct tape, using the original jungle boots as a basic framework. They were waterproof and protected his feet. He wore them for his remaining time in the rainforest.

It was June and time for the birders to come back from the northern hemisphere. John Terborgh, Nina Pierrepont, and Scott Robinson arrived late one afternoon, unloading special treasures such as Chilean red wine, cartons of Sublime chocolate bars, and D-cell batteries.

Dave Sivertson, finished with his three months of vocalization research, had only one evening to finalize his packing for the return voyage. With tears in his eyes, he placed his tapes and tape deck into a duffel. Although there wasn't much left in good condition, Dave donated the rest of his possessions, including his tiny tent, to the Cocha Cashu research house storeroom. That night, we went out to the clearing to hear the hoots of the distant owl monkeys resounding over the lake in the rising moon. After these months of stumbling in the dark, we knew much more about what the calls meant. We suspected that we could tell males from females and that these calls were an auditory dating system.

Early in the morning, I walked down Trail One with Dave one last time. Dave, towering over me as ever, now had blond shoulder-length hair held back by his purple bandanna headband and a full Viking beard. He wore his *Star Wars* T-shirt, now bloodstained from squashed mosquitoes, his hiking shorts, his purple socks, and his moon boots. The Piro Indian helped him load his gear, and started the motor. As he waved from the boat, teary eyed, I waved back to my hardened, high-tech field assistant.

CHAPTER ELEVEN

HARPY EAGLE AND BIG FIG

(Cocha Cashu, 1981)

JUNE MEANT THAT there were only three months left for me to solve the owl monkey mysteries. Both Charlie and I felt the clock ticking as we entered the final quarter of our dissertation year. I needed to clinch the advantages of nightlife to *Aotus*, and Charlie needed to understand what factors in the life of *Cebus* engineered their social grouping patterns. Tensions mounted for the monkey watchers. The return of the bird watchers just reminded us of how little time we had left.

In the middle of June, I trudged back to the cabin, exhausted but exhilarated after a long day with the *Callicebus* Lake Group. I was eager to report the battle between the Lake and South Groups.

The only audience in the cabin were Scott and Patrick, but before I could begin to recount my day's adventures, Scott said, motioning to the fire out back of the cabin, "We have visitors. Zakarias and his wives arrived by canoe this afternoon from Tayakome."

"Interesting fashions out here in the rainforest," Patrick commented.

I had no idea why he made this remark. The Indian cushmas were usually made out of brown hemp, sort of drab like a monk's robes, although some of them were decorated with sewn-on seeds.

I went to the screened window to see what was going on out back. JT, Charlie, and Zakarias were squatting by the fire, in deep discussion. I saw piles of bananas and some very big catfish near the woodpile. Behind the fire squatted two Indian women. But they weren't wearing the traditional brown woven cushmas. Instead, they were wearing transformed bedsheets: bright red, white, and yellow caped super cat cruising over the skyline of New York City. If only Amanda was here to see this! I looked back at Patrick and Scott, who were grinning at my shocked expression. I went out to greet my old friends.

The two women smiled at me shyly, and not being able to say anything that they would understand, I gave them my biggest grin. They were proud to show me their new skirts, and I admired them.

The next morning, my *Callicebus* were feeding on fruits near the cabin when I heard Charlie's voice. When I reached the cabin he was inside, head on the dining room table, in tears. He pounded his fist on the table, jumped up and kicked the wall, paced back and forth, and collapsed again at the table. He didn't even notice me at the door.

I glanced around, looking for clues. Had something happened to Patrick? Then in the corner of the room I saw a small capuchin monkey, limp, with a six-foot-long black arrow through his heart.

I gasped, left the cabin, and walked to the lake, trying to assemble my thoughts. The Machiguenga had shot Charlie's monkeys. We had made an agreement with Zakarias that he would never hunt at Cocha Cashu. For years, this Machiguenga family had visited the research station, with no problem. Why now had they hunted here? Poor Charlie. He'd been studying this group since 1975. If someone had murdered my monkeys, I would have wanted to get retribution. There was potential for big trouble here. I went to find JT, who was writing in his tent.

After I told him what had happened, JT went to find Zakarias. He returned to the cabin over an hour later and sat down next to Charlie and me.

"Zakarias was very upset. This is the story he told me. He had decided to bring his fifteen-year-old son to visit us this year. The son had remained down at the beach camp and had been told the rules about no hunting at Cocha Cashu. Zacharias was adamant about that point. But his son heard the monkeys feeding on the river trail and went to investigate. He'd never seen habituated monkeys before. These monkeys were just a few yards away and they weren't running! Automatically he reached for his bow and arrows."

Charlie winced, and JT hesitated, then continued.

"The male group leader, probably remembering from decades ago, sounded an alarm when he saw the bow and arrows, and he and the females disappeared. But three young capuchins, about six months old, were killed by arrows. It was all a mistake, Zakarias explained. He assured me that it would never happen again. He said he had prohibited his son from ever coming back to Cocha Cashu, and neither he nor any member of his family would ever hunt at Cocha Cashu again. He was upset and ashamed that his son had dishonored him. I don't know what to say, Charlie, but that's the story." And JT lapsed into silence.

There was nothing really to be done. The Machiguenga left that day, paddling back up to Tayakome. Charlie spent hours alone in the forest, trying to reconcile himself with the loss. We felt his pain. All of us prided ourselves that Cocha Cashu was a pristine forest, one of the few places where you could study real animal behavior, unaffected by human intervention. What we were recording was evolution in the making, the daily lives of our monkeys in a true natural state. This snapshot year of their behavior and ecology could lead us to understand how generations of monkeys became what they were. But Charlie feared that losing these monkeys in an unnatural way would throw off his models and predictions.

Scientific discoveries can be serendipitous, and within two weeks Charlie realized that he had a major problem of a different sort on his hands. Even I heard the whining of the female capuchin monkey, which carried all the way to where I was studying *Callicebus*. Low, simpering, continual whining. An annoying sound that I had never heard before. And it didn't stop all afternoon.

When I came in for dinner, Charlie was not back yet. When he arrived, he was exhausted and exhilarated. Female A was in estrus. She had whined the estrus call all afternoon. Charlie had never observed capuchin monkeys mating before, and it is a fairly rare event. Birth spacing between capuchin births is two or even three years. Nursing mothers do not return into estrus, and each female may mate only once in three years. In fact, no one had seen capuchins mate in the wild before.

Most people think that sex in monkeys is sort of a rude affair. And indeed, in Old World monkeys such as baboons and macaques, females advertise their sexual attractiveness with large, red, bulbous swellings that dominate their hindquarters. This flamboyant advertising attracts males from miles around, and multiple copulations with many males occupy a female's daily schedule for almost a week. However, once pregnant, an Old World monkey female probably won't return to that "neon" state and mate again for two or three years.

In contrast, New World monkey females are much more subtle and do not advertise their receptivity in visual ways. There are two main reasons for that. All New World monkeys live in trees, not the savannah, like baboons in Africa do, and visual signals are difficult to detect amongst the greenery of the rainforest. In addition, male primates in South and Central America do not have the color vision abilities that African and Asian monkeys and apes have. Therefore, colorful signals are replaced with smells or calls to "market" sexual readiness. In many species, such as *Callicebus* or *Aotus*, it's difficult to tell when sex is on their mind. That is one reason mating is not observed very often. But even when New World monkey females mate with many males, such as with woolly spider monkeys, it is a relatively civilized affair, males quietly waiting in line to take their turn. Once a female New World monkey is pregnant, she will not mate again until her infant is weaned, which may be as long as three years.

But no one knew about mating in wild capuchins, until Charlie made these observations at Cocha Cashu. Charlie shared with us a graphic description once: "Sex must be a pretty labor-intensive event in capuchins. At least, that's the way Big Male acted. Female A had to follow him around, whining, approaching him, running away, approaching him again. All afternoon, Big Male ignored her flirting. Finally, at 4:32, he gave in and they mated. It didn't take that long, a minute or two. Afterward Big Male collapsed on a branch, exhausted. He just lay there on this wide branch for half an hour. But Female A seemed happy to sit next to him. What a day! Females certainly seem to choose their mates. Scarface sure wasn't her choice. And the three subadult males weren't either."

But that was just the beginning for Big Male. Charlie found out that estrus lasts three or four days in capuchins. Female A followed and whined at Big Male for three days. She hardly ate a thing for those days, spending all her time shadowing her partner. But the next day, Big Male had a real problem. Both Female B and Female C came into estrus. The whining in the forest was unbelievably loud and insistent. And Big Male was unbelievably hounded by these two females. Patrick and Charlie had their hands full trying to track them. The data were amazing. Female soliciting was seen every time. Female choice was firmly documented. The timing of estrus, number of copulations, number of thrusts, all were recorded for the first time. It was a whole chapter on capuchin sexual behavior for Charlie's dissertation. But there was more than that.

"Why are all the females interested in Big Male? What's his charm? It sure isn't his good looks," Nina asked, teasing Charlie.

Charlie countered, "Big Male is tough enough to open up the tasty, rich palm clusters. Big Male shares food with the youngsters and his favorite females. Big Male babysits while the females forage. Big Male is the one who faces down predators and protects the group. He's a great guy, Nina, and he isn't ugly like Scarface. He's a great choice."

The implications of this to our understanding of primate sex was dawning on me. My discussion with Charlie was very insightful. "Charlie, the females are calling the shots in the relationship. The females are choosing who their sexual partner is. This is a far cry from the vision of our primate ancestors' sex life I know from the literature. Did you read Robert Ardrey, Desmond Morris, and Irv DeVore? Big baboon and chimp males beating up the other males to mate with the female of their choice. Charlie, are things different in the Americas?" I asked, thinking back years ago to my earlier readings and similar questions.

"Or are the scientists just seeing themselves in their study animals?" ever-cynical Nina asked.

"Female choice is something Darwin thought was important in 1872," I said. "But primatologists have been focusing on different questions. They emphasize how warlike and male-dominant our primate cousins are, implying that all these behaviors are encoded in our genes. Well, there are other messages in our genes, too. Father care and female choice are there. And with our big brains, we might have a choice among this menu of genes." I decided to bring the conversation back to Cocha Cashu.

"Charlie, this sex thing has never happened before. Nobody has ever seen a capuchin mate in the wild, and now we have three females in estrus within a week. It's crazy. What's happening?"

"I've been thinking very hard about this," Charlie replied. "It isn't the food, and it isn't the season, and it isn't the rains. Capuchins aren't seasonal breeders. I think it was what Zakarias's son did. All three of those juveniles he shot were still nursing. Losing their infants must have brought the females into estrus immediately. They have a sixteen-day estrus cycle." And with a sardonic grin, he looked at me and said, "I can thank Zakarias's son for one dissertation chapter."

"Yes, Charlie," I said, thinking of all the dark moments in my own life. "Failure can be the best fertilizer for success."

June was nearly over and now I had less than two more months to figure out why the world's only nocturnal monkey was nocturnal; to put all these clues together and come up with a reasonable understanding. I was seeing that during the day, *Callicebus* was different in some ways from *Aotus*. *Callicebus* traveled low and were difficult to see hiding in vine tangles, and they moved slowly and deliberately. They rested a lot more than *Aotus*—Scott called them the "Brown Blobs." In contrast, *Aotus* was energetic and fearless as they noisily leaped through the trees, especially on bright moonlit nights. The majority of the diet of both species was fruit. As for the extra courses, *Callicebus* ate more leaves, *Aotus* more insects, but of course, as Dave Sivertson had pointed out, there are more insects active in the night.

Then the harpy eagle made a cameo appearance at Cocha Cashu. During the June five-day sample, the *Callicebus* River Group was quietly selecting fruits in a riverside tree when the whole forest came alive with alarm calls. The ruckus came from the north: spider monkey barks, capuchin caws, tamarin and squirrel monkey crescendo whistles, howler monkey roars. Staccato and urgent, these calls meant business. In a split second, the *Callicebus* parents looked up, the baby (now more than half grown) jumped on father's back, and the whole family dropped to within three feet of the ground. And they didn't move.

I looked up. Silhouetted against the sky to the north was an enormous bird. A giant eagle with a seven-foot wingspan was soaring upward, and in his talons was a limp squirrel monkey. With its black chest band, white undersides, and black-and-white striped tail, it must be a harpy eagle. The largest raptor on earth. The forest continued to erupt in monkey alarm calls all day, more to the west, then more to the south. The River *Callicebus* sat frozen for three and a half hours straight, then fed fifteen minutes on leaves, and at dusk rushed to their sleep tree. That night at the dinner table, everyone was talking about the harpy eagle.

Scott was particularly keen on discussing it. He especially liked the idea that a raptor could strike terror into the hearts of monkeys. "Neil Rettig sat under a nest and documented all the prey items of the harpy eagle in a rainforest in Surinam. They ate monkeys and sloths, and loved male capuchins the best. They can kill pigs up to seventy pounds, and can fly off with catches up to thirty-five pounds. They even eat porcupines."

"I've seen one kill a spider monkey once," Charlie mused. "And spider monkeys weigh twenty-five pounds and have big teeth."

"Raptors kill by surprise, from the back of the neck. Teeth don't help," Scott replied.

"Can you imagine being a monkey and knowing that thing can come down from the skies and kill you at any moment?" Patrick asked.

"Just think about all those crested eagles and hawk eagles in addition to the harpy," I said. "Little monkeys like the tamarins and *Callicebus* have to think of seven different species of hawks and eagles being able to eat them at any moment."

My words pointed to the obvious. My little *Callicebus* hid in the shadows, moved slowly so as to not bring much attention to themselves, spent so much time in vine tangles, rarely fed on fruit in canopies open to the sky. With seven different raptors trying to spot a good dinner, the *Callicebus* had better be furtive and careful.

"Scott," I continued with my train of thought, "what about owls? I've only seen barn owls and reddish owls, and they're pretty small. Are there any big owls here?"

"Nope, owls in rainforests are pretty small worldwide. The great horned owl, snowy owl, eagle owl, all those big owls are in the temperate zones and the Arctic. They need open places—fields, savannah, or tundra to see and hear their prey."

"Interesting." I started to think about how brave and feisty *Aotus* was in the night. Playing noisily in the treetops, unabashedly whooping at neighboring enemy groups, hooting loudly, drawing attention to themselves from long distances in the bright moonlight. Totally fearless and brave, but maybe this plucky courage was backed up with the knowledge that they had escaped day-active hawks and eagles. No owls were big enough to eat *Aotus*!

There had to be a reason for owl monkeys to turn to the night. Maybe it was a life without fear. As long as they were asleep in a tree hole or dense vine tangle, they were safe where no hawk or eagle could find them. I was very pleased with my explanation. But as with any discovery, there are always more questions. Was that enough incentive for a monkey to retreat so completely into the night? If fear of day-active predators was the answer, why weren't all small monkeys nocturnal?

July in Manú National Park was the cold, dry season. Even in the rainforest, winter evenings are chilly, and fruits became harder to find. My day-active monkeys began eating more leaves to compensate. Even under all that brown fur, the monkeys were looking thinner and I worried about them getting enough to eat. Daily temperatures dipped to just above freezing and the *Callicebus* monkeys huddled together with their tails entwined, trying to keep warm. In fact, some days they were very lazy, not getting up for the day's activities until nearly noon, and after a binge or two on leaves or bamboo leaf bases, they would find a good sleep tree and retire at 3:30 P.M. This cut their traveling down to a quarter of a normal day range at any other time of year. Faced with so many hours of sleeping monkeys, I was actually getting a bit bored. But I didn't admit that to anybody.

By contrast, Charlie would come in exhausted at the end of those July days. "My capuchins are going crazy," he would say. "We must have traveled one and a half, maybe two miles today. We went right out of their range as I know it and kept on going. Finally, we found a huge fig tree, maybe a hundred feet across, and it was filled with figs, most of them ripe. The capuchin monkeys just pigged out. I was there the rest of the day, but it's far from here. I'm going to have to get up well before sunrise to make it out there before those capuchins wake up."

During the second *Callicebus* sample in July, the Lake Group found one of those gigantic fig trees in their territory. Because of its canopy diameter of forty yards filled with millions of tiny red figs, I named this feeding tree "the Big Fig." There were just a few ripe fruits, and the *Callicebus* Lake Group entered the same tree several times that first and second day, searching for the few ripe figs. It looked like their lean salad days were over.

By the end of the third day, a squirrel monkey group traveled by. Thirty-five hyperactive, chattering squirrel monkeys spread out searching for fruits, and of course they found the

Big Fig and whistled with glee as they all clambered into it to feast. Four or five juvenile squirrel monkeys spotted the *Callicebus* and leaped over to playfully chase them. The quiet *Callicebus* retreated from the tree to wait their turn, after the boisterous squirrel monkeys had moved on up the lake. But it was too late. Charlie's *Cebus* House Group had heard the calls of the squirrel monkeys and arrived to enjoy the banquet. Immediately, they chased the *Callicebus* out of the tree, who had waited over an hour, and the *Callicebus* at last munched on some vine leaves and retired to their sleep tree.

The *Callicebus* family slept near the Big Fig and woke up unusually early in the morning and were into the tree by 6:00 A.M. Ten minutes after they started feeding, a big group of a different and rarely seen species of *Cebus*, the white-faced capuchin, chased the *Callicebus* out of the Big Fig, and these lankier, bigger *Cebus* monkeys noisily ate the figs. Hearing the feeding commotion, a squirrel monkey group arrived again. The white-faced capuchins chased the small squirrel monkeys out of the tree, but the group was so big that the individuals just kept coming back and entering from a different side. I sat quietly with the *Callicebus*, waiting in a small tree about twenty yards from the Big Fig.

When the squirrels and white-faced capuchins, with their stomachs full, left together for the south, it was already 11:00 A.M. The *Callicebus* family quietly headed into the Big Fig for a late breakfast. Before they could get their first mouthful, Charlie's burly *Cebus* group appeared and Big Male chased the four *Callicebus* out of the Big Fig. When the capuchins had fed for an hour, spider monkeys swung by and started feeding. I knew

Callicebus were afraid of spider monkeys and wouldn't challenge them. By mid-afternoon the spider monkeys left and up loped a group of six red howlers. They roared a warning to the approaching *Callicebus*, and the *Callicebus* retreated, watching the howlers feast on figs. Once the howlers had curled up for a nap, *Callicebus* entered the Big Fig, and I was relieved.

Then I heard the capuchin food call, and another group of capuchins, different from Big Male's group, came storming up to the Big Fig, chasing *Callicebus* out before they had time for a mouthful. I had forgotten that not only do both species of capuchin monkeys have large home ranges, they also have overlapping home ranges, so that different groups of the same species can share food trees. In contrast, *Callicebus* families guard their fruit trees from all other *Callicebus* families, and there can be many territorial disputes at the borders when fruit trees were ripe.

By four in the afternoon, the *Callicebus* monkeys looked desperate. They had tried all day to get into the Big Fig to eat fruits. But all those other monkeys had chased them out. So the *Callicebus* went into the bamboo patch to browse, and never did eat any figs that day.

That night at supper, I told Charlie about all the groups of *Cebus* monkeys. "My monkeys never had a chance to feed," I complained. "My monkeys are small, quiet, and nice. Other monkeys are big bullies."

"Interspecific interference competition." Charlie shrugged.

I continued to follow that *Callicebus* group for an extra five days while Big Fig was in fruit. The same pattern of "interspecific interference competition" continued, and my monkeys never got into the fig tree again. Instead, they substituted leaves and bamboo bits, the famine foods of these second-class citizens.

When I watched the Big Fig at night, things were different. At dusk, the tree became like a Fourth of July firework, surrounded by fireflies and fruit bats. Then came the owl monkey family. They moved quickly into the tree, munching the figs with breakfast hunger. Nobody complained about their presence. The bats never came close. When they were full, the monkeys rested in the tree, and then began to eat again after their two-hour siesta. Yes, this was the best restaurant in town, and the owl monkeys planned to enjoy it for the month it was available. Then I realized another advantage of living in the dark. Large monkeys couldn't harass them. In a world where "might means right," it might be a good strategy for a little species to avoid fights by time-sharing the resources. Avoid the bullies and feast in the dark.

"What do you think of this idea?" I asked Charlie at breakfast. "*Callicebus* is a victim of interspecific interference competition, especially in times of the year when fruits are scarce, and those available are only found in big patches like fig trees. But *Aotus*, with the same problems of a small body size, small group size, and territorial boundaries keeping groups apart, goes nocturnal in desperation. Once capable of living in the night, all those fig trees are available to gorge on to a night monkey's heart's content. Another reason to be a nocturnal monkey."

I was pleased to put the keystone piece into the puzzle. In addition to escaping the talons of the hawks and eagles, *Aotus*

could avoid eleven species of bullying and elbowing monkeys
at the banquet table by going nocturnal.

It was August and my time was up. I packed up the year in
twenty-four little black books containing the information for
a dissertation. These mildewed books were my jungle treasure,
to be guarded like gold during the journey home.

My impending departure weighed heavily on me. I woke
up sweating in my tent, startled by nightmares of racing down
concrete alleys that ended in concrete walls. Later that week,
I was finishing my last *Callicebus* sample on the River Group.
Unexpectedly, I heard a plane flying high overhead, a rare
event, and a chill of fear made me shiver. Irrationally I thought,
They're going to take me away from here. I won't go. I won't
leave this paradise! But I knew that there was no choice. I had
been in the field so long I had lost my perspective, and even
thinking about Amanda didn't help.

The next week, we packed the boat, and I climbed into the
canoe to leave Cocha Cashu. Once on the muddy, meandering Manú River, the breeze dried my silent tears, as the motor
churned the water. I spent starry nights on the white sand
shores and endless days watching birds fly over the unbroken
canopy, mesmerized by the drone of river travel, trying just to
look and not to think.

At Diamante at the mouth of the Manú River, already the
Green Cathedral with its moonlit nights seemed like a misty

reverie. The world had been transformed with sounds of roosters crowing and dogs barking.

The next morning, JT reported to us news from his late-night conversation around the fire. "First of all, Father Antonio of Shintuya has solved the puzzle of the wild women. They found the oldest Piro in the region—he's nearly a hundred years old—and Father Antonio brought him out to speak to the women. The old Piro said they were speaking the Mashco language. These women are indeed from the Mashco, the Lost Tribe who were driven into the interior by the rubber barons. The women said there is a large village three or four days' walk from the Manú River. This part of the story gets vague, but it seems that the middle-aged woman's husband was killed in a dispute and the three women—grandmother, mother, and daughter—went crazy and were driven out of the village and kept walking until they hit the Manú River. One mystery solved."

Then JT shifted gears. "Second of all, there's a change in plans. The road is blocked by a landslide above Shintuya and we must travel down the Alto Madre to the Madre de Dios and out to Cuzco from there."

Only two hours along our new route, we had motor troubles. Our motor coughed, sputtered, and stopped, and we docked for repairs at the frontier mining town at the mouth of a tributary of the Madre de Dios called the Colorado River. They had struck gold here and the gold rush was tearing the land apart, filling the pristine rivers with mercury, pitting man against man in the struggle for mineral riches. Over lunch, I heard gunshots and later learned that an Amahuaca Indian had been killed over a minor dispute. Drunken frontiersmen staggered out of the shanty bars recently constructed from scrap lumber and tin roofs. Competing music blared from every shack. When I went into a grocery store I saw a gold-digger sitting in a corner, shivering from malaria. There was no malaria in Manú National Park. Malaria mosquitoes live in the rainforest canopy and only bite humans when the forests are destroyed and mosquitoes breed in mud puddles.

In the middle of this decay I also saw a blurry-eyed Indian with a scarlet macaw on his shoulder, bargaining with a drunken prospector. The other man showed us a bedraggled squirrel monkey in a burlap sack. The animals had been ripped from the rainforest, and I could sympathize with them.

CHAPTER TWELVE

DARKNESS BRIGHTENS

(New York, 1982–83)

I T WAS DAYBREAK, and I looked out the window at the snow-covered cornfields of Livingston County in western New York State as I sipped my coffee. I was in the process of writing my dissertation. The snowflakes miraculously stitched themselves into a white blanket upon landing, effortlessly making an integrated whole. As the coffee warmed me, the wind whistled and harsh reality hit my early-morning consciousness. Unlike the snow, my dissertation was not going to effortlessly stitch itself into a completed whole. My data needed more diligent weaving.

My gaze turned from the window to the plank stretched between two sawhorses, my makeshift desk. Two-dozen black field notebooks were piled on the plank, each one identified by strips of gray metallic duct tape on the cover marked with the month, year, and species. Each book was mildewed at the edges, and from the inside, with its precious, handwritten scribbles blurred from the rain, emanated a musty odor from smashed mosquitoes, pressed flowers, and stains of fruits once tasted by monkeys. Those field notebooks were all I had left of the rainforest.

My brother Ted, knowing that I needed a place to live and work uninterrupted to write my dissertation, had offered his hospitality.

"I'm still in the midst of renovating this silo into a home," he told me on the phone after I arrived in New York, "but it has running water and electricity."

"It's a lot more than I'm used to," I replied.

"And it's peaceful out here, not a house for miles around. A few white-tailed deer, red fox, and some pheasants. Oh yes, and groundhogs. You won't be too distracted from writing your 'monkey business.' And Mom has found an old typewriter for you, donated by one of her librarian friends."

Indeed, it was very peaceful where Ted lived. I wondered if it was the peacefulness that made me want to go south as a young kid, or was it the snow? Whatever it was, it certainly inspired interesting projects. While I had been away in the Amazon, Nancy Mulligan, the local woman who had been my benefactor, had invited Ted for afternoon tea at the farmhouse homestead. This usually meant she had an interesting idea she wanted to mull over with someone. I could picture the comfortable living room surrounded by portraits of fox hunting in the English countryside, and Mrs. Mulligan reclining on the gigantic tapestry sofa, wrapped in the throw her mother had crocheted for her. As usual, Mrs. Mulligan would ring the bell, and, miraculously, tea in white porcelain teacups decorated with pink roses would be carried from the kitchen, with a plateful of homemade sugar cookies and gingersnaps.

"Do you know the cathedral barn?" she asked him.

Ted nodded. A construction manager, for years on his way to work he had admired the cathedral barn located near Avon, New York. Constructed by J. T. Wells and Sons in 1922 using their patented barn truss, the barn had a wooden beamed ceiling with arching rafters like those in Notre Dame or Chartres.

"How about the silo next to it?"

He shook his head.

"Louis Thomson built it in 1888 and he wanted it to have eight sides. Maybe it was more practical to build straight-sided forms to pour the concrete into, and that's why he made it octagonal. It's such a special building, it's a shame to let it go to waste. Maybe it needs a transformation. It could make a nice place to live for someone single. What do you think, Ted?" And the silo project started the next day.

In December, I moved into the second floor of the silo with my sleeping bag and air mattress. The floor was still makeshift plywood, but deep-set windows had been carved through the thick concrete walls. The exposed wiring along the walls and the pipes for the plumbing were visible like the nerves and tendons of a skeleton. Ted slept at the top of the silo in the loft covered by the custom-made Plexiglas dome. He worked from dawn to dusk on other people's houses and then returned at night to continue on the silo project. During the December nights he replaced the plywood floors with oak boards and laid down the spiral staircase with steps of cherry, maple, and black walnut wood. But, like my dissertation, the silo was still a long way from being finished.

I had taken up a monk-like existence, isolated from the distractions of "civilized" life in order to finish my dissertation as frugally and efficiently as possible. Robin was no longer in the picture, having moved back in with his old botanist girlfriend in Chicago. Amanda was living nearby with my parents. Every week we had Sunday dinner together. Usually, family dinner conversations were light. Sometimes, along with the apple pie, came some subtle questions to me from Dad. Dad and I were the two in the family that loved natural history. And he was very supportive of my adventures in South America. After all, he had been brought up near the Canadian wilderness and appreciated nature wherever it was found. But he had also lived through the Great Depression, and he was worried about the financial future of his oldest daughter and his only grandchild. It seemed incredible to him that anyone could actually make a living by studying monkeys.

"So, have you heard from your advisor this week?" Dad asked at dinner one night.

"Yes, I heard from Dr. Kinzey this week," I answered cheerfully, but I knew what he was getting at. "He sent me two publications on monkey feeding behavior, an article about interference competition—that's when several different kinds of monkeys are fighting for the same food trees—and he also sent some encouraging words."

"Encouraging words?" My father was quick to pick up any indication of employment. "Does that mean a job prospect?"

"Well, no, he just said it sounded like if I kept working at this pace, I might have my dissertation defended by the end of next year. I think it's too early for me to be thinking about jobs." I sort of bravely muttered the last sentence and continued to pick at my pie.

Of course, questions of how I was going to be able to live and support Amanda were always lurking in the air. My mother had encouraged me to follow my dreams, but the reality of being able to follow them was catching up to me. My family had supported me in many complex situations resulting from this dissertation for a long time. And although I was the oldest of all the siblings, I did not own a house, a car, or even have enough money for that week's groceries. Not wanting to pursue the obvious, my father changed the subject.

"Amanda, that new horse is really a beauty. Let's go see him after supper."

Amanda still loved horses, and the fact that her grandfather owned two trotters created a real bond between them. Later in the evening, when I was saying goodnight to Amanda, we would sometimes chat about the future.

"Mom, someday when your dissertation is over, what's going to happen? Are we going to live in a house together?"

"That's right, Amanda," I said.

"And Mom, the best plan would be for us to have all the monkeys with us for you, and then maybe one horse for me. What do you think?"

"That sounds like a great plan, Amanda—monkeys for me and a horse for you, and a big house with lots of trees in the yard!" And we both would laugh and she would nestle into bed. But as I left the room, there was always a moment when I wondered to myself, Will that dream really ever come true?

Will I ever finish this dissertation? Will I ever get a job? Will we ever have a home?

But I couldn't think too deeply. There was no time to get discouraged. And with blind faith I would return to the typewriter and all those sheets of carbon paper. But always in the back of my mind there was four-year-old Amanda skipping down Forty-Second Street, chanting "A house, a horse, monkeys, and chocolate, of course."

One Sunday dinner in early February, my mother reported that she'd received a telephone call months ago from the Director of the Duke University Primate Center. "He wanted to know where you were, and I told him. But we had no way to reach you. Then yesterday he called again. He asked to speak to you and I gave him the number in the silo. Did he call?"

"No, Mom, but what did he want? Why would he want to talk to me?"

"I don't know, but he insisted that he needed to talk to you soon. I'm sure he'll call back."

It was late the next day when the phone rang inside the silo.

"Is this Patricia Wright?" a low, slow voice with a trace of Texas drawl demanded.

I responded in the affirmative.

"This is Elwyn Simons, Director of the Duke University Primate Center."

I knew who Dr. Simons was. I had learned about him in graduate school. A member of the National Academy of Sciences and a professor at Yale, and then a professor at Duke University, he had discovered some of the most famous fossils of our primate ancestors, the earliest monkeys, in Egypt.

Before I could respond, Dr. Simons continued. "I have a serious problem, and they tell me only you can help me." There was another pause.

"That's why I am calling you."

I waited, puzzled.

"I have a National Science Foundation grant to find tarsiers. Do you know what tarsiers are? They're small night primates that live in a few Asian islands—Borneo, Sumatra, and the Philippines. They're small enough to fit in the palm of your hand, and have eyes as big as their brain. And some people say that tarsiers are the key to our primate ancestry. But in order to understand anything about tarsiers, we need to study them. We know almost nothing about them, except that there are three species. I want to establish a breeding colony of tarsiers here in North Carolina at the Duke Primate Center so we can understand their behavior."

Dr. Simons stopped to clear his throat. "I've had this grant for three years and have sent five men to find the tarsiers. And they've all failed. We don't have one tarsier at the Duke Primate Center, and that is why I need you. They tell me that you can accomplish this task. I can offer you a three-year job here at Duke University. I can pay you $18,000 a year. It's not much, but the cost of living here in North Carolina is not as high as in New York. I want you to take this job. Preferably by March 1. I want you to go to Borneo as soon as possible, maybe in three or four months after you move here."

Again a long silence. I was too stunned to say anything. Eighteen thousand dollars a year was a decent salary for a post doc, and Duke University was a prestigious school.

"One more thing," Dr. Simons said. "I've heard you have pet owl monkeys. At the Duke Primate Center we only keep lemurs. No monkeys allowed."

Then there was another pause.

"But we could make your pets honorary lemurs. We could put them in a large outdoor enclosure, big enough for the whole family."

Foggy from months of writing my dissertation, and stunned by visions of the rainforests of Borneo and a possible permanent solution for my owl monkeys and my daughter, I was at a loss for words. Finally, I said, "Yes, thank you, I'd like to take the job."

After I hung up, I turned, dazed, toward my piles of notebooks and stacks of hand-typed manuscript pages filled with the story of night monkeys in the rainforest. My mind was racing. Had I just been offered a job studying monkeys? In the south no less, and with a place for my monkeys? North Carolina was famous for being horse country, so Amanda would be happy there. No more vagabond living. I would have a real job, with primates.

I looked out the window and saw the full moon rising above the snow, and somehow following my dreams didn't feel so foolish anymore.

AUTHOR'S NOTE

On March 7, 1983, I moved to Durham, North Carolina, with Amanda following at the end of the school year. Although we started by living in a trailer on the grounds of the Duke University Primate Center, I eventually purchased a four-bedroom house on Mossdale Avenue, with a front yard full of azaleas and a large fenced backyard with eighteen trees. Amanda's pets included a Belgian sheepdog named Aries, a gray tabby named Frisky, two parakeets, our owl monkeys, and a family of red-handed tamarins. We owned a half-acre and I built a thirty-foot square cage outside. With the mildness of the North Carolina winter, the monkeys could be outside most of the year. Yes, Amanda did get her horse, a quarter horse named Boz, and boarded it at the same farm where Cornelia, Dr. Elwyn Simons' daughter, boarded her horse. Cornelia and Amanda became fast friends. Friderun Simons, Elwyn's gracious wife, was kind enough to drive both daughters to their horsey passion.

From Borneo I brought back twelve tarsiers, and then I traveled to the Philippines and brought back twelve more tarsiers of a different species. The Duke Primate Center, however, was most famous for its lemur collection. There were twelve species kept in outdoor cages, and I learned to love their elegant charm. And it was a trip to Madagascar that changed my life course.

That island had so many mysteries that it has occupied my last twenty-six years. I discovered a new species of lemur, as well as rediscovered one in 1986 that was thought extinct. I was the first person to bring the world's weirdest primate, the aye-aye—a large nocturnal lemur with long skinny fingers to extract beetle larvae out of wood, evergrowing incisors like a beaver, and long hairs like a opossum—into the United States. These four founding aye-ayes at the Duke Primate Center started the successful breeding program that now boasts thirty-two offspring. In 1986, I became an assistant professor at Duke's Biological Anthropology Department. In 1989, I won the John D. and Catherine T. MacArthur Fellowship, "the Genius Award," and my parents realized that being a primatologist was legitimate after all. I became a tenured professor at Duke the following year, but then decided to move to Stony Brook where I became full professor in 1995.

In 1991, I helped found the Ranomafana National Park in Madagascar, its fourth national park. This park now protects thirteen species of lemurs and became a UNESCO World Heritage Site in 2007.

I have never returned to Manú National Park and have only seen Robin Foster occasionally at professional meetings about tropical biology.

Amanda, who had spent my sabbatical year with me creating the park, attended the celebration. In 1996, Amanda graduated from Boston University with a major in international relations and a minor in French. She is married to Miguel Poston, a ship's captain, and they have two children, a daughter, Arianna, and a son, Issan. Amanda worked as Science Education Coordinator at the Marine Biology Department at the University of the Virgin Islands, St. Thomas, for eight years, and now is Africa and Pan Tropical Grant Administrator of a Democratic Republic of the Congo development project based at the Woods Hole Research Institute on Cape Cod.

Amanda's father, Jamie Wright, passed away on July 7, 2013, after a year of battling throat cancer.

Unfortunately, Herbie and Kendra, the monkeys that started it all, have passed on, but their offspring now live in Santa Barbara.

ABOUT THE PUBLISHER

LANTERN BOOKS was founded in 1999 on the principle of living with a greater depth and commitment to the preservation of the natural world. In addition to publishing books on animal advocacy, vegetarianism, religion, and environmentalism, Lantern is dedicated to printing books in the U.S. on recycled paper and saving resources in day-to-day operations. Lantern is honored to be a recipient of the highest standard in environmentally responsible publishing from the Green Press Initiative.